POST-TRANSITIONAL JUSTICE

CATH COLLINS

POST-TRANSITIONAL JUSTICE

HUMAN RIGHTS TRIALS IN CHILE AND EL SALVADOR

The Pennsylvania State University Press
University Park, Pennsylvania

Library of Congress Cataloging-in-Publication Data

Collins, Cath, political scientist.
Post-transitional justice : human rights trials
in Chile and El Salvador / Cath Collins.
p.   cm.
Includes bibliographical references and index.
Summary: "Analyzes how activists, legal strategies, and
judicial receptivity to human rights claims are constructing
new accountability outcomes for human rights violations
in Chile and El Salvador"—Provided by publisher.
ISBN 978-0-271-03687-8 (cloth : alk. paper)
ISBN 978-0-271-03688-5 (pbk. : alk. paper)
1. Transitional justice.
2. Crimes against humanity.
3. Criminal liability (International law).
4. Transitional justice—Chile.
5. Human rights—Chile.
6. Transitional justice—El Savador.
7. Human rights—El Salvador.
I. Title.

K3240.C5935 2010
345.7284'0235—dc22
2009053929

The Pennsylvania State University Press is a member of the
Association of American University Presses.

It is the policy of The Pennsylvania State University Press
to use acid-free paper. Publications on uncoated stock
satisfy the minimum requirements of American National
Standard for Information Sciences—Permanence of Paper
for Printed Library Material, ANSI Z39.48–1992.

For Pedro and Pablo

ganaremos nosotros,
los más sencillos
ganaremos,
aunque tú no lo creas,
ganaremos

—P. NERUDA

CONTENTS

ACKNOWLEDGMENTS

Particular thanks to Rachel Sieder, Alex Wilde, and Anne Perotin, who have been a source of inspiration as well as generous friendship since this project began. The University of London's Institute of Latin American Studies (ILAS), now Institute for the Study of the Americas, provided support and assistance way beyond the call of academic duty from part-time postgraduate studies through to visiting fellowship. I have long suspected my good fortune in falling into the world of scholarship through that particular trapdoor, and nothing seen since has altered that opinion.

This book was begun and ended in the same Bloomsbury attic, but many miles were covered in the interim: my various "families"—the Collins, Reyes-Cortez, and Olmos households in Spain, the UK, and Chile—have seen me through my own personal "Pinochet effect" with great forbearance for over a decade now. Thanks and more are due to them, as to Lal and L'Arche, Jesuits diverse and particular, and, perhaps unexpectedly, to Phil Marsh, CSSp: you are where I came in.

Some extraordinary people who contributed to and encouraged this project will be long remembered: among them are Margaret Popkin, Alejandro González, and Gladys Marín, QEPD. Ernesto Ledjerman meanwhile became, and still remains, the very human face of this litany of sadly unrightable wrongs. Heartfelt thanks to them, as to everyone else so willing to help make new sense of sometimes all too familiar terrain. In Chile, SERPAJ offered work space and more, while CODEPU provided not just data but the wherewithal to understand why it mattered. David Holiday, Mo Hume, and the Arriazas helped me to understand El Salvador, while Ana Maria Chávez, Martin Abregú, and colleagues at CELS in Buenos Aires helped me to see why I might never understand Argentina. Any remaining misapprehensions are of course my own.

Some of the arguments that appear in this book have also been developed in the articles "Grounding Global Justice: International Networks and Domestic Human Rights Accountability in Chile and El Salvador," *Journal of*

Latin American Studies 38, no. 4 (2006): 711–38; "State Terror and the Law: The (Re)judicialization of Human Rights Accountability in Chile and El Salvador," *Latin American Perspectives* 35, no. 5 (2008): 20–37; and "Human Rights Trials in Chile During and After the 'Pinochet Years,'" *International Journal of Transitional Justice* 4, no. 1 (2010): 67–86. Many of the authors cited for Chile took part in the conference "The Pinochet Effect: Ten Years On," held at the Universidad Diego Portales in Santiago in October 2008. The author is grateful to participants for their generous sharing of insights and ideas, published in summary form as Brett (2009) and available via http://www.icso .cl/. Financial support from ILAS and the Central Research Fund of the University of London made field research possible. Final thanks to Transporte Urbano (http://www.transporteurbano.cl/), without whom this book would have been finished much sooner. *Nos vemos en el calderón.*

ACRONYMS AND ABBREVIATIONS

Some countries or regions are coded as follows.

ES   El Salvador
LA   Latin America
UK   United Kingdom
U.S.   United States of America

Organizations not geographically ascribed are international.

Acronym and full title, country or region:

AFDD   Agrupación de Familiares de Detenidos-Desparecidos,
            Chile
AFEP   Agrupación de Familiares de Ejecutados Políticos, Chile
ANEPP   Agrupación Nacional de Ex-Presos Políticos, Chile
APDHE   Asociación Pro-Derechos Humanos de España, Spain
ARENA   Alianza Republicana Nacionalista, ES
ATCA   Alien Tort Claims Act, U.S.
CDE   Consejo de Defensa del Estado, Chile
CDHES   Comisión de Derechos Humanos de El Salvador, ES
            (nongovernmental)
CELS   Centro de Estudios Legales y Sociales, Argentina
CEPES   Centro de Estudios Penales de El Salvador, ES
CIHD   Comisión de Investigación de Hechos Delictivos, ES
CJA   Center for Justice and Accountability, U.S.
CNI   Centro Nacional de Información, Chile

CNRR	Corporación Nacional de Reparación y Reconciliación, Chile
CODEFAM	Asociación Comité de Familiares de Víctimas de Violaciones a los Derechos Humanos "Marianella Garcia Villas," ES
CODEPU	Corporación de Promoción y Defensa de los Derechos del Pueblo, Chile
COMADRES	Comité de Madres y Familiares de Presos, Desaparecidos, y Asesinados Políticos de El Salvador "Oscar Arnulfo Romero," ES
DICOMCAR	Dirección de Comunicación de Carabineros, Chile
DINA	Dirección de Inteligencia Nacional, Chile
EAAF	Equipo Argentino de Antropología Forense, Argentina
FASIC	Fundación de Ayuda Social de las Iglesias Cristianas, Chile
FESPAD	Fundación de Estudios para la Aplicación del Derecho, ES
FLACSO	Facultad Latinoamericana de Ciencias Sociales, LA
FMLN	Frente Farabundo Martí para la Liberación Nacional, ES
HIJOS	Hijos e Hijas por la Identidad y la Justicia contra el Olvido y el Silencio, LA
HRO	human rights organization
HRV	human rights violation
HRW	Human Rights Watch (formerly Americas Watch)
ICC	International Criminal Court
IDHUCA	Instituto de Derechos Humanos de la Universidad Centroamericana José Simeon Cañas, ES
IEJES	Instituto de Estudios Jurídicos de El Salvador, ES
IPS	Institute for Policy Studies, U.S.
LCHR	Lawyers' Committee for Human Rights (now Human Rights First), U.S.
MINUGUA	Misión de Verificación de las Naciones Unidas en Guatemala, Guatemala
MINUSAL	Misión de las Naciones Unidas en El Salvador, ES
MIR	Movimiento de Izquierda Revolucionaria, Chile
NACLA	North American Congress on Latin America, U.S.
NGO	nongovernmental organization
ONUSAL	Misión de Observadores de las Naciones Unidas en El Salvador, ES
PC	Partido Comunista, Chile

PDDH	Procuraduría para la Defensa de los Derechos Humanos, ES
PNC	Policía Nacional Civil, ES
PS	Partido Socialista, Chile
SERPAJ	Servicio de Paz y Justicia, Argentina, Chile
TVPA	Torture Victim Protection Act, US
UCA	Universidad Centroamericana José Simeon Cañas, ES
UDI	Unión Demócrata Independiente, Chile
UDP	Universidad Diego Portales, Chile
UN	United Nations
UNICEF	United Nations Children's Fund
US-AID	United States Agency for International Development

INTRODUCTION

International Human Rights Day, December 10, will forever carry a peculiar charge for many observers of Latin American affairs, since it now marks the anniversary of the 2006 death of former Chilean military strongman Augusto Pinochet. Although never formally convicted of a crime, the archetypal and once all-powerful Latin American dictator died while under investigation for dozens of counts of murder, torture, tax fraud, and corruption. In neighboring Argentina, former junta leaders were meanwhile under house arrest for kidnapping and forcible adoption of the children of the "disappeared." Fifteen hundred miles to the north in Lima, Peru, lawyers were busy seeking the extradition of disgraced autocrat Alberto Fujimori, finally handed over by Chile to become the first former head of state ever extradited to stand trial at home for human rights crimes. In Uruguay, first steps were being taken toward the imprisonment of half a dozen military officers for similar offenses. The country's two living former presidents were already in jail. In each of these countries, dozens of high-level former regime agents were worriedly revising their foreign travel arrangements and calling their lawyers. The trend toward calling former torturers to account now seems unstoppable, and yet it represents a major turnaround for a continent that for most of the 1980s and 1990s had been a byword for impunity. Why this seismic shift? Are these changes being willed by the societies themselves, or are they, as some claim, the result of meddling by former colonial powers? Are the new trials a symptom of crisis or a sign of the robust good health of Latin America's fledgling democracies?

Overview of the Argument

This book is among the first serious efforts to account for the recent "re-irruption" of attempted prosecutions over past human rights violations in Latin America. It suggests that the classic transitional justice school of thought is no longer adequate for understanding the resurgence of justice claims in post-transitional societies. The book proposes a new, "post-transitional justice" framework for describing and understanding post-transitional accountability trajectories. This framework is then applied to justice politics and the fate of emblematic legal cases in post-transitional Chile and El Salvador. These in-depth studies help to establish why and under what conditions transitional impunity outcomes can be expected to break down. They also show what particular combination of actors, strategies, and judicial-institutional arrangements seem to favor or inhibit post-transitional justice. In particular, the book tests the supposed demonstration or domino effects produced by transnational networks, whereby prosecutions in third countries—such as the frustrated 1998 attempt to extradite former Chilean dictator Augusto Pinochet to stand trial in Spain—are believed to spur domestic judicial activity.

The central question addressed by the book is: "what happens to human rights accountability after transition?" and, in particular, "what are the conditions under which transitional human rights settlements are likely to change?" A subsidiary question is how, how much, and how successfully national groups, norms, and initiatives have interacted with international ones in recent attempts to bring about this kind of change. Based on the experiences of Chile, which has recently seen substantial accountability change, and El Salvador, which has not, the book argues that recent developments need to be distinguished from earlier, state-level efforts to resolve outstanding justice dilemmas. This early transitional justice thinking and practice foregrounded the role of state-led truth-telling exercises and amnesties in resolving the "human rights question" in democratic transitions. Justice in the form of trials was generally considered unlikely or unwise, for a whole host of theoretical as well as practical reasons. In the words of one longtime human rights professional, "They told us the options were democracy or justice because we couldn't have both."[1]

This book analyzes how these early constraints on justice shift over time, responding to national political trends as well as changes in international law and the end of cold war geopolitics. It proposes the new conceptual framework of "post-transitional justice" for understanding contemporary domestic justice outcomes. This framework focuses specifically on the continued pur-

---

1. Argentine lawyer Juan Méndez speaking at the 2008 "Pinochet Effect" conference in Santiago, Chile, quoted in Brett (2009). Many of the classic texts expounding this view are collected in Kritz (1995).

suit of justice for past human rights violations via legal systems—henceforth termed "judicial accountability" or simply "accountability." It asks who, if anyone, acts in favor of this type of accountability after political transition, and draws attention to particular institutional and actor configurations that stimulate or constrain the ongoing pursuit of criminal or civil liability. Comparing and contrasting outcomes to date in Chile and El Salvador, the book concludes that strategic action by legally literate, domestic, pro-accountability actors, plus domestic judicial change over time, have been the primary drivers of the reinvigoration of domestic accountability in the Southern Cone of Latin America since the late 1990s. While acknowledging the growing internationalization of civil society activism on this issue, the book suggests that it is important not to overemphasize the relative contribution of international, or "outside-in," dynamics to national change. Accordingly, post-transitional accountability is approached through close attention to domestic trajectories, seeking to identify the specific role(s) played by national, international, and transnational actors in particular domestic outcomes.

Aims and Structure of the Research

The research on which this book is based surveyed developments in "post-transitional justice" from the perspective of domestic pro-accountability actors in two Latin American countries, focusing primarily on their interaction with national courts. Undoubtedly other analytical approaches can and have been employed. Studies by international legal scholars of amnesty legislation and recent transnational accountability activity tend to concentrate on institutional—legislative or judicial—outcomes across a wide range of settings and over time. It is proposed here, however, that a political science approach to understanding the outcomes of pro-accountability actions requires: first, detailed analysis of particular domestic trajectories; second, more sustained attention to legal *processes* as well as outcomes; and third, an understanding of legal processes as political processes. In other words, the experiences actors have of the legal process itself, the significance they attach to its outcomes, and the motives and goals they assign to their use of it are of primary analytical importance. The book therefore takes as its departure point the post-transitional justice framework set out in chapter 2, testing and refining this framework further through its application to the study of the internal accountability narratives of Chile and El Salvador. This in-depth focus on two domestic settings allows for detailed contrasts and comparisons of the effects on transition-era compromises of four interacting elements that the framework highlights as likely to be of particular significance. Systematic comparison of the interplay of these four factors—levels of domestic activism, accountability-actor strategy, changes in the stance of the judiciary, and presence of internationalized (transnationalized) initiatives—in the two settings throws light on precisely how they interact. It also allows us to consider which element, if any, can be identified as the strongest determinant of stability or change in accountability outcomes after transition.

One of the contentions of this volume is that the post-transitional justice framework presented here is of substantial comparative utility and can be applied to a variety of settings, though Chile and El Salvador were selected as the initial research areas. The two countries, certainly distinct in many ways as contexts, nonetheless offer very fertile terrain when paired for present purposes. Firstly, they share a roughly equivalent date of transition (1990 for Chile, 1991/92 for El Salvador), offering a chance to add a longitudinal dimension to the observation of post-transitional change that would not have been possible for a more recent case such as Peru. Chile has also seen almost continuous legal action over accountability since 1973, offering the chance to observe how pre-transition litigation patterns were affected by regime change. El Salvador offers the useful contrast of a country whose legal institutions, virtually moribund during political violence, were given a major overhaul at transition yet proved unequal to the task of challenging the imposition of amnesty. The contrasting effects of high continuity, and of radical discontinuity, in transitional legal institutionality can thus be observed.

As regards the "path-dependent" theory that transitional conditions are highly significant for justice outcomes, Chile and El Salvador again offer useful contrasts. In Chile, a formal handover of power masked a highly pacted transition offering little immediate room to reform compromised institutions. El Salvador's transition, via a negotiated peace agreement, did not include political replacement. The close involvement of the UN nonetheless permitted much more radical institutional overhaul. These cases thus offer a chance to evaluate the effects of gradualism versus institutional engineering as approaches to democratic institution building. Additionally, the two countries share extremely broad formal amnesty provisions, perhaps the broadest anywhere on the continent. These have been accompanied by—indeed, have perhaps provoked—both domestic and international attempts to challenge their effects in blocking accountability. Accordingly, the final and decisive factor making Chile and El Salvador attractive subjects for this initial study is the existence in both cases of recent (1990s) transnationalized accountability action, aimed at redrawing the domestic justice equilibrium. The eventual fate of these transnational actions offers clues as to how and under what circumstances such actions can have discernible domestic impact.

Methodology and Data

The research presented here spans a time period from 2000 to 2008, whose most concentrated period was a continuous stretch of fifteen months' fieldwork, carried out primarily in Chile and El Salvador, between 2002 and 2003. During this phase approximately 150 interviews were carried out with key accountability activists, lawyers, legal scholars, and policymakers in six countries.[2] Semi-structured interview material was complemented with secondary literature, monitoring of main media outlets, and analysis of case documents facilitated by lawyers and litigants, much of the latter previously unseen. This research has subsequently been updated and complemented by additional face-to-face interviews (Chile), telephone interviews (El Salvador), and monitoring of secondary sources (both countries). The original temporal scope of the detailed study runs to 2008 (Chile) or 2004 (El Salvador), although particularly significant recent developments have been incorporated where possible.

Research explored two principal aspects of accountability activity in each country setting. Firstly, the overall trajectory of the accountability issue at and since transition was traced. Initial resolution of the justice question by state authorities was analyzed, and accountability "milestones" were subsequently identified for each country. These consist of the principal events and actions that have shaped the evolution of the debate over past human rights violations, and justice for them, since transition. Secondly, three notorious or particularly well-known ("emblematic") human rights crimes were identified for each country, and attempted legal actions surrounding each one were studied in depth. This allowed for a detailed examination of the perceptions, goals, and strategy decisions of private actors, the policy choices of institutional figures (including policymakers and justice system operatives), and the

2. Peru, Argentina, the UK, and the United States, in addition to Chile and El Salvador. The fact that study of "domestic" processes in Chile and El Salvador required close attention to events and actors in three of these other countries is itself evidence of the internationalization (transnationalization) of present-day accountability.

construction, (re)negotiation, and operation of the legal opportunity context in specific accountability processes within each national setting. Although these individual legal case studies are not presented in detail in the chapters that follow, observations drawn from them inform the general analysis of actor, strategy, and judicial issues that is presented for each country. Since these emblematic cases often attracted international or transnational activism, detailed tracking of them also illuminated the dynamics of interaction between domestic and external accountability actors, allowing conclusions to be drawn about the relationship between external intervention and the domestic evolution of accountability issues over time.

Plan of the Book

Chapter 1 examines the transitional justice school of thought that underpinned theoretical and policy approaches to issues of justice in Latin American transitions in the 1980s. In particular, it reexamines the assumptions and predictive power of this school, questioning its adequacy for understanding contemporary developments in accountability. Chapter 2 sets out the proposed post-transitional framework and argues that commonplace state-level transitional justice choices such as amnesty mean that post-transitional accountability is taken forward, if at all, by private actors. In particular, it is suggested that private accountability actors and national courts are the key actors and sites in post-transitional justice. In chapter 3, these and additional constituent elements of post-transitional justice are discussed in detail. The framework is subsequently applied to analysis of post-transitional justice trajectories in Chile and El Salvador, two countries that similarly adopted or preserved broad transitional amnesties, but which have very different experiences of post-transitional accountability claim-making. Chapters 4 and 5 examine the transitional justice context and then the post-transitional accountability scenario in Chile, while chapters 6 and 7 do the same for El Salvador. Chapter 8 draws comparative conclusions for the two country settings, and reexamines the validity of the proposed framework for these and other possible comparative settings. It also reflects on the theoretical value and potential contribution of the notion of post-transitional justice in a variety of scholarly disciplines and in future policy debates.

1

TRANSITIONAL JUSTICE: WHY WE NEED A NEW FRAMEWORK

This book argues that an analytical framework of "post-transitional justice," outlined in the following chapter, better explains the presence, absence, persistence, or renewal of accountability claims in post-transitional societies than does the preceding "transitional justice" school of thought. To explain why a new approach is needed, and to examine the roots of judicialized post-transitional claim-making in transitional justice settlements, this chapter discusses scholarship and practice surrounding early (1980s to mid-1990s) Latin American political transitions. The general theoretical debates are illustrated with reference to specific Latin American country settings (see Appendix A).[1] The aim is to identify the common elements of transitional justice thinking and practice that emerged from early experiences. As will be seen, the combination of some form of truth-telling mechanism with the abandonment or severe limitation of the pursuit of justice through the courts came to constitute a transitional "blueprint" applied extensively in Latin America and beyond.

The term "transitional justice" is used to refer to and analyze how societies undergoing political change address the issue of human rights violations[2] (henceforth HRVs) committed by former regimes. Works by Kritz (1995),

---

1. Principally Argentina, Chile, Uruguay, El Salvador, and Guatemala. Peru and Paraguay are also included in table 1, for comparative purposes. Transitional justice in Chile and in El Salvador is also discussed in more detail in chapters 4 and 6, respectively.

2. The term "human rights violation" is chosen over a host of less specific alternatives found in the literature, such as "past wrongs," "atrocities," or "evil." The issue of which past acts a democratizing regime should take action over is itself a complex one. Adopting the term human rights violation(s) implies a focus on acts carried out by state agents, even though truth-telling measures, in particular, often also consider political violence by non-state forces. Although in some sense a limitation, this choice follows prevailing usage in international human rights law: while insurgent forces may be held accountable to international humanitarian law, only nation-states in the strict sense contract human rights obligations.

McAdams (1997), Roht-Arriaza (1995), Teitel (2000), and de Brito, González-Enríquez, and Aguilar (2001) were among the first major contributions to what is now a substantial scholarly canon, reflecting the wide range of historical, geographical, and political contexts in which the question of "reckoning with past wrongs" has arisen. Méndez (1997) suggests that new democracies are both impelled and invited to draw a thick line under the past to throw into relief their own credentials as radical departures from that past. When an authoritarian regime is replaced in a democratizing transition,[3] the new government is faced with deciding what to do with, for, and about perpetrators and victims/survivors[4] of HRVs committed by that regime. The options pursued depend substantially on the room for maneuver the new government enjoys over former holders of power, as well as the level of demands from survivors and society at large for punitive action over HRVs.[5] Since a major preoccupation of new authorities is to establish effective control over the state apparatus, a certain amount of concession and compromise toward still-powerful elites and institutions associated with the repressive period has generally been considered necessary, and has in turn restricted the pursuit of punitive sanctions against them.[6]

Thus state-level transitional justice policy is overdetermined by what de Brito terms "the stability v. justice dilemma" (2001, 345). This means whether and how much new governments consider justice measures to be compatible with goals such as securing the irreversibility of democratic change, (re)constructing democratic institutions, or asserting civilian control over the military. Possible responses range from doing nothing, to pursuing a "maximalist" policy of identifying individual perpetrators and applying punitive criminal sanctions to them. In practice, many or most incoming democratic governments have pursued a middle ground, mixing and matching possible

---

3. The Latin American cases dealt with here all follow this pattern, with "authoritarian regime" used for both overt military dictatorships and the civilian-façade regimes that ruled the Southern Cone and Central America for much of the 1970s and 1980s. Significant differences of course exist between and within these categories, and particular regimes are analyzed in more detail in the later, country-specific chapters.

4. A distinction is drawn here and throughout between "victims," who died or disappeared after suffering repressive political violence, "survivors" of it, and relatives' and other activist groups, including nongovernmental organizations (NGOs), who act on behalf of or in support of the first two groups.

5. See Elster (2004, 77) and Garretón (1994, 224) on how the "human rights question" often loses political salience over time, reducing the mobilizing and lobbying power of the human rights movement.

6. See Huntington (1991, 165–69) on how the dynamics of negotiated transitions tend to exclude radical demands from non-elite social groups.

and desirable measures along three main axes: truth, justice, and reconciliation. Incoming democratic governments generally identify all three as desirable social and political goals, yet the priority placed on each and the measures considered necessary to achieve them can vary widely. Consequently, the potential also exists for measures taken toward one goal to either complement or obstruct the others.

Truth and Reconciliation

TRUTH COMMISSIONS AND THEIR LIMITATIONS

Truth-telling—the production by the state of what Zalaquett calls "complete . . . officially proclaimed and publicly exposed truth" (1995a, 6) about HRVs committed by a former regime—has increasingly come to be seen as both a positive end in itself and a prerequisite for more comprehensive transitional justice initiatives. Truth-telling as a state undertaking has often been pursued via the truth commission, a product of 1980s Latin American transitional processes that later became an almost ubiquitous tool applied to regime transition and post-conflict situations worldwide.[7] Hayner (2001) provides a comprehensive survey of early truth commissions, usually temporally limited bodies charged with collecting, verifying, and making public data, testimony, and other evidence about past political violence. Initial mandates spelling out scope and powers almost invariably specify that commissions are not to be considered a judicial or quasi-judicial instance; in other words, they cannot assign criminal responsibilities or sanctions.

The genuinely revelatory value of state commissions may in fact be minimal. Many have relied heavily on testimony previously amassed by other actors such as human rights organizations and journalists.[8] Weschler (1990) argues that the particular symbolic value of official truth-telling may reside more in the function of "acknowledgement," when common knowledge "becomes officially sanctioned"[9] by the same state that previously denied or covered up its crimes. Hayner (2001, 106) has argued that truth commissions can in this way constitute a form of justice. She also claims that the establishment

---

7. See Tepperman (2002) for a critical approach to this new "fashion" in world affairs.
8. See da Silva Catela and Jelín (2002) and Hayner (1995, 26); truth commissions often formally recognize knowledge already "in circulation" rather than revealing entirely new facts.
9. Thomas Nagel, quoted by Weschler (1990, 4).

of an accurate and undisputed historical record can lay the groundwork for more specific justice endeavors, such as criminal prosecution or the removal of known perpetrators from public office. In practice, though, these uses have led to disputes about the legal status of truth commission findings. Some commissions have also short-circuited the link between truth and consequences, providing incentives for perpetrator testimony such as anonymity or the possibility of immunity from prosecution via amnesty. This constitutes one of the most controversial aspects of truth-telling initiatives: an apparent willingness to contemplate a trade-off between truth and justice.[10]

TRIALS AS AN ALTERNATIVE TRUTH MECHANISM

Resource constraints on time-limited commissions, restrictions on their access to sources of information, and political considerations related to likely reactions from perpetrators or their sympathizers all reduce commissions' ability to elaborate a genuinely comprehensive record and to attribute responsibility for the HRVs they document. Most commissions have, for example, been expressly forbidden to name individual perpetrators. Additionally, the breaking down of military "codes of silence" and the lessening of the fear of reprisals on the part of survivors and witnesses may not be possible in the immediate transition period. The emergence of further revelations via testimonial, confessional, and other literature that appears long after truth commissions have ended can expose omissions or inaccuracies in these supposedly authoritative accounts. These future revelations are condemned to remain outside the canon of validated and acknowledged truth that the state truth commission report has already established.[11]

Such limitations weaken Hayner's contention that the early transitional period and the truth commission model are the most appropriate for the creation of a comprehensive record. Osiel (2000a, 2002) and Malamud-Goti (1995) suggest that trials may be a better source than commissions of detailed truth. It is true that commissions often attempt overall explanatory treatments of the scale and origins of political violence, while trials generally do not. But these treatments are often hotly contested, whereas "specific

---

10. See Brody (2001, 27–29), Roht-Arriaza (1995, 286), and Hayner (2001, 86–106).

11. See Payne (2003, 2007) on how the later emergence of confessional material from former perpetrators helped re-ignite the justice debate in Argentina. Chile has even felt the need to complement its initial truth commission with a substantial new report—published in 2004—dedicated solely to political imprisonment and torture. See chapter 5.

factual findings" from criminal trials "shrink the room for political specula-tion" (Malamud-Goti 1995, 199). Trials often produce new information even many years after the incident, and can force individual perpetrators to finally provide their own versions of events. Thus "judicial truths" produced in legal settings have their own place in the creation of a comprehensive historical record, raising important practical and strategic issues about the relationship between truth-telling and judicial accountability.

RECONCILIATION

Reconciliation has been invoked as an aspiration in almost all post-conflict or post-authoritarian situations. The term indeed appears in the titles, mandates, or reports of many truth commissions.[12] Notoriously difficult to define, let alone to provide detailed blueprints for, reconciliation is referred to by Little as "the restoration of social harmony" (1999, 65). Crocker out-lines a more minimalist understanding of the term that aspires to little more than coexistence: "former enemies comply with the law instead of killing each other" (1999, 60). Some, including the self-serving, have suggested this can be achieved by a policy of "forgive and forget"—*borrón y cuenta nueva* or *olvido*. Thus reconciliation can be and has been invoked to suggest that attempts to hold perpetrators to account are unwise or counterproductive. In Argentina, claims Méndez, "reconciliation was a code word for those who wanted nothing done."[13]

Reconciliation is sometimes understood to require truth measures but preclude punishment. Little (1999) describes how the South African truth commission institutionalized this understanding, giving itself power to grant individual amnesty in return for full public "confessions." He also discusses, as does Minow (1998), how reconciliation is often eventually defined in essen-tially relational, interpersonal terms as "forgiveness," thereby raising ques-tions about how far forgiveness is or can be a state concern. The pursuit of reconciliation has motivated the provision of reparations to survivors or to relatives of victims. Forms of reparation that have been mooted or under-taken range from the practical—usually financial—to the symbolic, including

---

12. See, inter alia, Argentina's "Nunca Más" report, Chile's Rettig report, and El Salvador's Chapultepec Accords of 16 January 1992.

13. Quoted in Brody (2001, 28). See also Lira and Loveman (2000a) on how "reconciliación" has been invoked throughout Chilean political history to support amnesty and "olvido."

formal apologies and commemoration via public memorials. It has also been suggested that truth initiatives can have reparative effects, restoring the "good name" of victims whom regimes had discredited as somehow deserving of their fate (Zalaquett 1995a, 10).

Justice

Justice, like truth-telling, is viewed by some as a moral duty for post-authoritarian governments.[14] Others present it as a legal obligation of states, a method of preventing future atrocities, or a path toward the dismantling of authoritarian legacies and the construction of democratic institutions.[15] The debate is highly complex, since enthusiasts of distinct models and measures give widely differing meanings to the term "justice."

RESTORATIVE AND RETRIBUTIVE JUSTICE

One influential model turns on a distinction between "restorative" and "retributive" justice. Restorative justice focuses on the interpersonal consequences of crime and the need to restore relations between the perpetrator and victims or society at large. Retributive justice, by contrast, sees crime primarily as an offense against the state, deriving an automatic right and indeed duty of the state to isolate and punish the offender: it is, says Teitel, essentially "crime-focused" and "backward-looking" (1995, 146–48). Restorative justice, then, is more likely than retributive to place a priority on "forward-looking," or preventive, measures such as the rehabilitation of offenders or the adoption of institutional and legislative reforms. A restorative emphasis may therefore downplay the role of exemplary prosecution and punishment in transitional justice policy. Zalaquett, for instance, suggests that "clemency . . . may also have a preventive function," and proposes a range of non-judicial measures. These include reinforcement of human rights protection in legal codes, the establishment of human rights "ombudspersons," and the dismantling of security services particularly associated with past repression (Zalaquett 1995a, 11–12).

---

14. See, for example, Malamud-Goti (1995, 200).

15. Teitel (1995, 147–53), Malamud-Goti (1995, 197–98), and Méndez (1997) provide useful summaries and critiques of these claims.

VICTIM-CENTERED JUSTICE

Advocates of retributive justice are more likely to argue for punitive sanction of offenders, making reference, for instance, to the obligations that states acquire under international treaty law. These obligations, after all, often spell out supposedly non-derogable obligations to prosecute that override ordinary sovereign discretion (Teitel 1995, 147). It is also argued that punishment, far from being simply vengeance, may also have preventive effects. Furthermore, punitive measures need not consist exclusively of criminal prosecution and sentencing. Roht-Arriaza (1995) discusses other possible civil or administrative sanctions, including purges or "lustration"—the removal and sometimes banning from political or public office of perpetrators or their accomplices.

An alternative justice model that has gained ground in recent times in general criminal theory has also become influential in the transitional justice field. Seils (2003) explores the merits of the "victim-centered" model. The term is often associated with a restorative understanding of justice and the requirement to build policy from the starting point of "what victims need." But victims and survivors can themselves have widely differing needs, characteristics, and beliefs about what kind of justice they wish to see the state pursue. The expressed views of victims of crime are, moreover, only one element to be considered in the response the state gives. Roht-Arriaza discusses the view that "criminal acts transcend the harm to any one individual, harming the entire society and requiring punitive action by the state."[16] When, as in the case of transitional justice policy, HRVs are at issue, this state responsibility takes on an additional dimension. The very concept of HRVs owes much to the notion that certain behaviors constitute a more serious wrong when committed by state agents than when carried out by private individuals. For this precise reason the state is charged with special duties to prevent or punish, duties that are theoretically operative independent of the expressed views of survivors. The victim-centered model can usefully draw attention to the justice claims of private citizens in a transitional justice debate more often focused on institutional or elite considerations. Care needs to be taken,

---

16. Roht-Arriaza (1995, 8). The concept of "crimes against humanity," developed during the Nuremberg trials, applies this logic at the supra-state level, defining a category of violation so serious that it is considered an offense against all. The related notion of "universal jurisdiction" confers a duty on not one, but any and all states to act against such crimes.

though, to ensure that a victim-centered approach does not instead "privatize" accountability as an issue to be pursued solely between survivors and perpetrators, omitting the question of the appropriate state response.

Justice as Judicial Accountability

The most controversial justice question for transitional democracies has been that of whether to prosecute and punish members of outgoing authoritarian regimes for their actions while in power.[17] Truth and reconciliation measures, even where these have been contested or difficult to implement, appear to be relatively soft alternatives when compared to the dilemma of whether to confront outgoing authoritarians with the threat of trial and imprisonment, especially when they have residual political or military strength. The incoming democratic regime, as the main transitional justice actor in the initial period, has to answer a series of questions in relation to judicial accountability: Is it desirable? Are prosecutions really possible? If so, who is to be held accountable and for what?

DIFFICULTIES, DEBATES, AND LIMITATIONS

First, why prosecute at all? The debate often centers on the supposed positive or negative impact of judicial accountability on democracy. But the precise relationship between early accountability and democracy is itself an unresolved question. Some theorists posit a positive relationship between the two; others believe that the securing of democracy and the pursuit of judicial accountability are separate, and in some circumstances contradictory, goals.[18] Second, is it possible to prosecute? The structural and political prerequisites for justice through prosecution cannot be taken for granted in many post-authoritarian or post-conflict situations. Zalaquett (1995a) and Seils (2003)

---

17. Transitional justice literature principally understands judicial accountability as criminal prosecution, and further focuses on initial state decision-making about whether to prosecute. Judicial accountability is defined more widely here, however, to include civil claim-making as well as private attempts to bypass state prosecutors and directly trigger criminal investigation. Both have become increasingly prevalent in post-transitional periods, challenging executive and legislative authorities' previous monopoly on decision-making.

18. See Siegel (1998, 437–41) for a comprehensive overview of this and other main arguments for and against prosecutions.

list some of the political and practical obstacles that may arise. Where former rulers, although politically defeated, still have access to arms, or where controlled—"pacted"—transitions have enabled outgoing regimes to secure exit guarantees,[19] it may be difficult to conceive of prosecuting without provoking seditious and violent reactions. The sheer scale of widespread abuses or the lack of competent, minimally credible investigative and judicial capacity can also make domestic trials difficult or unlikely. In such circumstances the use of international tribunals has been both proposed and practiced.[20] Third, who to prosecute? Supporters, collaborators with, or apologists for authoritarian regimes may conceivably be affected by truth-telling, purges, and institutional reform, but judicial accountability cannot usually reach them, and rarely even tries. Both Zalaquett (1995a) and Huntington (1995) note that justice measures typically cover only a small percentage of the multiple ways in which authoritarian regimes infringed constitutional, legal, democratic, or moral boundaries in seizing and exercising power: "authoritarian regimes were prosecuted not because they killed constitutional democracy but because they killed individual people" (Huntington 1995, 66).

Zalaquett (1995a) highlights one important corollary of this fact: institutional-level sanctions are rare even where judicial accountability is pursued. This is because accountability principally uses the avenue of criminal law, designed to establish and sanction individual rather than collective guilt. Evidently state repression is much more than the sum of individual criminal acts, and indeed truth-telling initiatives often emphasize the need to expose the systematic, institutional nature of authoritarian repression. But efforts based on criminal law can only provide verdicts about individual responsibilities. Thus even where prosecutions have been carried out, institutions can continue to deny that repression was ever systematic policy, attributing HRVs instead to the "aberrant acts" of particular individuals (see Malamud-Goti 1995, 197–99). Where prosecutions are selective or symbolic, as in practice

---

19. Huntington (1991, 116) suggests that outgoing military regimes always seek, and often obtain, two crucial guarantees. One: securing continued autonomy for the military as an institution. Two: impunity—"no prosecution, punishment or other retaliatory measure against military officers for any acts they may have committed while in power."

20. Such bodies include the International Criminal Tribunal for the former Yugoslavia (ICTY), established by the UN Security Council in 1993; and the International Criminal Tribunal for Rwanda (ICTR), established in November 1994 in response to a request from that country's government. These constitute the first international criminal tribunals since the post-WWII Nuremberg and Tokyo trials.

they almost always are where violence was widespread, some have therefore argued that higher-ranking officials rather than low-level agents should be prosecuted in order to maintain the focus on state policy and responsibility. This can present practical difficulties, however: evidence of the direct participation of commanders in specific criminal acts can be elusive. Responses have included the use of conspiracy charges as well as "command responsibility" prosecutions,[21] both devices employed at Nuremberg. Seils, however, recommends a slightly different strategy: the prosecution of "illustrative" rather than "paradigmatic" cases, by which he means those that demonstrate the pattern of violations rather than focusing solely on high-profile incidents, victims, or perpetrators (2003, 22–23).

LEGAL CONSIDERATIONS

Where initial judicial accountability seems feasible, accountability strategies must not only define who is to be prosecuted and for what, but also establish the legal framework within which to prosecute. Distinguishing the morally censurable from the legally actionable is a complex task, and extant national law at the time of transition does not always provide a sufficient basis. The alternatives for states pursuing accountability are fourfold. They may, first, invent entirely novel judicial frameworks for "special prosecutions"; second, focus on infringements of basic constitutional guarantees; third, prosecute domestically via the direct national application of international human rights standards and legislation; or, fourth, allow international tribunals to do so.

Each alternative presents problems. The first risks perpetuating a kind of legal exceptionalism more commonly associated with the authoritarian period itself. Teitel has critically examined what she calls "transitional jurisprudence," the hybrid justice principles and practices often produced by attempts to transform repressive legacies (1997, 2010–14). Elsewhere she spells out precisely why these practices often prove wholly unsatisfactory for long-term democratic prospects: "the jurisprudence of these periods does not follow . . . core principles of legality . . . the very essence of the rule of law in ordinary times" (Teitel 2000, 215). Perhaps paradoxically, then, the more quickly basic principles of democratic legality are restored in the judicial system, the less room may be left for discretionary "political trials," even

---

21. Essentially, those that hold a commanding officer responsible for what he or she reasonably "ought to have" known or done about the actions of subordinates.

of former authoritarians.[22] The second alternative, reliance on constitutional guarantees, is problematic since even where such guarantees previously existed they rarely survived authoritarian periods unscathed. Some authoritarian regimes actively exploited the selective suspension of constitutionally mandated fundamental rights via states of exception, or engineered entirely new constitutions to provide a veneer of legality for repression. The status given by subsequent democratic administrations to laws passed or modified by authoritarian regimes has therefore become a key question in accountability debates.

As regards the third alternative, international human rights law does not always provide specific bases for domestic prosecutions, and international treaties do not necessarily commit states to undertake criminal prosecutions in fulfillment of their obligations.[23] At most, international treaties provide general principles of a duty to punish breaches of core rights, together with the understanding that certain acts ought not to be amnestied nor subject to statutes of limitation.[24] One major innovation of the Nuremberg trials was to establish the principle that individuals, rather than only states, had duties under international law and could therefore be held criminally liable for violations. Most domestic criminal justice systems do not, however, permit the direct national prosecution and penalizing of these "international crimes"— except insofar as these or some equivalent have been expressly incorporated into national criminal codes. Thus, "where international law is invoked in a [domestic] criminal setting, it is often used for its norm-establishing and reaffirming value rather than as a basis for the precise statutory definitions required for valid criminal conviction" (Roht-Arriaza 1995, 295).

22. See Osiel (2000a, 59–78) and de Brito (2001, 325) for discussion of trials as a form of "public political theatre," a concept that perhaps brings us uncomfortably close to the notion of the show trial.

23. Treaties vary on this point. For example, the Torture Convention of 1987 commits a state party to spelling out "offenses under its criminal law . . . punishable by appropriate penalties." The term "appropriate penalties" is, however, open to interpretation and in some views it does not automatically preclude amnesty. See the Convention Against Torture and Other Cruel, Inhuman, or Degrading Treatment or Punishment, UN General Assembly Resolution 39/46, UN Document A/39/51 (1984), entered into force 26 June 1987; and Zalaquett's discussion of it (1995a).

24. To encourage the prompt prosecution of offenders, most legal systems discourage delay or inaction by the device known as "prescription" or "statute of limitation." This stipulates that the possibility of legal action is forfeited once a certain period of time has elapsed after the commission or discovery of the offense. In relation to HRVs, however, international treaty law specifies that those which constitute internationally defined offenses can be neither prescribed nor amnestied. These kinds of treaty undertakings have been central to many post hoc challenges to transitional impunity.

Later transitional experiences do give some grounds for concluding that individual states are growing readier to admit international law commitments into the transitional policy mix. In particular, Guatemala's 1996 amnesty law explicitly reserved the prerogative and duty to prosecute internationally stipulated categories of HRV.[25] Roht-Arriaza (1995) suggests that the apparent aversion of states to the internationalization of accountability hides a gradual process of "norm creation and diffusion," which has increased the domestic salience of international standards. She gives various examples of national interpretations and legislation clearly influenced by, or indeed created specifically to implement, relevant international treaties. But international law has to date much more often been invoked by private accountability actors bringing post facto challenges to limited transitional accountability policies than by states wishing to reverse or limit impunity.

As regards the fourth alternative, the international tribunals for Rwanda and the former Yugoslavia and early International Criminal Court (ICC) prosecutions present perhaps the only modern examples of accountability based on the direct application of international law in an international setting. States have been notably reluctant to abdicate the right of sovereign decision-making on the accountability question to third parties, even where they have accepted intervention in other parts of the transition process.[26] The changing international political and legal climate over time has influenced both the formulation and durability of initial state accountability policy, with blanket amnesty laws increasingly outmoded.[27] The Latin American transitions considered here, however, mostly took place during a period when transitional justice decisions were still considered an essentially internal matter,

25. The South African government's Promotion of National Unity and Reconciliation Act no. 34 of 1995 declared a prima facie commitment to abide by international law in its truth commission process. Peruvian judges resoundingly rejected Fujimori-era attempts at self-amnesty in 2001, citing an Inter-American Court of Human Rights decision (the "Barrios Altos" case). The Peruvian truth commission, concluded in 2003, dealt extensively with the juridical dimension of HRVs from both national and international law perspectives (see the truth commission's final report, CVR [2003a], especially tomo 1, capítulo 4).

26. The UN, for example, played a key role as external broker of peace negotiations in El Salvador and Guatemala.

27. See table 1 for evidence of this in Guatemala and Peru. See Burke-White (2001) on the evolution of international law and practice concerning amnesty. Falk (2000) and Brysk (2002b) also trace how human rights discourse, specifically, has generated pressures for more effective suprastate enforcement mechanisms. Sands (2003a) and Charney (1999) discuss the impact on state sovereignty of developments in international criminal law, from the Nuremberg trials through the 1998 Pinochet prosecution and the 1999 Rome statute leading to the 2001 establishment of the ICC.

unfettered by largely unenforced international restrictions on the scope or legitimacy of domestic amnesty.

Conclusions

Méndez concludes that by the late 1990s, the new international context had sparked an urgent need to reexamine transition-bound theories of accountability. Such theories were—perhaps legitimately, given their context—"heavy on the political constraint side" (Méndez 1997, 258), tending to emphasize the obstacles to accountability. Much transitional justice literature was produced in the immediate wake of particular transitional experiences, responding to a desire to find practical solutions to a host of urgent governance dilemmas. One result was a perhaps undue sense of urgency, and a short-term perspective that contributed to efforts to "seal off" the accountability issue at or near transition. Two assumptions were commonly made that, when combined, proved fatal to accountability prospects. One was that authoritarian resistance and limited institutional capacity severely constrained initial policy options. The other was that, notwithstanding these constraints, new governments must act at once to carry out transitional justice measures.[28] Thus transitional governments were encouraged to act quickly and definitively, precisely at a time when their freedom of operation was in some cases extremely restricted. Where the outcome of this early action was amnesty, it became particularly difficult to envisage future high-level policy change (see chap. 2).

In sum, a general review of transitional justice theory and practice in Latin America in the 1980s and early 1990s suggests that transitional justice settlements close to transition itself usually privileged truth over justice, and institutionalized impunity. Settlements generally focused on what the state, rather than private actors, should do about HRVs committed by previous regimes. Although reconciliation was often recognized as a long-term goal, truth and justice were regarded as urgent issues that could and should be definitively resolved by immediate measures: in practice, by some combination of

---

28. See Hayner (2001) and particularly Roht-Arriaza (1995, 282): "A basic paradox of all measures against impunity is that such measures must be put into effect relatively quickly, before the new government loses the widespread legitimacy it enjoys . . . [and] before the old guard can reorganize. . . . At most, the window is usually about a year." The assumption that incoming governments enjoy a "grace period" after which resistance rises is questionable. Even where true, however, it would therefore seem particularly unwise or unnecessary to apply amnesty during this period.

truth-telling and amnesty. A perhaps excessive pessimism about the fragility of new democracies, together with reservations about the capacity of weak judicial structures to deliver justice via criminal prosecution, meant that amnesty was used to actively restrict or foreclose prosecutions. International norms restricting the possible scope and applicability of domestic amnesty legislation were largely ignored. There was a clear, and in some cases mistaken, expectation that the introduction or perpetuation of amnesty would lay to rest once and for all the question of judicial accountability for past HRVs.

2

POST-TRANSITIONAL JUSTICE

The resurgence of attempted claim-making over past HRVs in the late 1990s calls into question some of the central tenets of the transitional justice school, in particular the expectation of definitive closure of the accountability question by amnesty. Events, as much as theory, suggest the need for a new conceptual approach if recent developments in the region are to be adequately understood. The accountability impulse has proved remarkably resilient, resurfacing in different forms and with new agents after its arguably premature foreclosure in many initial transitional experiences. This chapter therefore sets out the possible components of what is termed here "post-transitional justice," contrasting it with the transitional justice school examined in the previous chapter.

It is proposed here that it is now both necessary and useful to think and theorize in terms of "post-transitional justice," involving the subsequent revisiting of transition-era human rights settlements. Under this model, the persistence of the justice question into the post-transitional period, or periodic "re-irruptions"[1] of it in the form of renewed accountability pressure, can be viewed as positive signs of democratic institutional health rather than as crises or breakdowns of transition. It is not only conceivable but logical to expect that private actors and even future democratic governments might pursue accountability more vigorously than transitional administrations.[2] As noted above, accountability through prosecutions is the transitional justice measure least often applied by the state at the point of transition. This means that

---

1. See Wilde (1999), and below.
2. Although in practice private actions have been in the majority. Political will has proved scarce, with the notable exception of Argentina from 2003. See below.

post-transitional challenges to earlier settlements, where they arise, generally focus on accountability as the least complete and therefore most contested element of the truth, justice, and reconciliation triad. Where initial state decisions have included the closing off of future justice claims by amnesty, however, future reversal of an initial anti-prosecution policy is made extremely difficult (see below). The nature and status of transitional amnesty provisions therefore become central to contestation over justice in the post-transitional period.

Characteristics of Post-transitional Justice

Post-transitional justice activity, in the form of continued or renewed contestation over accountability for past HRVs, can be observed in a number of present-day post-transitional settings in Latin America. Six characteristics of post-transitional justice distinguish it clearly from the transitional justice school of thought and practice analyzed in the preceding chapter. First, where transitional justice is centrally concerned with attaining and preserving the minimum institutional requirements of formal democracy, post-transitional justice focuses on subsequent questions of the quality, reach, and perfectibility of that democracy. Second, post-transitional justice accordingly questions the comprehensiveness and sufficiency of initial transitional justice compromises, particularly the renunciation of prosecution over HRVs. Third, since most subsequent administrations have regarded official renunciations of prosecution as irrevocable, post-transitional justice has been largely non-state, driven by private actors operating both "above" and "below" the state. Fourth, when contrasted with state-driven transitional policymaking, post-transitional justice is notably multi-sited, multi-actor, and multi-referential. A multiplicity of forms and sites can be used, depending on such factors as actor expertise, goals, resource access, and perceptions of likely success. Fifth, this multiplication of potential forms, sites, and actors means that post-transitional justice initiatives come to be adopted in pursuit of a wide variety of possibly divergent aims. Sixth: post-transitional justice activity is empirically more likely than transitional justice policymaking to have an "internationalized" character, encompassing norms and sites of contestation beyond the domestic sphere.[3]

---

3. Prior to 1996, transitional justice settlements virtually never incorporated restrictions proceeding from international norms, activism, or intervention. Teitel (2003, 88) nonetheless describes a late twentieth-century trend toward both "privatization" and "globalization" as the justice question was revisited.

What Has Changed? The Relationship Between Transitional and Post-transitional Justice Models

The transitional justice school clearly set out the exceptional context and corresponding limitations on what could be done about accountability in early periods. What it failed to address was the question of for how long those special conditions could be expected to obtain. In practice, most post-transitional periods saw substantial change to many of the objective conditions that had previously been considered to make accountability impossible or unwise. No Latin American transition succumbed to the threat of authoritarian reversal. Although the quality of subsequent democratic evolution has certainly been uneven, in no case can it be argued that old-guard military influence over civilian politics is undiminished, or that judicial structures are as beholden to authoritarian principles as they were in the past. This gradual internal evolution toward democracy, together with evolving international principles and practice mostly working against impunity, suggest that the passage of time can in fact improve accountability prospects. At the theoretical level, most of the initial obstacles to prosecution—fragility of democratic structures, lack of judicial capacity, military resistance—can be expected to diminish over time, as other transitional justice and democratization measures take effect. The mooted benefits of prosecution, on the other hand, largely retain their validity over time,[4] as do the duties under international law that require it. More recent transitional justice scholarship has itself begun to recognize the inadequacies of previous suppositions, reflecting a sense that something new and unexpected is emerging.[5]

Given the characteristics identified above, certain dimensions of post-transition polities can be expected to particularly affect the emergence of post-transitional justice activity. One is the quality and depth of subsequent democratization, particularly progress toward rule of law. The health and vigor of civil society organization in general and its ability to access the justice system, in particular, will also be relevant. The existence or absence of explicitly pro-accountability groups who are numerous, strong, or supported by political will or tactical national or international alliances is clearly significant. The extent to which such groups, where they exist, coordinate methods

---

4. The obvious exceptions are those that portray prosecution as an essential component of the initial securing of democracy.

5. See, inter alia, Roht-Arriaza and Mariezcurrena (2006), Elster (2004), and Teitel (2003).

and aims, or at least do not act at cross-purposes, must also be considered. The passage of time is a factor that can have varied and sometimes counter-intuitive effects. It may seem set to eventually consign the memory of victims and the concerns of survivors to irrelevance or even oblivion, but a look at the currently observable cases of post-transitional justice change suggests that other outcomes are also possible. The passage of time can serve to make the addressing of accountability more possible, perhaps less politically costly, even as it sometimes reduces both the personal (victim/survivor) and institutional (social) benefits. Late justice is not, in such matters, of equal value to its more timely equivalent.[6] Finally, as suggested above, the legal and legislative frameworks surrounding impunity, and the prospects for changing these, are crucial if anything new is to happen. Is amnesty explicit, how is it framed, and how easy is it to challenge? Is there constitutional, judicial, international-legal, or public opinion support for any such challenge?

Thinking About Post-transitional Justice

The remainder of this chapter identifies the main theoretical and scholarly approaches that can provide insights into the interplay of these dimensions in democratizing societies, with a particular focus on Latin America. The goal is to signal main thematic areas in post-transitional justice in the region, and to identify useful conceptual tools for its study. The interaction of national, regional, and international layers and spaces is also examined, and the preference for a national vantage point from which to view these eventually reaffirmed.

This book draws on a number of distinct and overlapping literatures. A globalization perspective often emphasizes the role of external factors in changing accountability outcomes. Transnational networks and "global civil society" are identified as key actors.[7] Accountability change is treated as one symptom of an emerging global human rights regime, challenging the traditional model of an international system composed of sovereign states and driven by state-led diplomacy. Scholars have put forward models such as

---

6. See Collins cited in Brett (2009). Research currently in progress on the human costs and lived experience of late prosecutions will address this point in more depth.

7. See, inter alia, Keck and Sikkink (1998), Risse, Ropp and Sikkink (1999), Burgerman (2001), Lutz and Sikkink (2001), Brysk (2002a), and Sugarman (2001a).

the "boomerang effect"[8] or the "justice cascade"[9] to describe mechanisms by which international human rights norms are imposed on states; by external activists, institutions, or governments acting "outside" and "above" the state in question; or by domestic activists. It is supposed that the latter, finding themselves unable to significantly affect state practices, ask like-minded outside actors to apply pressure to national authorities on their behalf. Such analyses accordingly tend to claim a central role for global civil society networks, which, it is said, promote and activate universal human rights norms using supra-state enforcement mechanisms.

It is certainly true that recent challenges to the principle and practice of domestic amnesty for past human rights violations have increasingly used external, including international, norms and settings to challenge justice compromises established during transition periods. Since internationalized accountability action has, as yet, no dedicated forum of its own,[10] however, it continues to operate through national courts (Sugarman 2001b, 941–42). These may be the courts of the state where the events took place, or they may be those of another country ("transnational" civil or criminal cases).[11] Even transnational cases, however, tend to return the issues to national settings: indeed, it has been suggested that their most significant impact to date has been in catalyzing new action from national judiciaries—the "Garzón effect."[12] Some even argue that this is precisely the aim of many such cases, driven by domestic actors reaching "around" blocked domestic judicial structures to provoke national change. Others claim that more complex alliances of national and extra-national activists now undertake accountability claims simultaneously at a multiplicity of sites and levels. Attempts to isolate or quantify the exact relative weightings of nationally or internationally driven change in this new accountability scenario are likely to founder in view of these increasingly fluid, and complex, interrelations between actors and sites.

Legal scholars, too, have attended to recent developments in the area of accountability for past HRVs. The growing incidence of universal

---

8. Keck and Sikkink (1998).

9. Lutz and Sikkink (2001).

10. As is well-known, the mandate of the ICC specifically prevents it from acting over crimes committed before its formal inception in July 2002.

11. As defined by Roht-Arriaza (2001, 40): "legal actions brought in the national courts of one country against civil or criminal defendants based elsewhere . . . rais[ing] the possibility of simultaneous [accountability] action in multiple arenas."

12. After Spanish "superjudge" Baltazar Garzón, responsible for Pinochet's 1998 arrest. See Brett (2009).

jurisdiction cases has been seen as one expression of an increasingly frontier-free, globalized justice system that finds its maximum expression in the 2002 establishment of the ICC.[13] From this perspective, the 1998 detention and attempted extradition of former Chilean dictator Augusto Pinochet for gross HRVs is often treated as the high water mark of global justice. There is, indeed, much force in the contention that efforts to prosecute Pinochet in Spain had a precedent-setting impact on international law over sovereign immunity, and a catalyzing effect on the subsequent bringing of similar cases worldwide. The "Pinochet effect,"[14] understood as ripples sent out by his 1998 arrest, certainly exists in many settings. Its manifestations, however, include a drawing back from the brink that has seen universal jurisdiction provisions actually narrowed in some European countries. In looking for its domestic impact, moreover, there is a danger of confusing sequence with cause, erroneously supposing that all accountability change in Chile after October 1998 happened "because of" Pinochet's arrest.[15] This book adopts a more agnostic approach to claims that transnational factors drive national events, be it in legal activism, government policy, or judicial performance. Accordingly, it argues that the mere existence of transnational legal cases does not necessarily signal a "justice cascade" or "boomerang effect" such as those outlined above.

Tracing the domestic evolution of accountability issues at and since transition is, it is suggested, an alternative vantage point from which to view the Pinochet case and others like it. There is no a priori intention to assert that domestic activity, or the lack of it, always trumps transnational activism or global norm change. Rather, it is proposed, the interaction of domestic actors with local judicial institutions provides a delimited and accessible field of inquiry within which elements of change and continuity over time can be identified. Transnationalized cases can then be viewed as part of a succession or trajectory of accountability events in specific settings. Their impact and incorporation within these settings is shaped by prior and parallel engagements with accountability issues at the national level, particularly by domestic human rights organizations. Where transnational network agency does exist, detailed study of domestic (national) contexts will discover it by

---

13. See Mertus (1999), Orentlicher (2002, 2003), Sands (2003b), Macedo (2003), and Dezalay and Garth (2003a).

14. See Roht-Arriaza (2005) and Brett (2009).

15. See particularly Golob (2002a, 2002b, 2003), Davis (2003b), and Orentlicher (2002, 56). See Brett (2009) for a corrective.

detecting the domestic "ends" of these networks. This in turn will allow for informed conclusions about the existence and density of such networks and their contribution to accountability change in particular settings. Adopting a domestic perspective also allows us to identify dual and multiple pathways and directions of interaction, since attention to domestic accountability histories quickly shows that "internationalized" incidents and legal cases are not a preserve of the recent period.

Close attention to the domestic setting means that the receptivity of national institutions to accountability claims—and, indeed, to other legally framed justice questions—becomes paramount. How does the quality of transitional institutions affect accountability trajectories? What is the role of later institutional change? Democratization theorists and "rule of law" scholars have studied the broad processes of institutional judicial reform undertaken by many Latin American states in the 1990s. Judicial performance in safeguarding and promoting individual rights in general, and international human rights standards in particular, has been suggested as one possible marker of judicial "liberalism" or "modernization."[16] But the particular place of accountability actions in this canon is rarely given sustained attention.[17] In general, the indicators and constituents of democratic rule of law, on the one hand, and progressive judicial change, on the other, are highly contested and poorly understood.[18] These debates and related policy measures are of concern here only insofar as they have shaped the context of citizen interaction with courts, and are traceable in the approach of judicial institutions to private accountability activity.

Amnesty

Amnesty, the suspension or renunciation by the state of its prerogative—some would say its duty—to investigate or sanction crimes was a major component of transitional justice policy in most Latin American transitions of the 1980s and 1990s (see chap. 1, table 1). While these amnesty laws proved in

16. See, for example, Domingo and Sieder (2001, 155) and Prillaman (2000).

17. Although Ruti Teitel, a transitional justice theorist, has done more than most to raise questions about the relationship between transitional exceptionalism and later rule of law. See particularly Teitel (2003).

18. See Dakolias (1996), Hammergren (1998a, 1998b, 2007), Domingo and Sieder (2001), and Hilbink (2007).

the long term not to be a watertight seal on the judicial accountability issue, they did represent the supposedly definitive state position on the question of prosecutions. The perpetuation or introduction of amnesty legislation represents, in this sense, the endpoint of transitional justice policy. Accordingly, it usually constitutes an obligatory referent or departure point for any post-transitional justice activity, which must address the legitimacy and validity of existing amnesty. An overview of the scope of domestic amnesty norms is therefore indispensable for understanding post-transitional justice developments in specific settings.[19]

The shape of amnesty legislation owes much to the kind of policy bargaining that surrounded transitions to democracy. Some legislative decisions, particularly the Chilean and Uruguayan, were directly attributable to the high bargaining strength of the outgoing regime.[20] In El Salvador and Guatemala, amnesty was agreed to in principle by both sides as part of peace negotiations leading to the cessation of armed hostilities. In Argentina, the eventual adoption of amnesty represented an almost complete policy reversal, sparked largely by military reaction against the vigorous accountability activity initially pursued. The fact that amnesty was the eventual outcome of transitional justice policy in each of these very different transition settings, however, suggests that the initial bargaining power of outgoing regimes was not the only consideration. Prevailing domestic and international assessments of amnesty's utility as a necessary, or the inevitable, price of peace or regime change also favored its adoption.

In contrast to transitional justice "inventions" such as the truth commission, amnesty has a long legal and political pedigree. Zalaquett (1995a and 1999a) draws attention to the latitude that international law provides for amnesty as a way to close chapters of insurrection or political violence,[21] or to persuade former authoritarians to hand over power. The Second Additional Protocol to the 1949 Geneva Conventions is often also cited to legitimate the principle: "At the end of hostilities the authorities in power shall endeavor to

19. What follows is a consideration of the general legal and conceptual issues surrounding Latin American amnesty legislation. The titles, dates, and principal features of the relevant legislation for each of the transitions discussed to date are set out in chapter 1, table 1, while chapters 4 and 6 will discuss the Chilean and Salvadorean amnesty provisions in more depth.

20. See Huntington (1991, 116–17) on the negotiation of "exit guarantees."

21. Amnesty can therefore play a genuine role in persuading non-state combatants to renounce arms by reducing the threat of retribution. See chapter 6 for examples from El Salvador. Chile also used partial amnesties to allow the release of political prisoners and return of exiles during the dictatorship.

grant the broadest possible amnesty to persons who have participated in the armed conflict, or those deprived of their liberty for reasons relating to the armed conflict."[22]

Burke-White 2001 describes a range of prevailing attitudes toward the principle and practice of amnesty. Retributive justice theorists "have argued that amnesty laws are per se invalid"; supporters of amnesty argue that "states have a right to grant [it] . . . on the grounds of state sovereignty"; while others take a pragmatic line, "finding amnesty valid when it leads to expedient political transitions" (Burke-White 2001, 468). Burke-White himself argues that amnesty should as a rule comply with domestic constitutional law as well as international obligations (467). The means, as well as the motives, of amnesty introduction seem to matter: amnesties introduced by democratically elected administrations tend to attract less censure. Thus the apparent political legitimacy of El Salvador's 1993 amnesty law is undoubtedly enhanced by the fact that an elected legislative chamber passed it,[23] while the credentials of the relevant Uruguayan legislation were boosted through submission to a national plebiscite.

The details of the categories of person and acts to which amnesty will apply are also relevant. Amnesties offered by states to former opponents are, says Roht-Arriaza, generally accepted (1995, 57). On the other hand, "self-amnesties," introduced by authorities in bad faith partly or wholly to protect themselves against sanctions for their own behavior, are widely regarded as illegitimate. Laws introduced by the Fujimori regime in Peru in 1995 were later overturned on precisely these grounds (see below). In practice, however, Latin American transitional amnesties to date have largely been for the benefit of former or serving state agents, even where the principles adduced for their adoption have suggested a more evenhanded intent.[24]

22. From Article 6(5). The principle is clearly operative for El Salvador and Guatemala. In other settings, including Chile, regimes often invoked the fiction of internal armed conflict to justify repressive strategies. In general, present-day accountability actors adamantly reject this "internal war" thesis. Some, however, have effectively accepted it as a legal fiction. They point out that it in turn imposes international legal duties, since the Geneva Conventions and the relevant protocols were designed to extend, rather than reduce, international legal protections into the arena of internal conflict.

23. Even though it arguably contains elements of "self-amnesty" (see below), having been introduced by the same political administration that had been in power before transition. This fact eventually became the basis for a partly successful domestic legal challenge (see chap. 6).

24. Not least because in all cases except Peru, official truth commissions found that state agents had been responsible for the overwhelming majority of fatal violence.

Amnesty and International Law

At the international level, a particular set of exclusions restricts the scope of legitimate amnesty. These include those HRVs that have been defined and specified in treaty law as international offenses for which an absolute obligation to prosecute or punish is stipulated. At the domestic level, constitutional protections of fundamental rights and physical integrity, plus provisions that establish the right of victims of crime to judicial redress, can and have been invoked to question the prima facie constitutionality of amnesty laws as well as their application to particularly grave crimes, including extrajudicial execution and torture.

Some relevant international treaty obligations, notably the 1987 Torture Convention, postdate the adoption of amnesty in certain of the Latin American transitional cases considered here. Orentlicher, however, claims that international restrictions on amnesty have always been more stringent than was generally understood by transition scholars and policymakers (1991b, 2540n6). Certainly many of the international obligations invoked in both past and recent challenges to amnesty predate all or most of the amnesty laws here considered. Examples include the 1948 Convention on the Punishment and Prosecution of the Crime of Genocide ("Genocide Convention"), which entered into force in 1951, the four Geneva Conventions of 1949 and their Protocols of 1978, and the American Convention on Human Rights of 1978. Roht-Arriaza likewise observes that national policymaking and even international peacemaking interventions prioritized sovereign discretion: "little or no reference [was made to] . . . norms of international law," even those unambiguously spelled out in treaties already ratified by the relevant state (1995, 295).

Although on-the-ground enforcement is always patchy, as far back as the early 1990s Orentlicher noted and welcomed a trend toward greater textual specificity in human rights instruments. In particular a duty to punish, rather than only to investigate, was more often stipulated. In effect, the application of domestic amnesty to internationally defined HRVs was gradually ruled out: "At the policy level, the international human rights community has moved from a widely-shared position of deference to the judgements of transitional governments to a generally assertive stance opposing whole-scale impunity" (Orentlicher 1993, 250; see also 1991b). The region does provide some evidence of increased observance of these international legal restrictions in newly arising amnesty choices: the 1996 Guatemalan law recognizes international exemptions, post-2000 Peru (and later, Paraguay) refused to institutionalize amnesty at all, and recent Colombian amnesty efforts were challenged and in some important senses reversed by the country's Constitutional Court. Regional and international trends toward limitation came mostly too late, however, to noticeably shape the content of amnesty in early Latin American transitions.

As regards the retrospective effect of the changing regional or international climate on amnesties already in place, Popkin and Bhuta were generally pessimistic. Although regional mechanisms—in this case the Inter-American Court and Inter-American Commission on Human Rights—consistently questioned the validity of domestic amnesties as drafted, Popkin and Bhuta pointed out that "no amnesty law has been overturned because the [Inter-American] Commission found it incompatible with the provisions of the American Convention on Human Rights" (1999, 102). This assertion has nonetheless since been superseded in Peru, where an April 2001 verdict of the Inter-American Court in the "Barrios Altos" case was taken up with some alacrity by courts and prosecutors to rule Fujimori's 1995 self-amnesty provisions as without legal effect. The Barrios Altos verdict has also begun to be cited by some national judges as one reason to find against domestic impunity, as in Argentina from 2001; while a similar, specific verdict against Chile in 2006 elicited at least the promise of change to bring domestic legislation in line with regional jurisprudence.[25]

Challenges to Amnesty

Most national courts are still reluctant to completely disregard existing amnesty legislation. Nonetheless, the contention that international law rules out amnesty for certain categories of crime has increasingly become a feature of post-transitional justice claims in both national and extra-national legal fora. Nationally, civil cases have tested whether amnesty can foreclose civil as well as criminal liability. Some national courts have shown signs of a greater readiness to use judicial investigation to at least discover facts, shifting the point of application of domestic amnesty to the end rather than the beginning of the judicial process.[26]

---

25. The 2006 "Almonacid" verdict of the Inter-American Court on Human Rights. See chapter 5.
26. See chapter 5 for examples from Chile.

Internationally, Popkin and Bhuta (1999) further point to the October 1998 Pinochet arrest as exemplifying a separate and increasingly significant transnational aspect to the debate: must the courts of another country respect domestic amnesties? The principle of territoriality of law suggests not, and increasingly criminal or civil charges brought in another country seek to elude or challenge the invocation of amnesty in the country where the violations took place. Sugarman (2002) and Roht-Arriaza and Jessberger, quoted in Brett (2009), list cases in the courts of Spain, Senegal, Belgium, the Netherlands, and elsewhere that have not only passively criticized but also openly disregarded other countries' transitional amnesty settlements. A separate but related development is the domestic prosecution of extraterritorial crimes. While countries routinely amnesty state agents for crimes committed on the national territory, there is no guarantee that even home courts can extend this amnesty to acts carried out in neighboring countries.[27] There is, then, evidence to suggest that the efficacy of amnesty in sealing off prosecution for past repressive crimes has been dramatically reduced, at both domestic and international levels, since the late 1990s. This development raises important questions, central to the principal concerns of this book, about the dynamic relationship among domestic petitioners, international norms and actors, and national courts in domestic post-transitional accountability settings.

Amnesty challenges have to date almost never originated from within successor governments.[28] Reluctance is often dictated by consideration of the political costs of dismantling complex and often-controversial transitional bargains. Additionally, legal and political obstacles to the retrospective application of a change in law limit the real, as opposed to symbolic, impact of

27. Investigations in several Southern Cone countries into the activities of Operación Cóndor, a region-wide collaboration among repressive security forces, have not only produced extradition requests from investigating countries for former security agents who are nationals of other states, but have also triggered domestic investigations and charges against those same agents in their home states. The signs are that, in keeping with the principle of territoriality, domestic amnesty is not being granted for crimes committed in another territory. Daniel Martorell, interview 23 April 2003; and see Dinges (2004).

28. The only apparent exception to date is Argentina, where in July 2003 President Nestor Kirchner overturned an anti-extradition decree imposed by his predecessor to protect military officers affected by transnational prosecution attempts. In August of the same year, the executive sponsored the annulment of the 1986 and 1987 amnesty provisions—with, uniquely, retroactive effect. The move nonetheless followed previous judicial findings of illegality plus a successful 1998 derogation vote, developments in turn attributable to renewed civil society activism on the issue since the mid-1990s.

overturning amnesty in a legislative forum (see below). Even where political will exists, governmental policy change in this, a legal area, is subject to the acquiescence or cooperation of the judicial branch. Thus the "state position" or "government position" over amnesty, even at a fixed point in time, must often be disaggregated to specify what actions and attitudes are discernible in different branches of government regarding the principle, practice, and future of amnesty. Perhaps unsurprisingly, though, post-transitional challenges to amnesty have in practice been driven predominantly by private actors, both national and—increasingly—external.[29]

Most recent domestic and international developments in post-transitional accountability, significant as they have been, have depended on exploitation of exceptions to or "loopholes" in amnesty legislation, rather than successful reversal or overturning of its provisions. Retrospective in-country challenges to existing domestic amnesty have taken two main paths. One approach is to directly challenge the legitimacy, usually constitutionality, of the amnesty when compared with internal or international norms that either directly impose a duty to prosecute or guarantee access to redress and justice for victims and survivors. These efforts have generally been unsuccessful. Alternatively, a case-by-case path has been attempted. This does not address itself directly to the general principle of amnesty, but rather exploits and tries to enlarge loopholes in and exceptions to it. So it may be argued that certain acts constitute exceptions as specified within the law itself, or that they constitute internationally defined violations that are exempt from amnesty under international human rights treaty law. This cumulative approach to narrowing the sphere of influence of amnesty seems to have had more success to date than efforts to undermine the principle entirely.[30]

29. Although the judicial branches or prosecutorial agencies of other states have sometimes initiated new activity in specific cases. See, for instance, chapters 4 and 5 for discussion of the Prats and Letelier assassinations, where the overseas deaths of Chilean victims were initially prosecuted outside Chile. The momentum of subsequent investigations was sustained, however, not by the Argentine or U.S. states, but by the adherence of private actors, including relatives. Sofia Prats, interview 7 February 2003; Fabiola Letelier, interview 21 January 2003.

30. This is particularly clear in Chile; see chapter 5. Only in Argentina has a judge taken up an exceptionalist argument in a way that clearly sought to broaden its impact. In 2001, federal judge Gabriel Cavallo made a paradigmatic case ruling asserting the per se nullity and unconstitutionality of the Argentine amnesty provisions (Poblete-Hlaczik case, ref. 8686/2000, copy on file with author, and see http://www.cels.org.ar/documentos/?info=detalledoc&ids=3&lang=es&ss=&idc=592). The Uruguayan Supreme Court similarly ruled the country's amnesty law unconstitutional in October 2009, but the scope of the ruling was at least initially limited to the case in which it was made.

In part, this state of affairs proceeds from the internal logic of amnesty as a political act—of legislatures or executives—that takes effect, however, principally in the legal terrain. There is considerable legal uncertainty over the eventual impact of a wholesale reversal of domestic amnesty on the national prosecution of past crimes. Indeed it could be argued that there is limited utility or practical effect to be gained from overturning or annulling amnesty per se. Even a case-by-case approach confronts real obstacles to reversing the effect of amnesty once granted for a particular crime. Investigations that have been closed under its provisions can only with great difficulty be reopened, and individuals who have benefited from it can even more rarely be brought back within the reach of domestic judicial prosecution. The commonplace legal provisions of *non bis in idem*—that a person cannot be tried twice for the same crime—and of the application of the law most favorable to a defendant where laws change or appear to contradict, are just two of the specific legal obstacles to reversing an amnesty once it is in place. These and other legal obstacles that have arisen in particular post-transitional accountability initiatives will be addressed in detail in subsequent chapters, as will the strategies adopted by private pro-accountability actors attempting to overcome them.

Conclusions

The introduction of amnesty was itself a powerful symbolic blow to the justice pretensions of potential or already-existing private accountability actors, such as human rights groups and survivors, particularly when it was imposed by democratic governments of whom such groups often had high hopes. Since accountability was usually regarded at transition as exclusively a high-level political prerogative, with new executives and legislatures alone able to instigate or prevent prosecutions, amnesty legislation had a substantial dampening effect even on private accountability activity. But the strong early sense of disillusion reported by many private actors served in some cases to fuel later legal challenges. Since amnesty typically exhausted or reduced the relative utility of political channels, it pushed any further pursuit of accountability into the judicial realm. Thus amnesty paradoxically judicialized accountability even while it seemed to rule out or severely restrict the pursuit of justice via the courts.

In sum, as we have seen in chapter 1, transitional justice theory and practice generally treated accountability as an exclusionary, state-led concern.

Potential justice actions were accordingly supposed to have been exhausted by what states chose to do in the period immediately after regime change: state-sponsored criminal prosecutions or, more commonly, amnesty. Few subsequent administrations substantially revisited initial transitional justice settlements of their own volition. The center of gravity for judicial accountability in the post-transitional period thus shifted to the private sphere and, additionally, to the legal setting. Private actors have become increasingly active in seeking accountability in both national and extra-national courts in the recent period. The space that domestic amnesty legislation leaves for private-actor intervention varies according to the text of the law—which, as we have seen, has largely not been open to subsequent revision—as well as to judicial interpretation and application of it, which has proved more malleable. Possible legal activism by non-state actors, on the one hand, and the attitude of the courts, on the other, therefore become central to accountability once initial policy choices have been made.[31]

---

31. Particularly since the practical effect of any government-initiated policy reversal over amnesty would always depend on judicial acquiescence.

3

STUDYING POST-TRANSITIONAL JUSTICE

In the previous chapter it was proposed that the closure of state transitional justice initiatives by amnesty gives way to post-transitional justice, a qualitatively distinct phase in the accountability debate. The present chapter sets out in more detail the theoretical and methodological approach put forward for studying post-transitional justice in national settings. It is suggested that a survey of the post-transitional trajectories of human rights organizations, combined with in-depth analysis of particular post-transitional accountability cases, is the most adequate procedure. The second part of the chapter describes in more detail the actors, sites, and dynamic relationships within and through which post-transitional justice develops and post-transitional accountability initiatives may be observed.

Research Themes in Post-transitional Justice

Accountability actors and national judiciaries have been identified as major objects of study. The term "accountability actors" refers to all individuals or bodies, domestic, external, or international, who promote judicial accountability measures in either criminal or civil form.[1] These actors are analyzed from an opportunity structures perspective. The primary research interest is in actors who have accessed or attempted to access judicial settings. Legal cases presented to domestic courts are therefore used as the prime identifier of post-transitional justice activity, although historical HROs that survived

---

1. Those who contest or oppose accountability claims, such as defendants or their representatives, will be excluded from this usage.

into the post-transitional period are also surveyed to identify what affected organizations' decisions to pursue or discount legal strategy at different times. Justice systems are approached as the principal institutional interlocutor and counterpart of accountability actors. The focus here is on their receptivity to accountability actions over time.[2] For reasons of space and scope, the impact of wide-ranging judicial reforms in many post-transitional Latin American societies is considered only with reference to those aspects most clearly identified by judicial actors, analysts, or accountability actors as of direct relevance to accountability outcomes.

As discussed in the introduction, research settings were determined with the desire to keep in view the framing issues of transitional amnesty legislation and subsequent domestic or transnationalized legal accountability activity. A single study of one national setting can permit a detailed analysis of domestic accountability activity. It does not, however, illuminate the extent to which transnational accountability activity both responds to and affects differing levels of preexisting domestic legal engagement—something only a comparative study could begin to explore. Nonetheless, the highly specific nature of transitional trade-offs and amnesty provisions means that domestic political contexts must be taken into proper account. They accordingly remain central to the exploration of post-transitional justice presented here. Meanwhile the dynamics of transnationalized accountability activity suggest a need to also attend to legal cases about—rather than those solely occurring within—a particular national territory.[3]

Chile and El Salvador were selected for both theoretical and logistical reasons as the best available, though not the only possible, combination of settings available and accessible for studying post-transitional justice. Some of the particular reasons for selection have been set out in the introduction to this volume. In addition to these, Chile displays comparatively high, although internally fluctuating, levels of domestic accountability activity, and moreover displayed often-overlooked domestic accountability change even before it was thrust back into the international spotlight by the 1998 Pinochet arrest. El

2. This without wishing to deny the extent to which actor-focused analysis of judicial opportunity structures, mobilization, goal and interest construction, and repertoire innovation might also be appropriate in a study more directly focused on the judiciary.

3. Thus cases about Chile and Chilean events have been heard in a variety of national court settings in recent years, and human rights crimes committed by Chileans on foreign soil have been the subject of court action in the United States and Argentina. Similarly, cases about events in El Salvador or involving Salvadorean plaintiffs, defendants, and victims have been heard in the United States. See chapters 5 and 7.

Salvador provides an illuminating counter-case of a setting in which legal activity could not or did not take root as a primary response to HRVs, while a recent revival of domestic accountability efforts has met with only limited success.

Both countries also provide opportunities to assess domestic perceptions of and involvement with transnationalized accountability actions prior to and during the late 1990s. In each setting, the involvement of U.S. citizens in violent incidents led to early official and private U.S. pressure for and involvement in criminal investigations.[4] A series of civil claims have recently been filed in the United States over HRVs in El Salvador, sponsored by a U.S.-based advocacy organization, the Center for Justice and Accountability (CJA).[5] Transnational criminal actions relating to Chile have included a fresh impetus in ongoing U.S. investigations into the Letelier-Moffitt murders following Pinochet's 1988 detention, plus one conviction and multiple extradition requests from Argentinian judges over the 1974 Buenos Aires assassination of General Carlos Prats—former head of the Chilean army—and his wife. The Spanish criminal investigation that produced the 1998 extradition request for Pinochet was ongoing against other defendants at the time of writing, as were criminal cases against former Chilean officers filed subsequently in several other European countries.[6]

In short, Chile and El Salvador were identified as of particular interest and suitability for researching post-transitional justice due to a combination of the shape of their internal accountability trajectories and the presence of transnational activity and interest. Correspondingly, one major object of research was to map national accountability developments over time since transition in both countries. The other main focus of inquiry was those legal cases that have been central to domestic accountability trajectories: "emblematic" cases, often attracting high levels of external involvement or attention.[7] Subsequent

4. The assassinations of U.S. citizen Ronnie Moffitt and prominent Chilean exile Orlando Letelier in Washington in 1976 eventually produced criminal investigations and trials in both countries as well as a successful civil claim in the United States for wrongful death. The assassination of four U.S. churchwomen in El Salvador in 1980 produced a criminal trial in El Salvador in which U.S. officials were peripherally, albeit apparently reluctantly, involved. Official U.S. involvement was more vigorous in relation to leftist violence, including the killing of a group of U.S. marines in 1985 and the "execution" of two U.S. airmen by the FMLN in 1991. For details in all cases see relevant chapters.

5. The CJA has filed or otherwise participated in five claims relating to El Salvador, as well as one relating to Chile. Salvador-related civil claims have to date been brought in the United States by relatives of U.S. citizens killed in El Salvador, by Salvadorean survivors, and by relatives of Salvadorean victims (see chap. 7). The Chilean case, prompted by approaches to CJA from Chilean exiles after Pinochet's arrest, was *Cabello v. Fernández Larios*, filed in 1999.

6. See Roht-Arriaza (2003, 191–212) and Brett (2009) for a fuller list of previous and ongoing transnational accountability actions.

7. These were identified from both secondary and domestic actor sources.

chapters therefore trace internal accountability trajectories in Chile and El Salvador through a survey of domestic actors and their interaction with the courts, and through consideration of each country as either a site[8] or a source[9] of emblematic legal cases.

The emblematic case approach adopted here required an in-depth tracing of particular legal processes and outcomes over time and across settings, since certain high-profile incidents have produced legal activity in more than one country and by more than one actor.[10] Complementing this tracing with a national trajectory approach rooted research firmly in the domestic actor perspective identified early on. It also acted as a corrective to the potential pitfall, particularly pronounced with respect to El Salvador, of taking the process and outcome of emblematic cases to be indicative of more general trends in domestic accountability.[11]

The preceding sections of this chapter have explained in greater detail the selection of Chile and El Salvador as research sites and emphasized the primary focus on emblematic legal cases plus general accountability trajectories. The remainder of the chapter explores principal considerations surrounding the study of those individual and institutional actors who take part in post-transitional accountability debates. The actors and sites through which post-transitional justice is played out are increasingly diverse and operate in a dynamic, shifting relationship articulated principally through the grammar of law and legal action. Major conceptual and definitional issues are accordingly explored below under the headings of actors, (legal) strategy, and judicial/justice system issues.

Actors

The range of actors potentially involved in legal accountability cases is paradoxically widened even as the political, public, or legal space favorable to such action narrows after transition. In effect, for each accountability case

---

8. Where emblematic incidents were prosecuted in-country.

9. Where emblematic incidents took place in a third country or were prosecuted in third-country courts.

10. Thus the Letelier-Moffitt assassination produced a criminal case in the United States and subsequently one in Chile. Both were reported in some depth and had marked political impact in Chile, and are in that sense emblematic. A related civil case in the United States is less well-known.

11. For El Salvador, there is a marked tendency for emblematic cases that attracted high levels of U.S. interest to be given some semblance of judicial resolution, while other HRVs were largely not even admitted to the judicial system. See chapters 6 and 7.

attempted or successfully pursued—as well as for each case abandoned, or put into abeyance by amnesty—there exists an "interested community" that may continue to press for accountability even after amnesty legislation has been adopted. These interested communities are contingent and shifting. They may, at least in principle, include state as well as non-state groups and individuals. The former may include prosecutors, investigating magistrates, or members of incumbent political administrations. At the supra-state level they can include international governmental organizations such as the UN. Regional mechanisms derived from associations of nation-states, such as the Inter-American Commission and Inter-American Court of Human Rights, have also been involved in the accountability debate both pre- and post-transition. The accountability actors focused on here are the "private" (civil society)[12] groups and individuals who have been key in recent accountability actions.[13] These often include relatives seeking civil redress or pressing for criminal proceedings; the aggrieved parties themselves in the case of survivors; individual lawyers and legal firms; individual politicians from incumbent or opposition parties; and national and international nongovernmental organizations (NGOs) and human rights organizations (HROs). As will be illustrated in subsequent chapters, the precise makeup of this interested community depends significantly, albeit not exclusively, on the level and forms of previous human rights organizing in a particular setting.

Popkin and Bhuta draw attention to the "pivotal role played by human rights groups and individuals in attempting to ensure that amnesty laws do not result in complete impunity for those responsible for egregious crimes" (1999, 99). Indeed, a recent resurgence of external interest in accountability has been most effective in reopening domestic transitional justice issues precisely where outside interest has been incorporated into the strategic repertoire of existing and new domestic accountability actors. These may include NGOs, structured organizations that provide resources for the channeling of particular civil society identities and demands and their linking to state and supra-state institutions.

The distinction between NGOs and other modes of social organization is imprecise, but is best illustrated by this focus on the capacity of NGOs

---

12. Civil society is defined here as the space of private associative activity of citizens, mediating the relationship between individual and state.

13. Outside of the justice system proper, there may be state functionaries whose involvement in accountability issues derives primarily from their institutional position in some branch of government. Such actors, including ombudspersons or political figures, are only considered where they have been significant in particular cases or national contexts.

to function as a kind of "service provider" to other groups and individuals (Brysk 2002b). The term "human rights organizations" is used here and
throughout to refer to dedicated, thematically specific NGOs; that is, those
whose discourse and practice are explicitly centered on the field of human
rights, but for whom legal work is one possible avenue rather than their only
or main mode of action. The term "advocacy organizations" is used to differentiate a subset of NGOs primarily staffed by lawyers and legal experts
and dedicated to activities such as the provision of legal support, advice, and
representation to individuals, other NGOs, and social organizations.[14]

The post-transitional accountability field has often involved the interaction of HROs and advocacy NGOs with individual relatives and survivors, as
well as with associations of the latter—such as relatives' groups and groups of
former political prisoners.[15] Individuals—including lawyers, Church figures,
and activists—have also participated significantly in accountability activity
from looser identities, that is, without a primary organizational affiliation.
In certain settings, political parties and Church organizations have also been
important actors at different periods. It is also necessary to consider the issue
of multiple and overlapping identities: some individual accountability actors
are also grouped into associations, but are operating individually in legal
claims. Some lawyers who have been active in post-transitional accountability cases are also relatives and survivors. Some political parties have, likewise,
participated in accountability actions from an ideological or party-political
commitment that is inextricably intertwined with the experience of having
been targeted by repression.

Studying Accountability Actors

It is necessary to look not so much at how particular social actors, such as
HROs, have changed over time, but rather at who has entered (and who
has left) the arena of legal contention over HRVs since transition. This
allows for a wide range of potential sites, and "creators," of contention over

14. Although they may also include efforts to alter the legal or legislative environment in favor
of their client groups.

15. It is usual in all the countries for which field data were collected for relatives' groups to be
considered, and consider themselves, as identifiably separate from professionals linked to organizations. In some places they have consciously adopted distinct policy positions and occupied
separate symbolic and interlocutory space from the latter.

accountability.[16] Such contention can, as will be seen in subsequent chapters, both persist and (re-)emerge even though large-scale human rights mobilization typically declines in the post-transitional period. Moreover, as we have seen, accountability and other human rights–based contention increasingly occupies legal terrain, suggesting a need to consider law as an alternative political site in post-transitional democracies.

McAdam, Tarrow, and Tilly remind us that the classic social movement agenda of the 1960s and 1970s asked questions about four major aspects of how groups mobilize: First, external circumstances that permit or prevent a group from acting: "political opportunities." Next, how such activity is internally organized: the group's "mobilizing structures." Third, "framing," "a collective process of interpretation, attribution [and] social construction [that] mediates between opportunity [and] action." Finally, "repertoires of contention": "the means by which people engage in contentious collective action . . . resource[s] that actors can use on behalf of their claims" (2001, 41). The same authors criticize a tendency of this model to treat claim-making as largely the expression of static, preexisting interests. In particular, they judge this approach inadequate to the task of accounting for demobilization processes. Better results, they claim, emerge from a focus on "the dynamic processes through which new political actors, identities and forms of action emerge, interact . . . and evolve during complex episodes of contention" (38).

Such a framework allows us to concentrate on questions of how actors in contention—an accurate, because sufficiently broad, characterization of protagonists in accountability cases—interact strategically with the post-transitional political and legal environment. That is, how they appropriate (rather than simply responding to) structures of opportunity and threat, construct interests and goals (rather than statically "framing" interests that exist prior to episodes of contention), and innovate in action repertoires, perhaps particularly in the legal sphere. Sikkink usefully suggests that the concept of political opportunity structure be expanded to encompass this sphere, drawing analytical attention to "how human rights activists take advantage of the interaction of international and domestic legal opportunity structures" (2004, 1). One virtue of the "movements" model thus refined is that it allows

---

16. McAdam, Tarrow, and Tilly define "contentious politics" as "collective political struggle where at least one interested party is a government, either as a claimant or as an object of claims"; and alternatively as "episodic, public, collective interaction among makers of claims and their objects" (2001, 5).

us to consider post-transitional accountability actors, in all their diversity, in terms of how and why each one has engaged in legal claim-making around past HRVs. Such actors do not necessarily display the cohesive identity or aims of a single social movement, nor do they necessarily engage in claim-making as a conscious collective enterprise. A strategic coincidence of repertoire and site—the legal sphere—can mask a diverse range of motivations, methods, and identities.

Domestic Human Rights Organizing Patterns and Post-transitional Accountability

Despite the reopening of political and civil space that transition provided, an apparently paradoxical reduction of social mobilization and contentious politics has been widely reported.[17] Social movements in general, and the human rights movement among them, tended to lose both ground and momentum to more traditional political negotiation.[18] Roniger and Snzajder (1999) trace a declining public profile for human rights groups in the Southern Cone, where the (re)emergence of competing, diverse political projects caused human rights claims to lose their centrality or their consensual character. In the Central American context, the urgent priority placed on securing peace and the immediacy of needs for postwar reconstruction provided competing claims on the energies of human rights groups and also reduced the political salience of the impunity issue.

In this climate it is understandable that some commentators have treated recent internationalized accountability actions as the principal or only vehicles for the reopening of an issue that was domestically moribund. But such analyses underestimate the resilience and protagonism of domestic organizations in both creating and exploiting accountability opportunities after transition. Roniger and Snzajder (1999) suggest that, although existing HROs gradually became marginalized from public life, inconclusive institutional closure of human rights issues converted the issues themselves into an ongoing legacy that periodically re-irrupts in both national and international public spheres. They attribute these re-irruptions largely to "legal changes."

---

17. See, for example, Foweraker and Landman (1997), Alvarez, Dagnino, and Escobar (1998), Eckstein (2001), and Hite and Cesarini (2004).

18. See Brysk (1994), Garretón (1996), Oxhorn (1995), and Jelín and Hershberg (1996).

Missing from their account, however, is a more detailed assessment of how these "changes" have themselves been produced, catalyzed, and capitalized on by domestic HROs and other accountability actors.

Accountability actors do not only appear with transition, though some may be new. Some emerge from the existing human rights movement, although certain elements of this movement may be largely satisfied by the achievement of transition itself, or by transitional justice outcomes such as truth commissions, and thus do not necessarily become pro-accountability actors in the post-transitional period. Other actors may move into the pro-accountability field for the first time, among them relatives and survivors wishing to press claims, emboldened by the opening of political and civil spaces or disappointed by the democratic state's limited accountability response. Transition is not necessarily the first time some of these groups and individuals have acted in broader human rights mobilization, or attempted to use legal strategies and international links to achieve certain goals. But the specific goal of accountability—civil or criminal legal action against perpetrators—may be new. Previous actions in the legal sphere may have been intended principally to expose HRV patterns, to reduce or end ongoing abuse, or to protect detained individuals via legal injunctions or international publicity.[19] It is necessary to examine in detail for each country context the identity of emerging accountability actors and what history of strategic engagement they have with the previous regime, with present political authorities, with outside actors, and with legal experts and institutions.

Strategy

The use of the courts by a variety of minority-interest groups to pursue or replace mainstream policy influence is a well-documented and growing phenomenon in modern democracies.[20] Post-transitional changes in the framing and practice of citizenship make the legal realm in theory increasingly available to citizens for claim-making.[21] In the immediate aftermath of transition,

19. A distinction between such "defensive" legal action and accountability claims per se is explored in more detail in later chapters. The distinction is necessarily inexact, since a single legal action often has multiple goals.

20. See Domingo (1999) and Sieder, Schjolden, and Angell (2005) on the "judicialization of politics." Sikkink (2004) specifically discusses the judicialization of human rights politics.

21. This redefinition has produced a growing emphasis on citizenship as an essentially rights-based paradigm that encourages individuals to place limits and make claims on each other, and on the state, through a rule-bound democratic matrix. The notion of the citizen as a legally constituted

however, relocation of the accountability debate to the courts is more often driven by necessity—the effects of amnesty—than by actors' perception of improved chances of success. The obstacles that the judicial route presents to accountability claims are still considerable and, indeed, have typically increased. Generic barriers include issues of access, cost, and system capacity. Specific barriers, aside from amnesty, can include the continuing legacy of collusion or tolerance previously displayed by most national judiciaries toward authoritarian repression. The beliefs and prior experience of potential accountability actors regarding the likely receptivity of courts can accordingly affect whether, when, and how these actors choose to access the legal system in the post-transitional period.

Actors' accounts of the decisions made and difficulties faced in attempting to initiate particular types of claims in specific settings are therefore central to the study of post-transitional accountability, as are the assessments of the prevailing opportunity environment that underlie decisions to desist or refrain from legal action. In this regard Abregú (2000) illustrates how domestic accountability actors can act as creators, rather than solely "clients," of post-transitional legal opportunities. He shows how one major Argentine HRO made explicit legal strategy choices that took careful account of the range of internal versus international sites and resources available. International law, he points out, can be treated variously as a *site*—when cases are pursued via regional and international mechanisms or in other countries' courts—or as a *strategic resource*, when pressure is brought to bear to have international standards incorporated into national legislation or given precedence in national courts. Abregú's account of the specific amenability of Argentina's constitutional structure and law to this kind of strategy reminds us of the need to factor in how specific legislative and judicial contexts both condition HRO opportunity structures and may be shaped by HRO strategy choices.

The alternatives open to and pursued by particular actors depend on a combination of the origin and status of those actors; their effective access to resources, relevant institutions, and strategic alliances; and the goals and meanings that they attach to particular accountability initiatives and avenues.

---

person with "the right to have rights" itself foregrounds law as a potential site for minority claims as well as a central mechanism on which aspirations of modern democratic citizenship depend. See the extensive literatures on citizenship in modern democratic theory and on democratic rule of law. For the former, see particularly Przeworski (1995), Jelín and Hershberg (1996), and Foweraker and Landman (1997). For the latter, see Méndez, O'Donnell, and Pinheiro (1999) and Schedler, Diamond, and Plattner (1999).

There are, in essence, at least five types of legal activity theoretically open to domestic post-transitional accountability claimants. These are: domestic criminal action; domestic civil action; the use of regional mechanisms; transnational criminal action invoking some variant of universal jurisdiction; and "transnational" civil claims,[22] such as those recently undertaken in the United States.[23] The section that follows briefly examines each of these alternatives.

DOMESTIC CRIMINAL ACTION

Although criminal prosecution has generally been the preferred legal route for domestic accountability actors, the space allowed for it varies in different legal systems. Many Latin American countries allow private individuals to bring or adhere to criminal complaints, acting in effect as a kind of subsidiary private prosecutor. Some systems limit such participation to individuals directly affected by the alleged crime. One possible result is a degree of "competition" for clients, with HROs and lawyers wanting to participate in accountability proceedings having to search out relatives or survivors on whose behalf to act. Alternatively, multiple representations can occur, with different groups of relatives appointing various lawyers to the same case. The Spanish system, on which many Latin American systems were originally modeled, allows a wider independent margin of action to organizations under the *acción popular,* effectively a version of public interest litigation.[24] In Argentina, since approximately 2001 HROs have been allowed to adhere as secondary parties in their own right, where the court considers them to have a demonstrable direct interest in the outcome of an existing case. This power has to date been exercised only in consultation with original individual

22. Although these cases are often discussed as examples of transnational action, I argue below that they should often be more properly classified as domestic civil claims. In particular, I argue that many have limited or no links with claimants in the country of origin, and additionally do not satisfy Roht-Arriaza's definition of transnational actions as being brought against "defendants based elsewhere" (2001, 40). See particularly chapter 7.

23. For reasons of space and definition, consideration is restricted to settings and institutions ordinarily available to private actors from the region pursuing criminal or civil accountability proceedings against individuals. The International Criminal Tribunals for Rwanda or Yugoslavia and the International Court of Justice are accordingly not considered, not least because they deal with cases initiated by states. Regional mechanisms, although they can find only against states and not individuals, are considered since the Inter-American system is accessible to individual claimants and has frequently dealt with accountability issues.

24. This provision was key in allowing the case against Pinochet and others in Spain to be brought initially by the Association of Public Prosecutors, with relatives adhering only once the case was under way. See Wilson (1999).

complainants,[25] but it could, in principle, be exercised independently of their consent or with differing or incompatible strategic aims.

The kinds of criminal charge that can be brought also vary.[26] If an attempted prosecution is to prosper, it has to use criminal offenses specified and penalized under national criminal codes. The issue of criminal codes is particularly relevant in combination with amnesty legislation: international or constitutional law, possible bases for arguing the inapplicability of amnesty, do not usually specify directly actionable criminal offenses. The nature and composition of the institution responsible for admitting and processing criminal complaints in a particular country is also relevant, and also varies. Judicial attitudes to accountability matter most in investigative magistrate systems, where judges often have sole discretion over admission of cases, formulation of charges, and sentencing. Many Latin American criminal justice systems, however, are tending toward assigning a larger role to a separate body of state prosecutors. Trends in judicial reform are moving this institution into the "gatekeeping" role of determining admissibility of complaints. The receptivity of the courts accordingly becomes of only secondary relevance, and the accountability attitude and performance of the prosecutor's office must first be considered.[27]

DOMESTIC CIVIL ACTION

No Latin American transitional settlement (except the Salvadorean) explicitly attempted to rule out private civil action over accountability. The fact that civil action is almost always tied to the demand for monetary compensation has nonetheless been a factor in making it controversial among accountability actors. In general, it has been regarded as a poor second best to criminal prosecution.[28] Such mixed or critical responses suggest the need to explore what civil cases mean in particular contexts and legal systems. Requirements, costs, and possible disincentives to civil—as distinct from criminal—claims

25. Carolina Varsky, interview 7 March 2003.

26. Thus, for example, although Spanish domestic courts admit the possibility of prosecutions for genocide, Chile's national criminal code does not even specifically penalize the offense of torture, despite legislative modifications in 2009 designed to update recognition of international HRVs.

27. El Salvador's Fiscalía (state prosecutor's office) has since 1998 had sole discretion over the admittance and investigation of complaints, and has consistently opposed the admittance of accountability claims. See chapter 7.

28. See, for example, the discussion of U.S. civil cases and their domestic impact in El Salvador in chapter 7.

vary from place to place.[29] In some Latin American legal systems, civil and criminal cases can run in parallel, permitting civil complainants to draw on criminal evidence previously uncovered by official investigators. Where criminal prosecution is vigorous, this can enhance the likely success of civil action and reduce its costs. But the opposite can also be true: half-hearted criminal prosecution, or its prohibition or abandonment through amnesty, can effectively extinguish the civil alternative.

Where a state has been unwilling or unable to prosecute, civil action may be primarily driven by frustration at a lack of criminal sanctions as well or instead of a genuine preference for private redress. Thus, although a rise in civil cases may in some instances be a product of criminal accountability progress, in others it may be a marker of its absence. The possible contribution of civil cases to ongoing accountability and truth recovery, and the strategic attractiveness of this alternative over time, thus has to be read within the context of particular legal traditions and accountability trajectories.

CLAIMS BEFORE REGIONAL MECHANISMS

Recourse to the Inter-American Commission and the Inter-American Court of Human Rights was a strategy pursued by domestic actors and HROs in Latin America well before political transition. Indeed, contact with regional or international institutions during the 1970s and 1980s provided alternative routes for denunciatory and legal activity when domestic institutions were unresponsive or hostile. The use of these mechanisms has continued into the post-transitional period. Such claims are treated here as essentially a strategic complement to domestic accountability action, since they are generally speaking only admissible if domestic legal action has already been attempted. An additional limitation is that claims before the Inter-American Commission or Court cannot in their own right produce findings of criminal or civil responsibility against individuals. Rather, they can at best produce censure of present-day state authorities for infringing or failing to uphold a right protected by the American Convention on Human Rights.

29. Thus, for example, Chile, having no equivalent of the U.S.-style class action suit, restricts the potential benefits of a successful claim to named defendants—rather than, as with the class action, to all individuals in the same circumstances. Other regulations have been invoked to argue that survivors must bring civil claims one by one even where defendants, witnesses, and evidence are the same, thus multiplying the cost burden of civil action. See also Roht-Arriaza (1995, 290) on disincentives to civil action.

The Commission can recommend measures that the state should take to rectify or to make reparation for violations, and can also recommend a case for further investigation by the Inter-American Court. The Court, unlike the Commission, can issue legally binding resolutions. But a case will only proceed if the state concerned has previously accepted the contentious jurisdiction of the Court.

Further, the real penalties for failing to comply with either Commission recommendations or Court verdicts are few, although Orentlicher (2002) does signal that the spelling out of unmet international obligations can provide useful leverage for domestic and external activists.[30] In general it seems that regional mechanisms' findings are most useful if they can contribute to a change in domestic legislation or jurisprudence. This kind of impact is difficult to measure, although direct citation of regional mechanisms' decisions in favorable verdicts by national judiciaries offers one possible indicator.[31] The beliefs domestic accountability actors hold about the real vulnerability of authorities to denunciation by regional mechanisms guide actors' evaluations of the relative utility of regional-level claim-making. Some regard the threat of regional cases as an alternative political strategy—a legal channel through which to wield policy influence on the executive and legislature for essentially extralegal goals.

TRANSNATIONAL CRIMINAL ACTION INVOKING UNIVERSAL JURISDICTION: THE "PINOCHET EFFECT"?

The Pinochet case will, claims de Brito, "be remembered as one of the most important case histories in the prosecution of human rights" (2003, 229). Indeed the dramatic, albeit ultimately unsuccessful, 1998 attempt to have Pinochet extradited from the UK to Spain made headline news around the world. Although it was neither the first nor the most successful transnational case of its type, the notoriety of its central protagonist and the circumstances of its unfolding meant that its reverberations seemed to run particularly

---

30. This potentially provides leverage for reformist tendencies within governments or in opposition parties.

31. For a useful overview of the operation and impact of regional mechanisms, see Farer (1997). Risse, Ropp, and Sikkink (1999) are equally optimistic about the power of regional and international institutions to provoke state behavior change even during authoritarian periods. A more region-specific discussion of access routes and the ratification status of relevant treaties is available in Lutz and Sikkink (2000).

deep.[32] The case has been described as "a catalyst stimulating the action of domestic courts" in both Chile and Argentina,[33] and it certainly brought about a significant increase in the number of transnational cases attempted.

Nevertheless, after a brief heyday in the 1990s, the prospects for international criminal justice in the form of transnational cases appear to be receding.[34] In some measure, the initiators of subsequent claims fell victim to their own enthusiasm. Attempted cases against former Israeli prime minister Ariel Sharon and former U.S. president George W. Bush for alleged war crimes surely represented a strategic overreaching for actors genuinely committed to the principle of universally enforceable human rights norms.[35] Reacting against what it viewed as the politically motivated misuse of such claims, the United States reneged on its commitment to the ICC, while a reluctance to be turned into default "world courts" led some European countries to restrict the admission of universal jurisdiction cases to their domestic courts.

Aside from these essentially political considerations, there are also technical barriers to successful transnational prosecution. Cases usually invoke the principle of universal jurisdiction, establishing the right and indeed the duty of all states to prosecute certain classes of crime (see Sands 2003b). The principle, far from novel, was applied to the prosecution and eventual execution of Adolf Eichmann in Israel in 1962. The proper use of universal jurisdiction is, however, neither uncontroversial nor clearly established (see Remiro Brotóns 2003, 232–39). Orentlicher points out that it is not clear whether universal jurisdiction permits prosecution of internationally defined HRVs only under *international* law in national courts, or whether it also permits prosecutions under the national law obtaining in the courts concerned (2002, 7). Extradition requests, which introduce a layer of political and diplomatic discretion to the judicial process, are also often a crucial sticking point for attempts at transnational prosecution.[36] Despite post-Pinochet efforts to invoke the universal jurisdiction principle, it remains true that "most states have been

32. See, inter alia, Wilson (1996, 1999), Brody and Ratner (2000), Davis (2000), Davis (2003b), Roht-Arriaza (2005), Collins (2006), and Brett (2009). See also chapter 6.

33. Davis (2003a, 15). See also Brett (2009) on the impact in Chile.

34. See discussions by protagonists of recent setbacks to the pursuit of "globalized justice" in IPS/ Washington College of Law (2004). See also HRW (2004) and Jessberger, quoted in Brett (2009).

35. A similar push to prosecute former Chadian dictator Hissène Habré provoked sharp criticism from African Union leaders, although it did eventually push host state Senegal to agree to try Habré rather than face multiple extradition petitions.

36. A government minister rather than a judicial figure took the final decision over the possible extradition of Pinochet from the UK.

reluctant to prosecute crimes committed beyond their borders, unless the victims or perpetrators include their nationals" (47). Host country courts continue to prefer some additional and more traditional jurisdictional connection such as citizenship or territorial links to the victims or perpetrators.

"TRANSNATIONAL" CIVIL CLAIMS IN THE UNITED STATES

A series of civil cases involving Latin American victims, survivors, or perpetrators has been brought in the United States under the Alien Tort Claims Act (ATCA) and the Torture Victim Protection Act (TVPA). This trend, beginning in the mid-1980s, accelerated after 1998 with the founding of a dedicated HRO, the Center for Justice and Accountability (CJA). The ATCA, a long-standing but formerly little-used piece of U.S. legislation, permits non-U.S. nationals to bring civil claims (only) against other non-U.S. nationals for internationally defined HRVs—including arbitrary detention, war crimes, crimes against humanity, and genocide—committed elsewhere. The TVPA allows both U.S. nationals and non-nationals to sue over torture and summary execution.

These cases may arguably be best regarded not as transnational cases but as domestic civil claims within the United States. Although the events they deal with usually took place elsewhere, claimants have predominantly been either U.S. citizens making claims for relatives who were also U.S. nationals, or foreign nationals—including exiles—who had become long-term U.S. residents. The domestic statutes invoked require that the accused also have close residence links with the United States. These requirements further limit the prospects of such cases triggering significant reverberations in the country where events took place, at least where links between U.S.-based claimants and "home" communities remain weak. The CJA, which has sponsored the cases, reports that plaintiffs' goals have included the hope that a civil case might "help put an end to the culture of impunity that exists in their home country." Perhaps tellingly, however, the CJA initially restricted its aspirations to "likely . . . interest and benefit to refugees in the U.S.,"[37] although by 2009 its list of possible or at least desired goals included immigration restrictions, social sanction, and deterrence.[38]

---

37. CJA's "case requirements" document on http://www.cja.org/cases/CaseRequirements .shtml, accessed 17 June 2003. But see below, chapter 7, for CJA's account of plans to develop closer links with "home country" activists.

38. CJA's "case requirements" document, accessed on 8 February 2009.

Strategy, Networking, and the Domestic-Transnational Interface

The quality and strength of relationships between domestic actors affects accountability strategy. Questions of overlap, coordination, and networking arise, in this as in any potentially multiple-actor field. Additionally, as shown above, the range of alternatives open to domestic accountability actors at least in theory includes access to institutions and courts elsewhere. Relationships, actual or prospective, with outside actors and institutions therefore also enter the equation. External actors may further elect to launch their own accountability initiatives, in third-country or even in domestic settings, although their access to domestic courts may be practically limited. The section that follows accordingly considers issues of strategic coordination and networking at domestic and transnational levels.

The previous history of human rights organizing in particular countries affects the extent to which legal expertise and support for the bringing of domestic civil or criminal accountability claims is readily available. Epp (1998) makes a central claim that the principal motor of effective rights change is neither judicial leadership nor legal codification, but citizen claim-making with a solid base in legal "support structures." Claim-making by private citizens must, he says, be predicated on a developed network of rights-advocacy organizations, lawyers, and finance sources if lasting change toward the judicial upholding of individual rights is to be secured. He further claims that "successful rights litigation depends on a steady stream of rights cases that press toward shared goals": advocacy organizations and lawyers who network, coordinating the sequence and nature of cases brought, are more likely to see favorable incremental shifts in judicial interpretation (Epp 1998, 18–19). Epp's emphasis on this advocacy "networking" leads us to search for evidence of how and where such coordination of strategies has taken place, and whether it has been demonstrably successful. Examination of attempts to overturn or otherwise overcome the amnesty barrier to accountability is particularly amenable to such an approach. The extent to which individual petitioners, lawyers, and advocacy organizations identify wider goals beyond the individual case result, and whether these reported goals have shaped the selection and presentation of particular accountability cases, becomes significant. The potential also arises for divergence or even conflict of goals between individual claim-makers and the lawyers or organizations representing them.

The international arena is one potential source of both advocacy and campaigning support for domestic accountability actors. It is also, increasingly, a site where accountability actions are taking place with or without domestic actor involvement. Accountability cases, both civil and criminal, can now appear in the domestic courts of countries far removed from the site of the events they concern. Many domestic actors reported an increase in external accountability interest in the post-1998 period, once the Pinochet arrest raised the profile of transnational cases.[39] They reported, however, that this interest differed from earlier international contacts. Funding and campaigning links between domestic HROs and third-country or international counterparts were often extensive during authoritarian periods; international networking, in this sense, is nothing new.[40] International support from external organizations during authoritarian periods was, however, often articulated as effective dependence. Domestic HROs provided information flows outward, while sympathetic international or specific other-country counterparts provided financial resources and lobbying/campaigning avenues. But domestic HRO representatives reported that new approaches after 1998 most often consisted of offers to bring specific cases in another country. Offers to provide financial or logistical support for domestic legal action by existing HROs, on the other hand, were few and far between.[41] Outside organizations or lawyers would instead ask for evidence or testimony to be collected for a transnational case already planned or under way. This new development may force domestic accountability actors to recast their traditional view of external organizations: no longer primarily providers of resource flows but rather—at best—potential strategic allies. External cases may, however, be viewed as irrelevant or even actively harmful by groups who prefer domestic strategies. Thus a coincidence of goals between domestic and external accountability actors should not simply be assumed.

Independent External Protagonism and Transnational Accountability

Keck and Sikkink (1998) suggest that apparently external pressure for state compliance with human rights norms often has national origins.[42] Lutz and

---

39. Interview data. The effect was generalized across countries.

40. Burgerman (1998) provides a useful reminder of the specific significance of exile communities in driving a transnational or multinational aspect to human rights organizing.

41. Approaches were reported as coming from previously unknown or uncontacted external organizations and, increasingly, from individuals. Interview data, principally from Chile.

42. Proposing the "boomerang model," whereby external agents are used to amplify and transmit to national authorities rights-based claims and pressure from domestic grassroots activists who find their own, direct access to state institutions blocked.

Sikkink take a similar approach to recent transnational claims, suggesting that "domestic activists bypass their states and directly search out international allies. . . . Outside pressure . . . serves to open previously blocked domestic avenues for pursuing justice" (2001, 4). Golob (2002b), discussing the Pinochet case in Spain, likewise claims that domestic accountability activists have taken the international stage principally to impose their own, minority, interests on their fellow citizens.

But these analyses risk overestimating the extent to which transnational cases are brought or driven by home-country activists.[43] Many transnational cases have in fact been initiated by the independent action of individuals and groups in the host country.[44] This book accordingly argues that transnational accountability cases, even where present and successful, do not necessarily signal connections between transnational accountability actors/outcomes and domestic events. In particular, transnational cases should not be assumed to be the cause of subsequent domestic accountability change unless specific points of contact or channels of influence can be detected.[45] At the very least, we may conclude that at least two kinds of transnational case should be distinguished: those initiated by home-country activists pursuing a conscious strategy of working through other-country activists or courts, and those brought by external groups at their own initiative and for their own reasons. The existence and operation of cross-border networking once legal activity is under way should not be allowed to obscure these distinctions, which can significantly affect strategy and outcomes.

The proliferation of transnational cases perhaps increases the potential diversity of actor interests. But coincidence or compatibility of goals cannot be assumed at the domestic level either. It might be supposed that individual relatives and survivors would be more interested in immediate case outcomes than long-term jurisprudential or institutional change, or that HROs with a broad, rights-based agenda would be more inclined to pursue "class action" litigation, eschewing exceptionalist accountability solutions or a case-by-case

43. "Home-country activists" refers to activists in the country where the violations took place.

44. Thus the Pinochet case in Spain grew organically from Spanish prosecutors' initiatives in bringing cases over Argentinian and then Chilean events. Relatives' groups in Chile quickly associated themselves with the Chilean case, but they were not involved in the initial decision. Similarly, Salvadorean HROs were asked to provide evidence for recent civil claims in the United States only once the cases were under way; see chapter 7.

45. For example, although it is often asserted that Pinochet's UK arrest "unlocked" Chile's frozen accountability scene, the domestic proceedings he faced on his eventual return to Chile had actually been initiated almost nine months previously, in January 1998.

•

approach. All such assumptions, however, must be tested through particular country and legal cases, not least since there is evidence of broadly similar categories of actors disagreeing over fundamental aims.[46]

Studying Transnational Accountability from a Domestic Vantage Point

As we have seen above, Keck and Sikkink suggest that emerging "international advocacy networks"[47] have come to constitute a new type of collective actor in the human rights field, becoming in their own right "sources of change in the international system" (1998, 199). It has been suggested that transnational accountability cases offer a chance to observe these networks in action. Keck and Sikkink's work does not, however, clearly spell out why networks in the modern period should be treated as anything more novel than simple (temporary) strategic alignments between existing groups. Brysk agrees, for instance, that although the sheer numbers and relative weight of "non-state actors" in international politics may be growing, this "increasingly interconnected transnational world"[48] is not necessarily to be treated as an entirely new paradigm of action (2000, 14). It rather constitutes both a context and a strategy: that is, a reality within which new alliances and projects are formed, yet also an arena that groups may choose to enter with locally (pre)defined goals (Brysk 2002b). Questions about what local groups take into and take from the wider arena can perhaps best be approached from the perspective of the localized, "component" actors in network relationships. Analysts interested in how new actors access (political) power should accordingly address themselves to "the impact of different features of globalization for local actors" (Brysk 2000, 11).

Yashar urges us to remain agnostic about causality, and ask not how globalization affects collective action, but rather "what causes collective action?" (2002, 360). Although she does not deny that "something is afoot," she

46. As an example, Guatemalan genocide cases currently before the Spanish courts were first instigated in 2000 by a particular Guatemalan NGO. Other national groups nonetheless expressed reservations, arguing that efforts ought rather to be concentrated on forcing a response from the national justice system.

47. In contrast to the legally focused definition adopted in this thesis, Keck and Sikkink (1998, 199) use the term "advocacy" to refer to "a subset of international issues characterized by the prominence of principled ideas and a central role for NGOs."

48. A world that permits direct, cross-border relations between "NGOs, corporations and individuals" as well as between states (Brysk 2000, 14).

suggests that this something may turn out to be in effect more politics. Thus, while agreeing that "an ever more integrated economy, networked society and binding global norms" do affect identity and collective action, she asserts that the analytical framework of political opportunity, mobilizing structures, and framing processes associated with McAdam, Tarrow, and Tilly (2001)—and outlined in chapter 2, above—"can quite profitably be applied to understanding globalization" (Yashar 2002, 370). Nor should we forget that movements' relationships with the state remain significant in shaping opportunity, mobilization, and identity (371). Hence not only the observable outcomes of transnational legal activity but also analytical and methodological considerations in the study of network models return attention inexorably to the domestic level, where international activity can be viewed as one component of national accountability histories.

The idiosyncrasies of individual legal systems shape opportunities for and limits to claim-making, guiding claimants' choice of system, where choice is available, and shaping outcomes when one particular national system rather than another is accessed.[49] This system-specific effect can be expected to persist, since international human rights enforcement seems to be definitively moving in the direction of reinforcing complementarity[50] rather than seeking to replace domestic prosecution with fully operative independent mechanisms. Thus the ICC, the first-ever permanent international tribunal empowered to try perpetrators of HRVs, carries a strong presumption of deference to domestic jurisdiction.[51]

Private accountability actors would also seem in the main to prefer domestic over fully internationalized or even third-country venues. The Lawyers' Committee for Human Rights (LCHR), a U.S.-based advocacy organization (now known as Human Rights First), was prompted by the 1998 Pinochet arrest to initiate gatherings of lawyers and HROs interested in accountability issues. In April 2002, individuals and groups from Africa, Asia, Latin America,

---

49. Sugarman (2001b, 2002) discusses how, in parallel with a "convergence" effect provided by the incorporation of global norms and practices, diversity persists in national legal systems. He illustrates his point by reference to traces of structural or procedural "determinism" in the trajectory of the Pinochet case in Spain and the UK. Chapters 5 and 7 below similarly describe how system-specific considerations affect domestic case outcomes in Chile and El Salvador.

50. Complementarity involves, in effect, the subsidiarity of internationalized to transnational or domestic claims to jurisdiction.

51. See the ICC "Rome statute," especially Article 18. It is for the present unclear whether the ICC will defer to states whose only claim is via the assertion of universal jurisdiction—in which case, any or all national courts could theoretically assert precedence.

and North America met for the fourth in a series of conferences with the avowed aim of "making universal jurisdiction . . . an effective legal reality" (LCHR 2002, 1). Although the use—or rather the threat—of transnational cases invoking universal jurisdiction was discussed, this option was presented principally as a strategic alternative for securing domestic prosecutions. The conference expressed a normative preference for the use of domestic courts for accountability claims wherever these were available, and for efforts to pressure them into being more available where they were not.[52]

Judicial and Justice System Issues in Post-transitional Accountability

Courts play a key role in accountability in the immediate post-transitional period, in the first instance, since it is judges who have to uphold, interpret, or apply amnesty legislation. Thus the role of national courts, and the attitude of judges, is significant regardless of the presence or absence of private accountability actors. Second, the national courts are as we have seen a key forum for domestic accountability initiatives after transition. Third, national courts have also had a role to play with regard to accountability initiatives that have come from outside the domestic setting. Successful transnational claims often result in extradition requests made to or through domestic courts; and in general terms, the possibility of transnational action pushes both political and judicial branches to justify or to review their previous accountability practice.[53]

Transnational accountability claims amount in essence to efforts to provoke the belated activation of long-standing international legal principles by national judiciaries. Advances in enforceability and receptivity have certainly been driven by the initiatives of accountability actors, both domestic and external. It may be suggested that the cumulative impact of these actors' undertakings in distinct judicial fora has reached a "critical mass" that is driving change in, or at least reexamination of, accountability scenarios across diverse national settings. As de Brito states, "the role of the courts is being

52. "It is generally considered that justice is best served when genuine and fair trials occur in . . . the territorial state of the crime, or the national state of the accused or of the victims. . . . National prosecutions are clearly better able to deter ongoing abuses and combat impunity within the country. . . . They have a much more direct ability to support the rule of law and restore faith in the legal system" (LCHR 2002, 14). See Gamarra and Burt quoted in Brett (2009) on how the Fujimori trial in Peru has served as a case in point. See also Burt (2009).

53. Discussions at the conference "El caso Pinochet," held at FLACSO-Chile, Santiago, 14 December 2003.

increasingly examined, given their greater role in the accountability process with the passage of time" (2001, 345).

Judicial branches of government in Latin America have often been characterized as essentially dependent on or subservient to executive interests.[54] This dependence goes some way to predicting or accounting for their generally deferential attitude to authoritarian regimes. Domingo suggests that complicity was additionally driven in some cases by an innate conservatism that made the individual and institutional value judgments of the judiciary largely consonant with those of authoritarian regimes.[55] During repressive periods, judicial structures sympathetic to or molded by authoritarian regimes were generally notorious for their abject failure to provide protection to victims of human rights crimes. They proved for the most part happy to suppress prosecution, either through simple inaction or through the vigorous application of amnesty where this device was already available to them. Judicial activism in favor of accountability has in practice been rare, though not unknown, before and during initial transitional periods.[56]

Many truth commission reports were accordingly critical of judicial complicity, recommending reform or purging of the judiciary as a necessary component of democratizing institutional change. The Salvadorean report was particularly scathing about the judiciary, calling on the entire highest court to resign (see chap. 6). Chile's truth commission report, more restrained in tone as befitted a highly constrained transitional setting, nonetheless also called for a judicial branch that "fulfils its role of guaranteeing the essential rights of persons" (Rettig 1993, 859). The capacity of those same judicial systems to subsequently act credibly regarding post-transitional accountability was necessarily questionable, not least because recommended punitive or reforming measures were rarely fully carried out.[57]

After transition, continued judicial indifference or even hostility to the subject matter of human rights prosecutions was tempered in some cases by an equally ambivalent attitude toward incoming democratic administrations. "Demarcation disputes" arose over the proper terrain of the judiciary

---

54. See Correa (1999, 284–85) or Estella Nagle (2000, 348–49).

55. Domingo (1999, 156). See also Garretón (1995) and especially Hilbink (2007).

56. But see Acuña and Smulovitz (1997) and Malamud-Goti (1996) on the role of the Argentine courts in transitional and post-transitional accountability. After the policy reversal represented by the introduction of amnesty, courts became, paradoxically, more effective accountability agents than the democratic legislature and executive.

57. See particularly Popkin (2000) with regard to El Salvador.

in interpreting and applying legislation, including amnesty. Osiel describes how such tensions can operate in favor of judicial accountability: "the need to keep criminal prosecutions within the realm of political possibility can quickly come into conflict with the desire of legislators and judges to assert their lawful authority" (2000b, 139). The opposite situation can and does obtain, with judicial systems hostile to the accountability impulse applying amnesty more vigorously than new governments would wish.

As will be demonstrated in subsequent chapters, changing judicial attitudes to accountability in general, and amnesty in particular, have been the single most significant factor, alongside private pro-accountability action, explaining change or stasis in accountability outcomes over time. Likewise, at the transnational level, legal norms such as universal jurisdiction are not new. Rather, they are only latterly being taken up and enforced by some host-country courts. Due consideration of the causes and direction of changing judicial receptivity is therefore essential in analyzing accountability histories and accounting for shifts in outcomes. Applicable laws have changed less often, and much less dramatically, than judicial receptivity, which has shown itself more malleable than relevant domestic legislation.

There are undoubtedly multiple factors at work in accountability change, including changing political climates, the explicit adoption and genuine assimilation of international rights norms, the impact of judicial reforms, and the effects of simple institutional turnover and replacement over time. A full account of broader changes in judicial performance, however, falls outside the remit of the present study, which concentrates on how judicial change has perceptibly altered accountability outcomes and therefore actor strategy. Actor perceptions of judicial receptivity are accordingly reported principally for their value in illuminating strategic choices. Assessment of the independent validity of these perceptions would require research targeted more directly at judicial behavior.[58]

Conclusions

This chapter has reaffirmed the contention made in chapter 2 that private accountability agents acting in relation to national courts are key to

---

58. Examples of such work include Huneeus (2010) or Hilbink (2007). Nonetheless, a total of almost thirty interviews with justice system functionaries or experts were carried out for this volume.

post-transitional justice. It has shown how accountability actors' strategy choices both respond to and mold the political and legal environments within which claims are generated and processed. Opportunity structure approaches to the study of social movements can therefore provide a useful lens through which to approach post-transitional mobilization over outstanding justice claims. Epp's notion that successful legal claim-making around rights is facilitated by the development of "advocacy organizations," legal support structures that can systematize and channel rights claims to the courts, suggests the need to pay particular attention to the role of legal expertise in facilitating post-transitional accountability.

Similar considerations suggest the need to examine critically the role of domestic and international networking: the international level has become an increasingly frequented and highly visible setting for transnational accountability. Nonetheless, and for reasons including very real legislative and practical limits on universal or international jurisdictional claims, national courts continue to play a central role in the increasingly wide-ranging accountability and international norm-enforcement scenario. The distinctive features of national legal systems—including the relative incentives and disincentives to criminal and civil claim-making these systems provide—accordingly shape post-transitional accountability. Judicial reform and other justice system changes should also therefore be expected to have an impact on levels and outcomes of accountability claim-making.

4

This chapter traces the outlines of human rights–related experiences and organizing in Chile during dictatorship and through the early transitional period. Dictatorship-era patterns of repression, organized response, and the legal strategies that lawyers and HROs evolved to combat HRVs are examined, since chapter 5 will demonstrate the importance of these early experiences in shaping Chile's post-transitional justice trajectory. In particular, the early (1978) introduction of an amnesty law is discussed, as is the early establishment of a pattern of human rights claim-making blocked by negative judicial response. Further, the emblematic human rights incidents whose related legal cases provided key research data for this book are introduced. Finally, the major transitional truth and reconciliation measures implemented from 1990 are outlined.

The Dictatorship (1973–1990)

The military coup that took place in Chile on 11 September 1973 was an exceptional event for a country of almost unbroken democratic-constitutionalist tradition. Political alternation had, however, given way to polarization and confrontation during the "socialist experiment" of the Allende presidency of 1970–73. Thus, although the military had little proven predilection for direct intervention in the political process, the 1973 coup had been widely rumored and was initially welcomed by the political right, the judiciary, the Catholic Church, and some sectors of the civilian population.[1] Most believed that the

---

1. See Arriagada (1998) or Vial (2002).

authoritarian interregnum would be brief. In fact, the coup ushered in seventeen years of military rule, presided over by one man: General Augusto Pinochet Ugarte. Although apparently lacking an initial ideological project beyond anti-Marxism, the dictatorship soon adopted a radical neoliberal economic project. Pinochet made adept use of military hierarchy and discipline to construct a presidential regime with little room for the emergence of rivals. This was not, however, a personalistic regime dominated entirely by individual whim: the regime could also be strongly legalistic, and complemented the ready use of repression with the observance of certain institutional formalities. Indeed, the government chartered a new constitution in 1980 that set out a vision for a future under "protected" (authoritarian) democracy.[2] Although intended primarily to prolong the regime and consolidate its project for enduring political and sociocultural transformation, the 1980 Constitution did, paradoxically, provide the framework for Pinochet's replacement, and the regime's eventual exit, at the end of the decade.

The Rettig report[3] identifies three distinct phases of human rights violations by the military regime. Well over half of officially recognized killings or disappearances occurred in the first, short phase between September and December 1973.[4] Under the fictional state of "internal war" decreed by the regime, military tribunals handed out death sentences to civilians. Despite official insistence that the country had to be "pacified," this initial violence was a one-sided drive to eliminate political enemies.[5] Violence was also employed for exemplary purposes: to compromise and intimidate military ranks and terrorize the civilian population (Escalante 2000, 13).

2. See Garretón (1995, 216). Barros (2002) aptly describes this as "rule by law," rather than "rule of law"; while Angell (2003b) points out that Chile's oft-invoked "legalism" is a characteristic that both predates and has outlived the Pinochet years.

3. The 1992 report of Chile's official truth commission, popularly known as the Comisión Rettig, or Rettig commission. The original text in Spanish is available at http://www.ddhh.gov.cl/ ddhh_rettig.html, last accessed 4 March 2009. The version cited here is the 1993 English translation published by Notre Dame University. Comprehensive data also exist in the archives of most Chilean HROs of the time, particularly those of the Vicaría de la Solidaridad at http://www.vicariadela solidaridad.cl/. See also Ahumada et al. (1989), Lira and Loveman (2000a), periodic international HRO country reports such as Americas Watch (1987), and the extensive bibliographic survey in Stern (2006).

4. Official figures consist of the Rettig commission's 1992 findings as supplemented by its official follow-up body, the Corporación Nacional de Reparación y Reconciliación (CNRR) in 1996. The CNRR's final report attributes 1,823 of a total of 3,197 accredited deaths and disappearances to the period of September to December 1973. See CNRR (1996, 579).

5. There was virtually no credible armed resistance to the coup itself. Armed resistance to the regime, such as it was, peaked in the mid-1980s.

The violence unleashed in the coup's early days gave way in 1974 to an apparent "legalization" of repression.[6] In fact, a rather schizophrenic state of affairs obtained. Less acute violations such as the suppression of political rights were simply rendered legal at one stroke by a declaration or decree, while grave HRVs became largely the preserve of the shadowy secret police, the Dirección de Inteligencia Nacional (DINA). Disappearance was adopted as a deliberate strategy to provide "deniability" for civilian deaths. DINA agents ran covert detention and torture centers to which no public authority had right of access. The DINA concentrated on the extermination of domestic left-wing militants, but exiles were also targeted. Overseas operations, coordinated through Operación Cóndor, a network of clandestine cooperation between regional security apparatuses, assassinated ex–army commander in chief General Carlos Prats in 1974 and ex-chancellor Orlando Letelier in 1976 (see Martorell 1999 and Dinges 2004).

The DINA reported exclusively to Pinochet himself, and operated virtually untrammeled until 1977. It was finally disbanded in August that year, in the face of growing internal and international pressure over its more flagrant atrocities. The official explanation was that the DINA had been a necessary response to "a situation of internal conflict that has now been overcome."[7] There followed a series of events designed to kick over the traces of DINA practices. Some clandestine burial sites were dug up, and bodies removed, in an effort to confound future investigations. Files and other physical evidence were destroyed (Rettig 1993, 640), and an amnesty law was passed (see below).

After 1977 the most violent manifestations of repression lessened, climbing again slightly after 1982 due to a rise in street protests, armed opposition, and related crackdowns. This third phase, 1977 through to 1990, also saw the DINA replaced by the Centro Nacional de Información (CNI).[8] The changes were slightly more than cosmetic. Although the CNI was far from innocuous, when confronted with genuine insurgent actions in the early 1980s it responded with less fatal violence than the DINA had in its time unleashed against a virtually imaginary armed threat.[9] Impunity to commit any and every type of atrocity—at least in full public view—also seemed to be on the wane. Perpetrators lacked the explicit impunity provided by amnesty, and judicial

6. See Brinkmann (1999, 33–38) and Americas Watch (1987, 21–24).

7. Text of Decree Law no. 1876, 13 August 1977.

8. Established 13 August 1977 by Decree Law no. 1878.

9. As one indication, only thirty disappearances, less than 3 percent of the official total for the whole dictatorship period, are attributed to the years 1978 to 1990 (CNRR 1996, 579).

tolerance for atrocities finally lessened somewhat.[10] Although no regime agent was convicted of a crime of repression, more assiduous investigations would serve as the basis for some convictions after transition.[11]

Human Rights Organizing During the Dictatorship

The Chilean coup attracted a remarkable degree of international attention, perhaps because Allende's shattered utopia of electoral socialism had itself captured the imagination of the left elsewhere. The coup also produced an exodus of articulate, politically experienced, and rapidly organized exiles. The human rights record of the regime emerged as the central plank of their campaigning.[12] In western Europe, a chain of "solidarity committees" kept Chile on the agenda, while pressure groups in the United States persuaded Congress to restrict military and other aid to the Chilean regime.[13]

The UN was consistently and strongly critical of the dictatorship's human rights record. Particularly during the U.S. presidency of Jimmy Carter (1977–81), there was unusual Great Power unanimity that human rights violations in Chile were suitable material for collective indignation (see Ropp and Sikkink 1999, 175–76). The Chilean regime regularly dismissed such criticism as politically motivated propaganda. Pinochet's response to a condemnatory UN resolution in December 1977 was to call a plebiscite to rally popular support against "international aggression" (Ensalaco 2000, 128). Chile's regime was not as materially or ideologically dependent on U.S. grace and favor as were later Central American variants. Nonetheless, cumulative external pressure was instrumental in certain improvements in the human rights situation after 1977. Ropp and Sikkink (1999, 179) conclude that the regime's defensive bluster cloaked concerns over its international standing, which did offer effective leverage for external human rights pressure.

Domestic human rights organizing in response to the Chilean coup was swift and robust. The ability of this nascent community to organize, sustain

---

10. Amnesty applied only to crimes committed before 11 March 1978 (see below).

11. See Correa Sutil (1997). For example, the *degollados* investigation (see below), launched in 1985, finally produced convictions in 1994.

12. See Ropp and Sikkink (1999), Ensalaco (2000, chap. 5), and UN resolutions and reports of the period at http://www.un.org/.

13. Congress was thereby set at odds with the administration in the era of Nixon and Kissinger, who actively supported the coup and the new regime. Such divergence between executive and legislative branches prefigured even more acute conflict over Central America policy a decade later.

itself, and generate reliable and comprehensive accounts of both repressive activity and its own responses was determinant in attracting high levels of international support. More recently, it has proved a key element in the renaissance of accountability activity in the late 1990s. Crucially, Chilean HROs did not only document and record repression; they also gave a response that was from the outset highly legalistic. Few if any cases of disappearance, for example, escaped being denounced to an HRO and brought before the courts at an early stage.[14]

These characteristics of Chilean human rights mobilization—its meticulous amassing of data, the legal shape to its activities, and the "paper trail" it thus left behind—were sustained by particular opportunity structures. One contributing feature was the concern of the regime to keep up the appearance of legitimacy and institutional functionality. Thus Chilean HROs used the courts because they could, while the authorities kept the courts open because it suited them to do so.[15] One consequence of this early habitual use of legal channels was that the Chilean human rights scene was, and remains, noticeably "lawyer-led" in comparison with those in other countries.

Second, the emergence and durability of the Chilean human rights community owed much to the early protective and formative role of the Catholic Church.[16] In accordance with a desire to be seen not as political opponents but as neutral defenders of certain values, the Church opted for a twin-pronged humanitarian and legal response, eventually channeled through the specially created Vicaría de la Solidaridad, or Vicaría. The Vicaría functioned between 1976 and 1992, and its centrality to popular experience of the dictatorship itself, let alone to the narrower field of the human rights movement, cannot be overestimated (see Cavanaugh 1998, 265). One striking and almost ubiquitous common denominator among present-day Chilean human rights lawyers and other professionals is early professional experience in the Vicaría. Loveman (1998, 488) distinguishes "generations" of Chilean HROs, suggesting

14. "Eventually everyone in Chile knew about the organizations, what to do . . . We put a full-page advert in the papers; even [right-wing newspaper] *El Mercurio* published it." Alejandro González, long-serving legal director of the Vicaría de la Solidaridad, interview 14 January 2003.

15. Alejandro González also reports: "When international visitors came here after being in, say, Central America, they were astonished that I could invite them to stroll round to the Supreme Court with me to register a criminal complaint. . . . They said, 'Call this repression?!' The government often invited its own international visitors to the courts, to make the same point" (interview 14 January 2003).

16. For the Church's rapid evolution from supporter to opponent of the regime, see Lowden (1996) or Cavanaugh (1998).

that a sequence of church groups, relatives' groups, then politically affiliated organizations created a human rights community progressively more diverse and more radically anti-regime. Many of the new groups were nonetheless launched and sustained through personal connections that overlapped in the Vicaría space. Those who did not have their own legal expertise additionally often depended on the Vicaría for legal services.

Ropp and Sikkink (1999, 181) and Burbach (2003, 31) emphasize how the Chilean human rights organizing experience was itself central to and formative for the international human rights community as a whole.[17] Dense personal and institutional connections fostered the early establishment of lines of international communication and funding support by a range of Chilean HROs, each with an international "constituency" corresponding to its particular identity. Significantly, the regime largely took the path of attempting to discredit rather than repress domestic HROs. Human rights defenders did not escape unscathed, but the regime generally preferred to wage a propaganda war against them. This regime practice of denial itself shaped HRO practice even more firmly toward meticulous documentation and case presentation in the courts.

Legal responses by HROs during the dictatorship were determined by the profile of repression but also by particular, sometimes multiple, strategic goals. In the first days, legal responses came largely from individual lawyers spontaneously mobilizing to defend civilians accused in military war tribunals. This experience led to the beginnings of coordinated response but also to the first strategic disagreements, over whether participating in the tribunals represented tacit legitimation of the regime's declared "state of internal war."

Legal response in the second regime phase from 1974, when systematic disappearance and torture were the principal concerns, was dominated by the presentation of habeas corpus writs.[18] The formal response to these writs, as indeed to legal actions in general, was notoriously poor. There were, however, potential secondary benefits. Released prisoners reported that the mere initiation of legal action was sometimes enough to improve treatment or speed

17. International HROs like Amnesty International or Americas Watch (now Human Rights Watch) cited Chile-related campaigns as having been central to their founding or early activities. U.S.-based interviewees often described campaigns over El Salvador as their next major formative experience. Interview data, third quarter of 2002.

18. Known in Chile as *recursos de amparo*, the purpose of such petitions is to safeguard the physical integrity of a detainee by having a judge review the conditions and legality of their continued detention.

release. The exhaustion of domestic legal avenues—a requisite for taking cases to regional mechanisms—was another motive for the routine submission of writs, which were hardly even expected to be successful. Presentation in court also represented a platform for domestic denunciation. The fact that a writ had been presented could conceivably be reported by an enterprising journalist, whereas a direct report of the alleged disappearance would certainly fall foul of the censor.[19]

There were also longer-term, cumulative goals or meanings attached to legal action by lawyers and HROs. Alejandro González, legal director of the Vicaría for most of its almost twenty-year existence, describes a shared secular faith in "law as a value, a guiding principle." There was also some intention to shame the judicial system into action: "These were judges I had had a hand in nominating [as minister of justice under the pre-Allende government]. One of them took me aside and said: 'Alejandro, these people are all dead. How much longer are you going to keep insisting?' And I said to him, 'Until you do something about it.'"[20] Finally, and perhaps most presciently, there was some notion of a future in which accountability would be possible and records would help.

Thus from the beginning, legal strategies were adopted to serve a multiplicity of purposes. Little of the legal activity of this early period can accurately be described as accountability action, since few people seriously believed that the judicial system could be persuaded to act against perpetrators. The majority of individual case activity was instead aimed at protecting the disappeared from death or torture. It was also "easier," or at least more common, for disappearance rather than other HRVs to lead to legal action, since relatives often felt an obligation to leave no stone unturned. Torture, on the other hand, produced relatively few legal actions of any sort, since survivors were often understandably too traumatized or fearful of reprisals.[21]

In general terms, the launching of formal legal responses during a time of illegality was a gamble,[22] since to use the courts at all implied accepting the risk of repeated defeats to preserve very limited horizons of victory. Thus the

---

19. Conversations with former Vicaría lawyer Roberto Garretón, September and November 2004.

20. Alejandro González, interview 14 January 2003.

21. Alejandro González, interview 14 January 2003.

22. Chilean lawyers tended to be prepared to gamble on a legal system that they did fundamentally believe in. In El Salvador, by contrast, one HRO pointed to its absolute conviction that the legal system could not be persuaded to defend victims as a reason for preferring alternative strategies such as international denunciation.

vast majority of legal actions actually undertaken were predominantly defensive. Situations where an immediate threat to life meant there was little to lose were the most likely to end up in the courts. Other issues, including political imprisonment and internal exile, were dealt with through other channels.[23] Legal strategy was, in other words, not always a reliable avenue even though it was the most widely available response. The rule of law was illusory and incomplete, with legal rules subject to unpredictable, autocratic change. Later, the space for full accountability—as distinct from defensive legal action—was narrowed hugely by the introduction of the 1978 self-amnesty law.

The 1978 Amnesty Law

Perhaps the most significant single regime act designed to institutionalize impunity was a self-amnesty law, Decree Law 2.191 of April 1978. This law, still in force (as of March 2010), provided that "an amnesty shall be extended to all persons who, as principals or accessories, have committed criminal offences during the period of the state of siege, between 11 September 1973 and 10 March 1978, unless they are currently on trial or have already been convicted."[24] The law was deemed necessary partly because in late 1977 human rights issues had provoked the most serious internal regime crisis to date. External pressure was acute, with the U.S. investigation into the 1976 assassination of Orlando Letelier in Washington at an advanced stage.[25] The law was designed to draw a line under the previous phase of the regime, associating HRVs with the past—and, conveniently, with the now-defunct DINA—and signaling a change of direction.

Textually, the law only suspends punishment for crimes.[26] That is, in itself it need not impede—and arguably, requires—that a judge fully investigate an incident, establishing what crimes have been committed and by whom, before applying amnesty. Lower-court judges vexed by unwelcome human rights complaints nonetheless seized on the amnesty law as a pretext for prematurely closing outstanding cases. Alternatively they passed cases over to the

---

23. One HRO, the Fundación de Ayuda Social de las Iglesias Cristianas (FASIC), specialized for years in obtaining the release of prisoners through informal political and diplomatic negotiations.

24. Decree Law 2.191, author's translation.

25. The amnesty law itself, at U.S. insistence, specifically excluded those responsible for Letelier's murder.

26. Although the Supreme Court has sometimes held that it erases the crime.

military courts, which enthusiastically applied amnesty as a matter of course. Up until 1985, regional courts of appeal were occasionally prepared to overturn these sentences, agreeing that amnesty did not preclude investigation. From 1986 onward, however, the interpretation became much stricter. The Supreme Court declared that a judge's only business was to discover if the alleged events fell within the chronological period covered by the amnesty law; if they did, amnesty was to be applied and the case definitively closed.[27]

The Judiciary During the Dictatorship

The Chilean judiciary's record on protecting human rights during the dictatorship was dismal. The judicial branch "did not respond vigorously enough" and was "largely, if unintentionally, responsible for aggravating the process of systematic human rights violations," according to Rettig (1993, 117, 119). Much judicial collaboration with the regime came about not through slavish following of regime diktat so much as genuine shared ideological conviction.[28] The courts were neither suspended nor more radically intervened in, largely because there was no need. Judges, particularly at higher levels, gave the regime every possible juridical support and were more than reluctant to cloud this mutual admiration by processing unwelcome human rights complaints.[29] The judiciary's single most glaring omission was its stubborn rejection of habeas corpus petitions. Judges rejected the petitions out of hand—finding some flaw in format or procedure—or simply stonewalled, obviating the whole purpose of the petition as a speedy defense. Of the thousands of petitions submitted from 1973, no more than ten were accepted by the courts. The Supreme Court president complained that the courts were being "inundated by these petitions, filed under the pretext of arrests. . . .

27. This doctrine arose out of a case in which Santiago Appeals Court judge Carlos Cerda was eventually suspended on two occasions for indicting, then refusing to amnesty, military officers including a former junta member.

28. See Hilbink (2003, 66, 76; 2007) on an innate conservatism that the judicial institution nonetheless construes as apolitical. See also judge Carlos Cerda, published interview at http://www .memoriayjusticia.cl/espanol/sp_home.html, consulted 11 April 2003.

29. Although there was an initial purge, the extent of which is often underestimated. About fifty judges or magistrates were removed—nearly 10 percent of the total (see Gallardo Silva 2003, 24). Gallardo Silva's book nonetheless takes as its title the *íntima complacencia* (profound satisfaction) with which Supreme Court president Enrique Urrutia officially welcomed the coup on 12 September 1973.

The truth is, these people have gone underground or have secretly left the country."[30]

There were various other practical manifestations of judicial sympathy with the regime. Judges sheltered behind a traditionally formalist approach to law (Hilbink 2007; Couso 2005, 122), according to which their role was solely to apply the letter of the law without concerning themselves as to its spirit—nor, it seemed, its legitimacy or constitutionality. In the early period, the Supreme Court voluntarily renounced its supervisory power over military tribunals, which were authorized to apply the death penalty (see Gallardo Silva 2003, 20). At the same time, the courts maintained the façade of an independent judicial branch supervising the regime's activities and finding nothing amiss. Despite the occasional hint of independent action,[31] the regime's very longevity meant that Pinochet gradually had the chance to mold a Supreme Court very much to his own liking. At transition, the new government accordingly faced a largely unsympathetic judiciary in which twelve of seventeen Supreme Court judges were Pinochet-era appointees. The court itself, meanwhile, was smarting over criticisms leveled at it by the Rettig report, which it resented and vehemently rejected. The prospects for opening a new front on accountability were correspondingly remote.

Emblematic HRV Episodes

No legal initiative or case brought during the dictatorship produced accountability, in the sense that no state agent was ever convicted of a human rights–related crime. But certain cases or episodes produced noteworthy reverberations, either at the time or later. The first of these took place between the end of September and mid-October 1973. Pinochet commissioned an official personal delegate, General Arellano Stark, to travel up and down the country by helicopter reviewing sentences handed out by military tribunals. He left a trail of bodies in his wake. At least seventy-two prisoners were summarily executed, some of whom remain disappeared. The operation later came to be known as the Caravana de la Muerte (Caravan of Death). Some

---

30. Enrique Urrutia, 1 March 1975. See http://www.chipsites.com/derechos/dictadura_poder_3_esp.html, last accessed 4 March 2009.

31. Widespread judicial passivity was occasionally interrupted by rare but courageous individual rulings that defied the application of amnesty to circumvent investigations. See below and Gallardo Silva (2003).

legal proceedings were initiated in 1985 over individual Caravana episodes,[32] but the connection between the clusters of deaths only became widely known after investigative journalist Patricia Verdugo published a book-length exposé in 1989 (Verdugo 1989). In 1998 the episode leapt back to prominence, as it came to form the principal basis of the first domestic criminal investigation ever to be pursued against Pinochet himself.

In 1974, General Carlos Prats and his wife were killed by a car bomb in Buenos Aires. The former head of the Chilean army had been forced into de facto exile in Argentina after the coup. The couple's efforts to then leave for Europe were repeatedly frustrated by the refusal of the Chilean embassy to issue them valid passports. The delaying tactic allowed DINA agents to arrange one of the first of many assassinations of regime opponents living outside Chile. The killing was an early action of Operación Cóndor.[33] Criminal proceedings opened in Argentina were swiftly overtaken by Argentina's own descent into military dictatorship, and remained stagnant even after both countries had undergone political transition. Much later, the couple's three daughters and even the Chilean government finally associated themselves formally with a reinvigorated Argentinian investigation, under a new judge. A former DINA agent was convicted and imprisoned for the crime in Buenos Aires in 2000. In 2002, extradition requests from Argentina to Chile over the crime led to the opening of the first-ever domestic investigation into the crime in Chile.

In September 1976 Chilean exile and former chancellor Orlando Letelier was killed in Washington, together with U.S. colleague Ronnie Moffitt, by a car bomb planted by DINA operatives. The ensuing federal investigation caused substantial political embarrassment in both countries, and the eventual denouement rocked the Chilean regime in 1977.[34] The real nature of the episode, as only a single chapter in Operación Cóndor, was not fully exposed. But DINA agent Michael Townley, a U.S. citizen, had to be handed over to the United States, where he and several Cuban coconspirators were sentenced to prison terms. The episode brought DINA chief Manuel Contreras to public prominence and notoriety, initiating his fall from favor and contributing to the downfall of the DINA itself in 1977. The incident also sparked an early

---

32. Typically for the time, most were turned over to military courts and closed. See Escalante (2000).

33. See above, chapter 5, and Dinges (2004). For a full account of the Prats assassination see González and Harrington (1987).

34. For detailed accounts see Dinges and Landau (1980) and Propper and Branch (1982).

civil claim in U.S. courts by relatives of both victims (which was won, but not settled until after transition). The most spectacular national legal ramifications of the incident came in 1993, however, when the reopened domestic investigation saw Contreras and his deputy sentenced to prison terms for murder (see chap. 5).

In March 1985, DICOMCAR[35] agents operating in Santiago abducted and slit the throats of three Communist Party members, in what became known as the *degollados* crime. The contrast with earlier times, when the DINA had with total impunity wiped out two entire Central Committees of the Communist Party, could hardly have been greater (see Ensalaco 2000, 142; and Caucoto and Salazar 1994). An initial investigation established police participation, although convictions were not forthcoming until 1994. The public furor produced by the incident even at the time suggested that such atrocities were no longer accepted with equanimity, and perhaps signaled that Chile's long transition was at last on the horizon.

Transition, Truth, and Justice (1990–1993)

Chile's transition to democracy finally took place at the very end of the 1980s. This was certainly no case of regime collapse. The dictatorship exited largely on its own terms, and its economic and institutional projects survived virtually intact, safeguarded by the 1980 Constitution, which served as the blueprint for transition-from-within. This constitution specified that a plebiscite be held, by the end of 1988, to confirm or deny eight more years of Pinochet's "presidency." The regime's human rights record—heavily identified with the figure of Pinochet himself—became the dominant theme of a sophisticated and eventually successful opposition campaign. The "no" vote finally triumphed, by 55 percent to 43 percent, in the plebiscite on 5 October 1988, although full elections were still over a year away. The opposition coalition, the Concertación de Partidos por la Democracia, managed to negotiate minor constitutional changes in the interim.[36] For the most part, however, a framework of military-supervised "democracy" with a built-in right-wing legislative majority was preserved. Pinochet also introduced new *leyes de amarre*, "binding" or

---

35. DICOMCAR was the intelligence unit of the uniformed police (Carabineros).
36. These included an amended Article 5 setting out the incorporation of ratified international treaties into domestic law.

"mooring" laws. These confirmed the tenure of regime loyalists in the Supreme Court, and of Pinochet himself as army commander in chief until 1998. Other measures betrayed concerns about accountability: secret police archives were destroyed and future congressional powers to investigate or sanction official acts were reduced (see Wilde 1999, 480; and Angell 1993, 198).

Concertación candidate Patricio Aylwin won the December 1989 presidential election by a comfortable margin, and in March 1990 Pinochet finally handed over the usurped presidential sash. Aylwin then held a second inaugural ceremony in the National Stadium, at which former exiles, political prisoners, and relatives of the disappeared all featured prominently. This highly charged gesture augured well for those who had high hopes for an active justice stance from the new government.[37] Concertación efforts were much more focused, however, on carving some semblance of democratic functionality from the unpropitious constitutional and institutional conditions the administration had inherited. Moreover, the outgoing regime had made it clear that Pinochet, in particular, was to be protected from any question of judicial reprisals.[38]

The new president, playing a complex and occasionally valiant hand in undoubtedly difficult circumstances, quickly coined a phrase that would forever be associated with his administration: "justicia en la medida de lo posible" (justice—insofar as is possible). From the beginning, Aylwin's campaign proposals had foreseen only a limited judicial response to systematic violations of human rights,[39] and the substantial element of compromise in his justice policy was rapidly made evident when a manifesto promise to repeal the 1978 amnesty law was quietly dropped. Aylwin perhaps did what he could, and more than some thought possible, to grapple with the human rights issue. But Chile's transitional justice package came to be dominated by a truth measure—the truth commission—that produced little if any justice activity.

Chile's truth commission, the Comisión Nacional de Verdad y Reconciliación, was established at Aylwin's personal insistence as one of the first acts

---

37. The stadium was itself a symbolic site strongly associated with victims of the regime, having served as a concentration camp and torture center immediately after the coup.

38. Human rights lawyer Héctor Salazar, interview 17 October 2002; and Enrique Correa Ríos, interview 22 January 2003. Correa, former Concertación "fixer" and a trusted go-between for Aylwin with the military, reports that at this time the anonymity of perpetrators in the Rettig report and impunity for the Pinochet family were the overt military preoccupations over accountability, although he categorically denies that truth-for-justice "deals" were struck.

39. "Criminal responsibility is individual; institutional responsibilities will not be pursued" (Concertación de Partidos por la Democracia [1989, 2]; author's translation).

of his administration. Its mandate was to investigate grave HRVs and acts of political violence carried out between 11 September 1973 and 11 March 1990. The initial decree stipulated that the commission should not "assume jurisdictional functions proper to the courts nor . . . interfere in cases already before the courts."[40] To this end the commission was not permitted to name perpetrators, although it was charged with passing any evidence of criminal activity to the courts. Further, the fact that the decree was presidential rather than parliamentary deprived the commission of subpoena powers. The commission functioned for a total of nine months, between May 1990 and February 1991. Its eight commissioners were professionals drawn from the fields of law and politics, politically identified with the center and right.[41] The commission and its report are usually referred to as the "Rettig" commission and report, after chairman and former Senator Raul Rettig.

The report acknowledged its indebtedness to HROs, particularly the Vicaría, in providing documentary evidence to supplement testimony from survivors, relatives, and witnesses (Rettig 1993, 19). Cooperation from the security forces was virtually nonexistent. Rettig's restricted mandate identified HRVs exclusively with their most serious manifestations—threats to physical integrity and the right to life. This meant that Rettig attended fully only to "absent" victims—the dead and disappeared. Torture was discussed only at a general level, since it was considered "unprovable" at the level of individual victims.[42] The commission concluded that 2,279 people had been victims of human rights violations involving death or disappearance, with the vast majority—2,189—killed or disappeared by "government agents or persons at their service." Ninety deaths—less than 4 percent of the entire victim total—were attributed to "politically motivated private citizens."[43] The report took no direct stance over the amnesty law, although it did note serious practical obstacles to prosecution. These included the Supreme Court's "emphatic" position in favor of amnesty and the fact that military courts were still claiming jurisdiction over many HRV cases (Rettig 1993, 885–86).

---

40. Article 2, Supreme Decree no. 355, 25 April 1990. See Rettig (1993, 7).

41. Right-wing political parties refused an initial invitation to be officially represented. Commission members included José Zalaquett, subsequently to become an oft-cited commentator on transitional justice associated with a conciliatory position. The commission's secretary, Jorge Correa Sutil, has written on the Chilean judicial system and went on to become a member of the Constitutional Tribunal.

42. José Zalaquett, interview 28 November 2002.

43. These deaths are, nonetheless, classified alongside the state-sponsored acts as HRVs, a technical anomaly since most were caused by the armed left.

The commission did, however, recommend that a successor body be set up, empowered to initiate judicial processes to locate the disappeared; and that withholding information about their whereabouts should be made a criminal offense.

Aylwin presented the report publicly to the nation in a televised address in March 1991 during which he tearfully asked forgiveness "on behalf of Chile" from victims and relatives. Tellingly, most critics steered clear of disputing the report's well-documented facts, although the army came close: it declared its "fundamental discrepancy" from the report, declaring the findings to have neither "historical [nor] juridical validity." The response of the judicial authorities was even stronger: they declared it "an absurd critique . . . tinged with political passions," and refused categorically to accept questioning of their probity by "an entity which lacks even the most tenuous of grounds on which to do so."[44] Plans for a national tour of truth commissioners and government officials to promote the report were suspended after the May assassination of prominent right-wing politician Jaime Guzmán. The spotlight shifted firmly back to potential left-wing political violence, and much of the impetus of the report was lost. The details of the report became perhaps better known and regarded outside the country than in.

Meanwhile, Aylwin's record on justice was mixed, despite his early promises to "procure the trial" of particularly "atrocious crimes" and "promote the derogation or nullification of the amnesty law."[45] Insiders claim that the legal obstacles to nullification were simply too great, pointing to the new administration's lack of a legislative majority in Congress[46] and the Supreme Court's clear sympathy for the law in its broadest possible interpretation.[47] Other versions suggest that the amnesty law was left untouched as a necessary concession to the military and the right, in return for cooperation over the pardon and release of remaining political prisoners.

What is certain is that just days after Rettig's publication Aylwin reiterated its criticism of judicial complicity or inefficacy, saying some judges had "lacked moral courage" (Correa Sutil 1997, 139). He had already exhorted the judiciary to reinterpret amnesty in a way that would at least permit the full truth to be discovered in the cases Rettig had sent to the courts. Thus the issue of judicial investigation was at least highlighted, albeit with truth rather

44. All cited in Lira and Loveman (2000a, 521–23; author's translation).
45. Concertación de Partidos por la Democracia (1989), 2, 3; author's translation.
46. This was due to the presence of nine designated senators, a legacy of the 1980 Constitution.
47. Enrique Correa Ríos, interview January 2003.

than accountability as the explicit goal. In these limited terms, the proposal met with some response: in April 1991 the Supreme Court indicated that lower courts should reopen cases involving the victims named in the Rettig report, even those previously closed by amnesty.[48] Around thirty such cases were indeed reopened during 1992 and 1993, although the Court itself issued directly contradictory interpretations of amnesty during the same period.[49] In the more immediate term, the successor body that Rettig had recommended was in fact created. The Corporación de Reparación y Reconciliación (CNRR) did valuable and often under-recognized work in making sure that some reparations were actually delivered, principally to relatives of the disappeared. Its legal work, however, was restricted to identification and location of victims, rather than accountability.[50]

Conclusions

In sum, the legacy of Chile's dictatorship period included a well-organized, often lawyer-led human rights movement that adopted a legally framed strategy from the earliest days after the coup. This twin legacy of judicialization and meticulous documentation laid the foundations of later persistent, and renewed, attempts to pursue justice claims in the national courts. During the dictatorship and even after transition, however, a combination of sustained judicial negativity and high levels of concession to the outgoing regime restricted the success of such claims. Significant transitional justice measures were largely limited to a truth-telling exercise, albeit itself undoubtedly an impressive achievement given the prevailing political context. Two tense standoffs with the military in Aylwin's first two years perhaps supported the contention that no more was possible given the circumstances. Nonetheless, the Rettig report came to symbolize an official preference for truth rather than justice measures, which would be a recurring theme of the later, post-transitional period.

48. The "Aylwin doctrine," as it became known, did not gain more widespread acceptance at that time. But its basic outline is the very same one that, being applied by the courts from 1998, has permitted the investigation of outstanding cases as well as the re-investigation of those deemed to have been prematurely amnestied. See chapter 5.

49. See chapter 5 and Hilbink (2007).

50. See chapter 5.

5

NO ONE WRITES TO THE GENERAL:
POST-TRANSITIONAL JUSTICE IN CHILE

It is tempting to read the dramatic Pinochet arrest of late 1998 as a bolt from the blue, an external and wholly unexpected lightning strike bringing a dormant domestic accountability debate back to life. Although the unexpectedness of events in Spain and London is beyond question, it will be argued here, however, that the undoubted post-1998 transformation of the Chilean accountability scene was in train even before those external events. This is shown by tracing interactions between domestic claim-makers and national courts over the period. In particular, it is argued that activity in the judicial, rather than political, sphere has been the main motor of accountability progress[1] in Chile since 1998. This chapter therefore examines the principal features of Chile's post-transitional accountability trajectory. The first section is chronologically organized, identifying accountability "milestones" in each of the four presidential periods from transition to the present. The second section analyzes the dynamics of accountability change thematically, dealing in turn with accountability actors, legal strategies, and judicial receptivity.

Chile's post-transitional era has to date comprised four completed presidential periods: Patricio Aylwin (1990–94), Eduardo Frei (1994–2000), Ricardo Lagos (2000–2006), and Michelle Bachelet (2006–10).[2] All have

---

1. Defined here as movement toward adequate judicial processing of HRV cases. "Adequate" processing, perhaps inescapably subjective, is defined as resolution of HRV complaints within the regular judicial system. This should include, where relevant, trials that seem to conform to generally accepted standards of rigor and fairness, with no perceptible pattern of "standard" judicial outcomes irrespective of evidentiary strength. It is a moot point whether the application of nationally valid amnesty laws falls within this definition. In this model, the role of other branches of state is to promote and facilitate, or at a minimum not to obstruct, judicial processing and claim-makers' access to it.

2. Bachelet's term ended in March 2010. She was replaced by right-wing candidate Sebastian Piñera.

represented the seventeen-party, center-left Concertación coalition.[3] An apparent official desire to avoid excessive protagonism over accountability was a constant throughout the four administrations, additionally and deliberately constrained by built-in legislative overrepresentation of the political right.[4] Wilde (1999) describes a resultant culture of cautious, elite-led politics, with governments aiming to "manage" rather than confront controversial issues, including the human rights legacy of the dictatorship. Although each Concertación president aspired to close the transition, none really wanted to grasp the nettle of outstanding accountability claims, on the one hand, and the very real residual influence of Pinochetismo, on the other. Nonetheless, says Wilde, official attempts to downplay the accountability issue have been frustrated by periodic "irruptions" in the form of specific incidents, cases, or turning points such as significant anniversaries. These shifts have largely not been the result of executive initiatives. Rather, says Wilde, they have been catalyzed by private groups or by state actors—particularly the courts and the military—operating outside or even in defiance of the authority of the elected government of the day (481–86).

Accountability Milestones

PATRICIO AYLWIN (1990–1994)

In March 1990, Christian Democrat[5] Patricio Aylwin took office as Chile's first democratically elected president in seventeen years. The human rights issue, central for the democratic opposition in the last years of the regime, was not quickly or easily forgotten. Long before the official truth commission reported, grisly discoveries like that of a mass grave in Pisagua in the northern desert, or mass anonymous burials in Santiago's General Cemetery,

---

3. Formed for the 1988 plebiscite, the Concertación has retained the presidency plus a majority of elected parliamentary seats ever since.

4. The 1980 Constitution bequeathed a binominal electoral system and (now abolished) unelected senator posts. See Portales (2000). Cavallo (1998) describes a specific set of behind-closed-doors deals and concessions over human rights that many believe were struck in the first few months of transition.

5. Aylwin's party forms part of the Concertación, which can select its presidential candidate from any of its member parties: subsequent president Eduardo Frei was also a Christian Democrat, while Ricardo Lagos and Michelle Bachelet were Socialist Party candidates.

countered the effects of clandestine military operations to remove all traces of the disappeared.[6]

Aylwin's initially bold words and actions were eventually circumscribed by the reality of continuing military strength. Pinochet—who had famously threatened that "if anyone lays a finger on one of my men, the rule of law is over"—resolutely refused to disappear from view. As commander in chief of the army, he had a predictably strained relationship with the new civilian authorities.[7] Aylwin also had to face two overt episodes of military saber rattling. In December 1990, the army retreated to barracks to protest the Pinocheques affair, a congressional investigation of Pinochet's eldest son for fraud. In May 1993, just after Aylwin had declared the Chilean transition officially over, the army took to the streets of the capital in full battle dress to protest human rights prosecutions.[8]

In such a climate, the 1991 Rettig report began to look like Aylwin's best and perhaps only possible contribution to truth or justice progress. Subsequently, two major sets of legislative proposals seeking variously to locate the disappeared, expedite outstanding judicial cases, and offer anonymity to informants, were criticized on all sides and were either modified or withdrawn.[9] Aylwin was likewise unable to achieve the transfer of outstanding cases from military to civilian jurisdiction. In practice, the main justice achievements of the period were the release of political prisoners[10] and the reopening of the Letelier case. Despite the extradition requests and convictions in the United States, a dictatorship-era investigation in Chile had covered only the minor offense of use of false passports. The 1991 re-investigation, prompted by a personal petition from Aylwin to the Supreme Court, was a very different affair. In just two months judge Adolfo Bañados had amassed enough evidence to charge Manuel Contreras and his former second-in-command Pedro

---

6. Army intelligence units also spied on and obstructed early attempts at investigation, spiriting agents and potential witnesses out of the country in a process known as Operación Control de Bajas (Operation Damage Limitation).

7. Enrique Correa Ríos, interview 22 January 2003. See also Cavallo (1998).

8. The incident, known as the Boinazo, was timed to coincide with Aylwin's absence on a European trip.

9. These measures were the so-called Leyes Cumplido proposal of 1990–91, named for the justice minister who drafted it, and the Ley Aylwin proposal of mid-1993. See UDP (2003, 151–52) and Lira and Loveman (2002, 37–77, 109–28).

10. This was done via a 1991 law allowing presidential pardon for those convicted of "terrorism offences." Only those guilty of the most emblematic acts of opposition violence, or who refused to renounce armed tactics, remained in prison.

Espinoza with crimes, including murder.[11] A guilty verdict, and sentences of seven and six years respectively, followed in November 1993.[12] The verdict undoubtedly represented the first major accountability milestone since transition.

EDUARDO FREI (1994–2000)

Still only a presidential candidate when the Letelier sentences were handed down in November 1993, Frei expressed personal satisfaction at the outcome. As president, however, he displayed a less ebullient attitude. The first symbolic setback came in early 1994, when police force commander in chief Rodolfo Stange refused to resign despite repeated presidential requests.[13] In May 1995, the confirmation on appeal of the Letelier sentences sparked a full-blown crisis in civil-military relations. Contreras was spirited away to a naval hospital, where he languished with a series of supposedly incapacitating ailments. The standoff was finally resolved by compromise, and by October, both Contreras and Espinoza were finally serving sentences in a specially constructed prison complete with military guards.[14] Yet the episodes did little for Frei's image as a decisive leader, nor that of the government as a confident democratic administration no longer beholden to its authoritarian past. During the rest of Frei's term, institutional engagement with the human rights legacy was distinctly muted. Human rights groups found him not so much antagonistic as uninterested,[15] and his only major legislative proposal with significant accountability implications failed to prosper despite careful courting of right-wing support.[16]

11. The pair were also the subject of a motion to recover US$2.5 million paid out by the Chilean government after transition to settle a successful civil claim made in the United States by relatives of both victims.

12. The verdict was reproduced as a special supplement of the national legal journal. See *Revista Fallos del Mes* 35, Edición Suplementaria, November 1993.

13. The requests were made in response to the *degollados* verdict, which clearly implicated Stange in attempts to cover up the crime.

14. According to Salazar (1995), the government agreed that no more than half a dozen other HRV cases should be "allowed" to proceed through the courts, while the army made only a vague commitment to the "gradual and prudent" retirement of officials closely linked to HRVs.

15. He notoriously failed, in the whole of his six-year term, to grant an audience to the main relatives' association, the Agrupación de Familiares de los Detenidos-Desaparecidos (Association of Relatives of the Detained-Disappeared).

16. This was the "Figueroa-Otero" proposal, also opposed by human rights groups who saw it as a step back after the Letelier case. See UDP (2003), 154.

Frei's contribution to accountability came largely in the form of incidental—even inadvertent—actions that proved significant only at a much later date. One such action was the preservation of the CNRR after it made its supposedly final report in December 1996.[17] Frei gave it a new incarnation as the rather cumbersomely named Programa Continuación Ley 19.123 (henceforth Programa).[18] Although it had a relatively low profile during Frei's period in office, the Programa became a more significant player after a 2001 relaunch. More important, Frei instigated the first significant judicial overhaul since the transition, which included the replacement of a substantial proportion of sitting Supreme Court judges. This transformed a Supreme Court predominantly staffed by Pinochet-era appointees to one where, by 1998, only four of twenty-one judges were from that era. The same reforms set in train the specialization of the court into *salas* (benches). The final relevant action of the Frei administration before it was overtaken by the event that would consume its final months—the Pinochet arrest—was to take soundings in military and Church circles as to the feasibility of a renewed effort to discover the whereabouts of the disappeared. This would come to fruition only later, under Lagos, as the Mesa de Diálogo (aka the Mesa).[19]

THE SPANISH CASE AND THE ARREST OF PINOCHET

In March 1996, a Spanish lawyers' association (the Unión Progresista de Fiscales) filed charges in Spain against former Argentinian military leaders over HRVs carried out against Spanish citizens during Argentina's 1976–83 "Dirty War." This was followed in July by a similar complaint against Pinochet and others, alleging genocide, terrorism, and other offenses against Spanish and

17. The "Informe sobre Calificación de Víctimas de Violaciones de Derechos Humanos y de la Violencia Política" (CNRR 1996). See chapter 4 for background on the CNRR itself.

18. A reference to Ley 19.123 of 8 February 1992, the original enacting law. The name change never took root, and press and other sources continued to refer to the institution as the "ex-Corporación." After yet another reorganization in 2001 it became known by its present title, the Programa de Derechos Humanos del Ministerio del Interior. For the sake of clarity "Programa" is used here as shorthand for all post-CNRR variations.

19. "Roundtable," see below for details. It has been suggested that the Mesa finally took shape even later than stated here, and only as a direct reaction to Pinochet's arrest (interview with human rights lawyer Héctor Salazar, 17 October 2002). Most analysts, however, place the Mesa's origins well before the arrest, albeit after the beginning of the Spanish investigation that would produce it. They suggest the Mesa was motivated principally by the accumulation of newsworthy and controversial occasions like Pinochet's accession to the Senate (March 1998), followed by the twenty-fifth anniversary of the coup (September 1998). José Zalaquett, interview 28 November 2002. See also FLACSO (2000).

(eventually) Chilean citizens. The jurisdictional basis of the complaints was, essentially, the invocation of universal jurisdiction over certain internationally defined human rights crimes.[20] The two cases were eventually subsumed into one investigation under the direction of judge Baltazar Garzón.[21] In Chile, the Spanish investigation was viewed even by accountability actors as quixotic at best, an action that might at most curtail the soon-to-be-senator's travel plans.[22] To the Chilean government it appeared, if anything, a mild embarrassment, badly timed in the run-up to Pinochet's imminent army retirement and accession to the Senate. The case promised to renew public controversy about Chile's compromised political past and the quality of its democratic present. Accordingly, Chile's public and military authorities registered their distaste for the Spanish investigation. Justice Minister Soledad Alvear traveled to Spain in March 1997 to this end, and former chief military prosecutor Fernando Torres Silva made a semi-clandestine visit in September. The resulting media commentary in Chile meant the trips had perhaps the opposite effect to that intended: they raised the profile of the case and put impunity back in the spotlight.

But the heat was really turned up on Pinochet by the turn of domestic events. In December 1997, Manuel Contreras declared that he had always acted "according to orders given by the President of the Republic," who, as the "maximum authority behind the DINA," was the "only one . . . who could order missions."[23] The declaration was the first public avowal from within Pinochet's inner circle of his direct involvement in atrocities. The statement finally spurred opponents exercised by Pinochet's post-retirement plans to take legal action. In January 1998 the first post-transitional criminal complaint against Pinochet himself was lodged in the Chilean courts by the Communist Party. As with the Spanish case, initial expectations in Chile were low, even from those who brought the complaint.[24] As if to underline the

20. Both complaints nonetheless foregrounded crimes committed against Spanish citizens, in the hope that this would make Spanish courts more likely to accept them.

21. When the investigation over Chilean events appeared to be running out of steam, lawyers had Pinochet included in the Argentine investigation by raising the issue of Operación Cóndor killings. The two investigations continued in parallel for a time, until the judge in the Chilean investigation renounced in favor of Garzón. For details of the Spanish cases, see various articles and dedicated volumes, inter alia, Wilson (1999), Pérez and Gerdtzen (2000), Brody and Ratner (2000), Rojas and Stefoni (2001), Ekaizer (2003), Davis (2003b), and Roht-Arriaza (2005).

22. Patricia Verdugo, interview 18 November 2002.

23. Contreras's appeal submission to the Supreme Court, p. 260, quoted in Pérez and Gerdtzen (2000, 46; author's translation).

24. Gladys Marín, interview 20 November 2002.

meager prospects, hard on the heels of this legal submission Pinochet became a senator,[25] acquiring a new layer of legal protection: parliamentary immunity (*fuero*).

Assigned judge Juan Guzmán, however, initiated a rigorous domestic investigation, unexpected given his own previously conservative record. By mid-1998 Guzmán was simultaneously investigating a number of different episodes. One of these, the Caravana case, soon emerged as the most viable. It involved legal issues—disappearance and extrajudicial execution—that straddled the increasingly questioned dividing line between those acts that could and could not be amnestied. Those issues were thrown into sharp relief in September 1998 by a landmark judicial ruling in the separate, and long-running, Poblete-Córdoba case.[26] The newly constituted Sala Penal (Criminal Bench) of the Supreme Court ruled that disappearance where no body had ever been found amounted to kidnapping. They further ruled that kidnapping, a so-called *delito permanente* (ongoing crime), was therefore not covered by amnesty.[27]

In the immediate aftermath of the Poblete-Córdoba ruling, attention was drawn away from domestic events by a drama unfolding on the other side of the world. Pinochet, in apparently reckless disregard of the advice of his own lawyers, had travelled to the UK for recreational purposes and medical treatment.[28] Getting wind of his stay, the Spanish judge Garzón had made a hurried request through Interpol for a UK arrest warrant to be served. The aim was to have Pinochet held in the UK long enough for a full-scale extradition effort to be launched. The warrant was duly served on Pinochet, convalescing in the London Clinic, on the night of 16 October 1998. The ensuing diplomatic

25. Pinochet himself had created this position via Article 45 of the 1980 Constitution, which reserved seats for "designated" senators, including former commanders in chief. On 10 March Pinochet participated in an emotional resignation ceremony from the armed forces. He was received into the Senate the following day amid protests from fellow legislators, including Allende's daughter, who filed into the chamber carrying portraits of the disappeared.

26. The case, over the 1974 disappearance of a young sympathizer with the far-left Movimiento de Izquierda Revolucionaria (MIR), had been shuttled between military and civilian jurisdiction since its inception. Contesting a renewed attempt by military courts to close the case, prosecuting lawyer Sergio Concha brought the matter before the Supreme Court.

27. This since the offense was technically still being committed right up to the present day, and amnesty applied only to crimes committed before 10 March 1978. Supreme Court ruling dated 9 September 1998, in Rol. (Case) 895–96.

28. Official claims in the immediate aftermath of the arrest that he was on a fully accredited diplomatic mission regarding defense supplies quickly faded, amid allegations that copies of supporting paperwork presented were hasty post hoc forgeries.

and legal drama outlasted the end of Frei's presidential term and cast a long shadow over the presidential elections of December 1999.

Official reactions are at one level difficult to unravel, and certainly to document, since, in accordance with Frei's typically cautious style, much was left unsaid. Although the administration contained a number of prominent former exiles, who might have been forgiven for displaying a certain personal satisfaction at the former dictator's plight, the executive branch was certainly unstinting in its efforts to have Pinochet returned to Chile. The official line varied little from Frei's initial protestations that national sovereignty had been violated and that law—including, apparently, international law—should not be applied extraterritorially.[29] This line was punctuated with veiled "offers" to ensure that Pinochet would face domestic justice if he returned home.[30] The dozen or so criminal complaints already generated, and Guzmán's ongoing investigations into them, were adduced as evidence. The aim was to counter the claim that Pinochet should be extradited to Spain precisely because of the unlikelihood that any domestic prosecution in Chile would prosper (Brody and Ratner 2000, 10–12).

The reasons for Frei's vigorous action on behalf of Pinochet's homecoming can be endlessly debated. It does, however, seem that a genuine nationalist instinct rejecting foreign, particularly Spanish, intervention in domestic affairs was at work. Left and right found themselves in unusual agreement over the undesirability of Chile's transition being, by implication, found wanting by the former colonial power. Domestic HROs and lawyers were torn between wanting to see Pinochet prosecuted somewhere—anywhere—and wanting to have him answer exclusively to domestic courts and charges. In the meantime, the prospect of domestic accountability progress was apparently strengthened when the Chilean Supreme Court, in July 1999, upheld Guzmán's definition of all as-yet unproven deaths in the Caravana case as (non-amnestiable) kidnappings. Additionally the Mesa promised advances in tracing the disappeared, with at least the theoretical possibility of legal action to follow.[31]

Chilean authorities gained a temporary respite when UK Home Secretary Jack Straw recommended Pinochet's return to Chile on discretionary medical

---

29. Interview with Enrique Correa Ríos, the policy's coauthor, 22 January 2003.

30. Chilean chancellor José Miguel Insulza declared that "if he were to be returned to Chile, justice would become the main issue. People would say 'Now we've reaffirmed sovereignty, let's reaffirm justice as well.'" Quoted in Rojas (2001, 27; author's translation).

31. Although as it turned out, the paucity of information meant the only legal action to follow was to be against military officials themselves for obstructing the process.

grounds. The issue of Pinochet's health provided, in the end, a neat route for the UK authorities to unburden themselves of Pinochet without having to enter into the legal substance of the extradition requests against him.[32] By the time Pinochet returned, on 4 March 2000, Lagos had replaced Frei as president. The most immediate official fear was that Pinochet would insist on attending the official inauguration, giving the lie publicly to protestations about his fragile state. After an initial show of defiance at the airport, however (where he was met by an unofficial military honor guard), Pinochet seemed willing to abide by the terms of an enforced retreat from public life, retiring from his recently acquired and hardly occupied Senate seat. During his stay in London, however, the previous trickle of domestic legal initiatives against him had picked up pace. Around sixty criminal complaints had been lodged against him in national courts by the time of his return, a number that would continue to grow.[33] Also, and quite deliberately, prosecuting lawyers had chosen the very day of Pinochet's return to press for formal charges in the Caravana case.

RICARDO LAGOS (2000–2006)

The furor over Pinochet's detention came at a particularly delicate time for Ricardo Lagos, the Concertación candidate in a close-fought presidential campaign. The desire to preserve electoral prospects by appeasing the center and right was contrasted with the symbolic weight attached to this first Socialist Party presidential candidacy since Allende's. Lagos initially seemed paralyzed by these conflicting pressures. Once elected, and with Pinochet safely back in Chile, Lagos adopted the time-honored Concertación policy of taking a backseat to the courts. Lagos, however, gave the practice a more positive spin, making statements about the separation of powers and the progress of democratization. In effect he declared the whole issue sub judice, presenting a refusal to venture an opinion as a positive executive virtue (*Qué Pasa*, 22 January 2000).

32. Under universal jurisdiction rules, Britain's obligations were to either extradite or prosecute. According to some versions, the medical issue was first raised by the Chilean embassy in London. See Brody and Ratner (2000), 18.

33. Reaching at least three hundred by October 2002 (HRO archives and http://www.fasic.org/juri/quere2002.htm), this exponential growth in complaints directly naming Pinochet responded to a deliberate strategy on the part of some HROs and lawyers: "We said, since the government keeps promising to make him face the courts if he comes back to Chile, we'll take them at their word" (Federico Aguirre, interview 24 October 2002).

José Zalaquett remarks that Lagos proceeded "like a card dealer," sending the human rights issue to the Mesa, the Pinochet case to the courts, and debates about the need for constitutional change to the Senate.[34] The card dealt to the courts, however, did not provide the hoped-for respite. For one thing, domestic courts were not the only threat to Pinochet's peaceful retirement. Appetites whetted by the Spanish investigation, U.S. prosecutors reopened the Letelier case. In Argentina, long-running investigations into the Prats assassination gained new momentum. Formal extradition requests were made for Pinochet and the still-imprisoned Contreras. Domestic prosecution increasingly seemed like not only the "least worst" but almost a necessary alternative to stave off outside pressure.[35] There was a certain onus on the government to live up to its previous statements about Chile's capacity to deliver justice, even though, strictly speaking, assurances about prosecutions had not been the government's to make.

Notwithstanding, the government did show itself ready to intervene in domestic proceedings, apparently making consistent and strenuous attempts to protect Pinochet from the full weight of domestic law. On 5 June 2000 the Santiago Court of Appeal surprised many by voting to strip Pinochet of his senatorial immunity,[36] clearing the way for him to be charged over Caravana. The Supreme Court upheld the decision on 8 August,[37] at which point the question of medical fitness resurfaced. Investigating judge Juan Guzmán ordered medical tests, carried out at a Santiago military hospital in early January 2001. Participating lawyers and even Guzmán himself allege that from this point a series of subtle and not-so-subtle pressures were brought to bear by officials, attempting to convince both the public and the judiciary that the case had gone far enough and Pinochet should not be prosecuted further.[38] Pinochet was formally charged on 29 January 2001 with various counts of murder and kidnapping, but the Santiago Appeals Court suspended the case against him on 9 July 2001. The court accepted the defense's contention that, according to new criminal code standards designed to improve fair trial

---

34. José Zalaquett, interview 28 November 2002.

35. Specifically, domestic investigations would almost certainly suspend extradition proceedings, since domestic jurisdiction is traditionally given precedence.

36. Santiago Appeals Court ruling dated 5 June 2000, in Rol. 136-2000.

37. Supreme Court ruling dated 8 August 2000, in Rol. 1920-2000.

38. Interviews with Eduardo Contreras, Hiram Villagra, and Juan Subercaseaux, 3 December 2002, 13 November 2002, and 18 March 2003, respectively. See also press reports, including *El Mostrador*, 13 September 2001.

guarantees, Pinochet was medically unfit to stand trial.[39] Prosecuting lawyers denounced this ruling since the standards in question—contained in reforms being phased in across the country—were not yet in force in the area where Pinochet was being tried. A definitive Supreme Court decision a year later went even further than its Appeals Court counterpart, however, suspending proceedings permanently rather than temporarily.[40]

Prosecuting lawyer Hiram Villagra claims that an initial Supreme Court vote favorable to prosecution was reversed by direct executive pressure on a single judge, Amanda Valdovinos.[41] Carlos Cerda, more elliptical as befits a serving Appeals Court judge, nonetheless commented: "certain sources gave [me] to understand that the Supreme Court ruling . . . was a way of producing an outcome that the Chilean state . . . thought appropriate, and, in that sense the most just . . . That's what would explain a decision which probably doesn't stand up to any juridical analysis."[42] Enrique Correa Ríos, even more elliptically, asserted that the suspension had been "the best possible outcome for the country." Asked whether the courts had fulfilled the government's wishes by coincidence or due to intervention, he responded: "Sometimes, when you are in government, you only have to want something badly enough in order for it to happen."[43]

Although some accountability actors were perhaps predisposed to believe the worst about government actions, even previously neutral figures from within judicial ranks were clearly persuaded that something underhand had been attempted. Here, however, it is perhaps helpful to distinguish actions against Pinochet from the broader thrust of accountability. Lagos and military authorities alike had shown signs before Pinochet's arrest of a readiness to take a different view of other manifestations of justice change. Indeed, the arrest of Pinochet arguably proved a setback in a military-civilian rapprochement. The arrest forced military authorities into a defense of Pinochet and his legacy, partly in deference to the more extreme pro-Pinochet sentiments within their own ranks (Rojas 2001). In more general terms, though, Lagos had long been cultivating cordial relations with new military leaders who

39. Perpetuating suspicions of undue intervention, one of the three medical experts who conducted the January tests later alleged that his diagnosis had been altered after the fact. Letter from Dr. Luis Fornazarri to Caravana case lawyers, dated 9 April 2001; on file with author.

40. Supreme Court resolution 1 July 2002, Rol. 2986-01; on file with author.

41. Hiram Villagra, interview 13 November 2002.

42. Carlos Cerda, interview 7 November 2002.

43. Enrique Correa Ríos, interview 22 January 2003.

seemed willing to accept that some concessions on justice issues were needed. Sebastian Brett, for example, considered that although there was never any indication that Pinochet would be allowed to end up in court, military and political authorities were attempting before his arrest to quietly "script him out of [Chile's] political future."[44] Pinochet's arrest initially threatened to upset this new understanding, which is one reason why it was vigorously resisted by the government.[45]

THE MESA DE DIÁLOGO (1999–2000)

The Mesa de Diálogo, mentioned above, was to be a public manifestation of the turning of a new page in Chilean accountability—or, at least, in truth-telling. Overtures begun under Frei were accelerated by the Pinochet arrest, which gave government negotiators ample grounds to suggest to military leaders that here was a problem that would simply never go away of its own accord. If new gestures were needed, why not start with the most acute and least defensible manifestation of the problem: the remaining disappeared, and relatives' decades-long quest to find them? The military had always denied holding any centralized information about what they still maintained were individual criminal acts. A formula was therefore needed that would not imply acceptance of institutional responsibility. The Mesa was accordingly inaugurated on 21 August 1999; military, government, and human rights representatives would meet under Church chairmanship to hammer out a mutually acceptable fact-finding plan. Unfortunately, no one thought to check that the intended beneficiaries of the measure would agree; relatives' associations came out in opposition to the measure and boycotted it. Both process and outcome began to escape Lagos's grasp.

It seems at least possible that the Pinochet arrest simply proved too destabilizing for delicately balanced efforts still in their early stages. The government's wholehearted play in favor of Pinochet's return had soured the mood among participating lawyers, as had the pomp and ceremony provided by military authorities for his homecoming (Pérez and Gerdtzen 2000, 306). Worse was to follow, in the shape of the Mesa's final outcome. The Mesa's concluding declaration, made in June 2000, just three months after Pinochet's

---

44. Sebastian Brett, interview 15 October 2002.
45. For an account of changes in civil-military relations since 1990, and of how the Pinochet arrest ushered in a new phase, see Fuentes (2009).

return, heralded a six-month period of data collection. Informants could talk to military or Church authorities, who were authorized to guarantee them anonymity. The final January 2001 report was a huge disappointment. It consisted of an almost desultory list of names and places, some bearing only the legend "thrown into the sea." The government was scenting a public relations disaster even before ongoing judicial investigations proved that the new information could not be trusted.[46] The disaster turned to farce when it emerged that a supervising officer had taken the opportunity to withhold testimony incriminating his own wife. Not for the first time, a judge appeared to move more decisively than government officials: the officer was detained for obstruction of justice, and his commander in chief forced to resign. In the final analysis the Mesa hardly counted as an unqualified success for any side. The military, for their part, seemed at times genuinely bemused that a simple answer to the long-standing question "¿Donde están?" (Where are they?) had led to such a furor. As far as they were concerned, they had kept their side of the bargain.

The Mesa report produced only two major collateral effects favorable to accountability. First, its somewhat meager contents were handed to the courts, who appointed special judges (*ministros en visita*)[47] to certain cases. Others were relayed to whichever court already had an open case file for that victim. It soon became clear that the cases given to *ministros en visita* were advancing much more rapidly. At the same time, the government was being publicly taken to task by the lawyers who had participated in the Mesa for the lack of progress. Discussions were held with the courts and it was agreed that more specialized judges would be assigned. It seems that the government had in mind the assignation only of the cases of disappearance mentioned in the Mesa report. The Supreme Court nevertheless went one step further, calling in records of all outstanding HRV investigations from every court. This provided a substantially bigger case universe, no longer restricted to disappearance (though still, importantly, omitting all cases being seen in

46. Individuals who appeared on the list as having been dispatched into the sea were identified in an illegal burial site in a different location. Testimony from survivors also showed that some of those on the list were alive and still in detention months or even years after the list showed they had been killed.

47. Literally, "visiting judges." This is a standard tool available to the courts to expedite the investigation of cases considered to be of particular urgency or social/political importance. The *ministro en visita* is a judge, normally from a second-instance (appeals) court, who is removed from normal duties and assigned exclusively to such a case.

military tribunals).[48] The cases were reassigned to a small group of judges who were relieved of all or part of their normal duties[49] for a renewable, fixed period. The measure was accompanied by an injection of additional resources to courts and complementary agencies, including the investigative police.[50]

A second outcome of the Mesa was the strengthening and reorganization of the Programa. HROs had extracted a promise from the government that the Mesa would culminate in extra juridical support for relatives of the many victims whom the government confidently expected would be located. But the internal disarray of the accountability-actor field after the Mesa (see below) meant that the AFDD, principal government interlocutor on the issue, was unable to decide how the legal support should be provided. The government finally decided to entrust the Programa with the task, giving it new staffing and a higher profile. AFDD members were initially reluctant. For one thing, lawyers at the Programa had always been restricted by mandate to a single task, the location of the disappeared. The institution had been expressly prevented from bringing subsequent criminal complaints on behalf of relatives.[51] The relaunched Programa did, however, become more active in adhering to existing criminal complaints. Lawyers from the Programa also began to work around the restrictions by representing relatives in a private capacity. The Programa, which had inherited much of the former Rettig commission's archive, had always been a port of call for judges investigating disappearances, and began to provide information to an increasing number of the newly assigned special judges.[52]

"NO TOMORROW WITHOUT YESTERDAY":
HUMAN RIGHTS POLICY IN 2003

After the Mesa, Lagos finally seemed to depart from the essentially passive official policy that had been the hallmark of the previous decade. Continued

---

48. A Supreme Court declaration of January 2005 insists that the 2001 survey included military courts also, but all protagonists interviewed suggest that military courts remained recalcitrant, with subsequent progress restricted solely to cases from civilian courts.

49. *Jueces de dedicación exclusiva* or *jueces de dedicación preferente*, respectively.

50. The investigative police's dedicated division, the Departamento V, has been instrumental in most successful HRV prosecutions since 1991.

51. The Programa was permitted to register *denuncias* (reports of a possible criminal offense) only for suspected illegal burial. The reports were moreover intended to produce exhumations and identification of remains, not the prosecution of perpetrators.

52. Raquel Mejías, then head of the legal department of the Programa, interview 17 January 2003.

case progress had brought, in 2002, the first sentences for theoretically amnestiable crimes. It seemed clear that the human rights question could no longer be "managed" back into stasis or obscurity, and on 13 August 2003 Lagos
launched a major Propuesta de Derechos Humanos (Human Rights Proposal). This included a second truth commission, to deal with torture,[53] as
well as "austere" and "symbolic" reparations for survivors and pardons for
remaining political prisoners.[54] Although some legislative aspects, including
a proposed reduction of penalties for informants, provoked controversy, the
proposals were the first in over a decade to broaden the HRV issue beyond
disappearance.[55] Lagos also made stronger symbolic gestures than Frei: an
unprecedentedly high-profile official program to commemorate the thirtieth
anniversary of the coup decisively rehabilitated the figure of Allende, while
studiously avoiding any mention of Pinochet.[56]

THE DECLINE AND FALL OF AUGUSTO PINOCHET: RIGGS BANK (2004)

July 2004 brought yet another unexpected complication to Pinochet's plans
for a quiet but lucrative retirement. The U.S.-based Riggs Bank, under Senate investigation over possible arms dealing, was found to have operated
secret accounts for various members of the Pinochet family. The revelation
triggered domestic investigations for possible fraud and tax evasion. Family
members told the judge that they knew nothing about the accounts because
Pinochet himself administered all money matters—a startlingly improved
picture of his mental and administrative capabilities. Allegations of financial offenses proved more damaging to Pinochet's reputation on the political
right than had criminal complaints for torture and murder. The dictatorship
had always been at pains to project itself as an austere, abstemious regime
motivated solely by the good of the country. Evidence of personal enrichment

---

53. The new truth commission became known as the "Valech commission." See below.

54. The first legislative package derived from it was submitted to the lower house in October.

55. Though some special provisions had been made for returning exiles, no previous government had recognized the very real present-day legacies of internal exile ("relegation"), blacklisting,
and imprisonment.

56. On the day of the anniversary, 11 September 2003, Lagos made a poignant solo walk around
the perimeter of the presidential palace. He re-inaugurated a doorway associated with Allende's
political martyrdom, which had been bricked up during Pinochet-era rebuilding. Surviving members of Allende's personal bodyguard later laid wreaths at Allende's statue, itself a conspicuous
recent addition to one of Santiago's most frequented public spaces. See Joignant (2007) on 11 September commemorations since 1974.

went down particularly badly with Renovación Nacional, the more traditional of Chile's two right-wing parties. Even former opponents seemed particularly exercised by money matters. Ex-president Patricio Aylwin, who was notably silent throughout criminal proceedings and had evaded testifying in the Spanish case, was moved to declare that Pinochet "ought to answer to the country." The liberal press gleefully drew direct parallels with Al Capone's final, ignominious downfall over tax evasion.

The fraud investigation also influenced the outcome of ongoing criminal cases. On 26 August 2004 the Supreme Court reversed its previous block on continuing efforts to have Pinochet prosecuted, recommending new medical tests to establish whether Pinochet's fitness to stand trial had altered since 2002.[57] The change was widely attributed to the combination of the revelation that Pinochet continued to personally direct family finances plus his apparent lucidity in a birthday interview broadcast by a Miami television station in November 2003. The ruling reversed a two-year track record of finding Pinochet "preemptively" immune from prosecution on medical grounds. On 13 December, Judge Guzmán accordingly processed (formally charged) Pinochet for his part in nine kidnappings and one murder.[58] Despite occasional wavering, from this point on the military and the mainstream right began to distance themselves slowly but inexorably from the tarnished figure of their former hero.

INTENTIONS OVER AMNESTY: SIGNS OF CHANGE IN 2004

Cases against agents other than Pinochet had also been moving ahead, and began to produce yet more signs of judicial innovation. Investigations into the 1975 disappearance of Miguel Angel Sandoval, as the first case to reach sentencing stage after 1998's key Poblete-Córdoba ruling, had become a test for the new doctrine of non-amnestiable kidnap. Blanket amnesty seemed to be definitely on the retreat after the initial, April 2003 Sandoval verdict imposed sentences of up to fifteen years for perpetrators, including the ubiquitous Manuel Contreras. By 2004 the verdict was up before the Supreme Court on appeal.

57. Majority ruling (9–8) of the Supreme Court, 26 August 2004, Rol. 2182-98, episode Operación Cóndor.

58. *Auto de procesamiento* emitted by the Santiago Appeals Court, 13 December 2004, Rol. 2182-98, episode Operación Cóndor. These were the first charges preferred against Pinochet since the Caravana case, also investigated by Judge Guzmán, had been suspended on medical grounds in 2001 (see above).

The outcome was being carefully watched as the first signal of likely Court intentions on the hundreds of other ongoing cases yet to reach this stage.

In the event, the Court's November 2004 verdict allayed the fears of lawyers and HROs. It upheld the view that amnesty should not be applied to disappearance, and for the first time firmly declared that the DINA and its installations, detention centers, and practices had all been manifestly illegal. In a less progressive vein, however, the verdict issued a "reminder" that the location of remains would convert disappearance into amnestiable homicide. Its acceptance of international law was also relatively weak, using international norms in a merely illustrative or supplementary manner.[59] But it was the line taken by the government, rather than the judiciary, that worried lawyers. The government's legal agency, the Consejo de Defensa del Estado (CDE),[60] had initially taken a prosecuting role in the case, arguing in favor of the 2003 convictions. In 2004, however, the CDE executed a remarkable volte-face. It argued that although the verdict should be upheld in this particular case, the loophole should be closed to future claimants. The CDE argued that an "alternative method" of legally establishing a victim's death should be sought, allowing future disappearance cases to be treated as homicides even where the body had not been discovered or eyewitnesses could not be found.[61]

Accountability actors believed the CDE's position reflected a new government plan to placate the military. Lawyers claimed that the "Insulza project"—so named for then chancellor José Miguel Insulza, rumored to be its architect and principal enthusiast—aimed to minimize future convictions. The principle of amnesty was to be reasserted, and reduced penalties encouraged for cases to which it could no longer apply.[62] The suggestion that the

---

59. A fuller acceptance would have recognized the direct applicability ("justiciability") of international legal principles in the domestic domain. Decision emitted by the Second Chamber of the Supreme Court, *recurso de casación* in Rol. 517-2004, 17 November 2004.

60. The CDE is a somewhat unusual state legal agency, quite distinct from the public prosecutor's office and operating in effect as a private legal chamber acting on behalf of the state. Thus the CDE defends the state against civil and other legal claims, and can also adhere to criminal prosecutions in cases deemed particularly significant to the national interest. In prosecutions it is given roughly the same status as a private adherent, although it has enhanced (because nondiscretionary) access to the judge's investigative record.

61. CDE, "Minuto de Alegato, recurso de casación forma y fondo," Sandoval case, dated 29 September 2004; on file with author.

62. *El Mostrador,* 5 October 2004. Penalties would be reduced using an existing criminal code provision allowing judges to apply discounted sentencing once more than half the set prescription (statute of limitation) period for a crime has elapsed. This same clause was invoked in 1993 to keep Contreras's and Espinoza's sentences for murder to a minimum, and would reappear in 2008 with some force.

government might be signaling to the courts a desire to see accountability progress slowed in this way was for some reinforced by developments in more minor cases in late 2004.[63]

THE "VALECH REPORT" (NOVEMBER 2004)

The Comisión Nacional Sobre Prisión Política y Tortura (National Commission on Political Imprisonment and Torture) had begun work in late 2003. Its report, published in November 2004, represented the first in-depth official account of the non-fatal HRVs not addressed by Rettig. Known as the Valech report, after its chairman, Monsignor Sergio Valech,[64] the report summarized approximately thirty-five thousand graphic testimonies received from survivors over a nine-month period. It found that over twenty-eight thousand people had suffered illegal detention or torture in over one thousand clandestine detention centers across the country.[65] The report caused genuine public consternation, and generated the first-ever official acknowledgement by the military that HRVs had been an institutional policy and practice. The renewed mea culpa emitted by army commander in chief Juan Emilio Cheyre on 5 November nonetheless exposed a growing gulf between even this moderate capitulation and more hard-line stances. Navy and police chiefs distanced themselves from Cheyre's statement, and the Supreme Court declared itself unmoved by the flurry of calls to public repentance that followed. Despite the obvious determination to redress some of the limitations of Rettig by addressing the subject of violence against survivors, the initiative could also be read as yet another essentially diversionary, truth-for-justice activity. In particular, the decision to place testimony under a fifty-year embargo and ban its use for judicial purposes[66] was noisily resisted by some HROs and by the organized survivors' groups that had begun to emerge.

---

63. On 21 October a first-instance judge amnestied a disappearance case, allowing uncorroborated testimony to convert the crimes into amnestiable homicide. The verdict contravened extant requirements for the establishment of a legal presumption of death, and rejected international law arguments with the statement that the relevant Inter-American Convention, ratified by Chile, was nonetheless "not a law of the Republic." *Santiago Times,* 21 October 2004. The author is grateful to David Sugarman for drawing her attention to this case.

64. Valech is a retired bishop and former Vicaría director, who was also a key figure in the 1999/2000 Mesa. The report is available at http://www.comisionvalech.gov.cl/InformeValech.html.

65. Additional later cases added a further one thousand victims, among them eighty-seven children under twelve years old.

66. Text of "Presidential Message to the Congressional Chamber of Deputies Nº 203–352," dated 10 December 2004, regarding pensions and other reparations and benefits (on file with author).

LAGOS AND THE MILITARY

Lagos cultivated generally positive relations with the military, although accountability change in the later part of his term made the relationship precarious at times. The high command attempted a delicate balancing act between acknowledgement and defensiveness, evidenced by its participation in the Mesa, efforts to differentiate the institutional armed forces from the "maverick" DINA, and a growing tendency to point to civilian culpability for the 1973 coup. Although the capacity of the armed forces to exercise political power has been dramatically reduced, it undoubtedly retains a symbolic potency, which means that its pleasures and displeasures in this matter do carry weight with the government of the day. Tensions rose and fell with the timing of particular irruptions or incidents, and the limits of military preparedness to traduce Pinochet and his legacy were repeatedly tested. In January 2005, dramatic and occasionally violent scenes surrounding the forcible removal of Manuel Contreras from his home[67] led military figures to talk publicly of "lynching" as they strenuously protested the government's handling of the affair.[68]

EFFORTS TO LIMIT OPEN ACCOUNTABILITY CASES IN 2005

On 25 January 2005 the Supreme Court issued an edict setting a six-month time limit for outstanding HRV cases. Judges with investigations at the final, *sumario* stage were ordered to prefer charges or to suspend (*sobreseer*) the case within six months. The move came only twenty-four hours before a similar, broader government proposal to facilitate justice system changeover by bringing cases opened under the soon-to-be-superseded investigating magistrate system to an end.[69] Accountability actors resisted the move, believing

67. Contreras was required to appear in court, to receive confirmation of a twelve-year sentence for his part in the Sandoval disappearance.

68. The scenes were reminiscent of earlier attempts to imprison Contreras, although the military response in 2005 was somewhat complicated by its own increasingly fraught relationship with the former DINA agent. Contravening the military code of silence, he had publicly accused both Pinochet and the institution as a whole of betrayal. Even as detectives ignominiously hauled him from his home, he was issuing thinly veiled threats of future damaging revelations. *El Mostrador*, 28 January 2005.

69. See below for discussion of the system and the main features of reform. The government's proposal, known as the *ley empalme*, would have applied to all ongoing criminal cases, while the Supreme Court's edict was specific to human rights cases. Their practical effects in HRV cases, however, would have been identical.

judges were bowing to government and military pressure for a speedy end to high-profile prosecutions. Even some judges rejected the idea, with the capital's magistrates association declaring it unacceptable interference with judges' freedom of action. The proposal was nonetheless welcomed by all 2005 presidential candidates, who claimed it was a simple "efficiency" move as likely to expedite as to frustrate final sentencing (*El Mostrador,* 26 January 2005). In the event, both proposals were quietly dropped—another common occurrence in post-transitional policy affecting accountability.

MICHELLE BACHELET (2006–2010)

Michelle Bachelet, Chile's first-ever woman president, took office in March 2006 to high expectations from many quarters. These included human rights groups, who believed that this former political prisoner and exile, with close personal links to figures in major HROs, would be more likely than previous incumbents to understand and support their demands. Bachelet certainly reached out to relatives' groups on a personal level: one of her first official engagements was the inauguration of a monument to the *degollados,* and in the first six months of her presidency she also made a visit to Villa Grimaldi, the reclaimed former torture center where she had briefly been detained back in the 1970s. A proliferation of private memorialization initiatives continued to be supported and in some cases funded by state bodies,[70] a process begun under Lagos. Bachelet also formalized and extended other initiatives first mentioned by Lagos, announcing plans for a national Museum of Memory and a state Human Rights Institute. But these efforts belonged largely to the realm of symbolic or memory politics, rather than accountability per se. They also ran into their own difficulties, with poor communication and lack of legislative support leading to conflicts with some HROs and the temporary abandonment of the Institute proposal.[71]

The major milestone of the first part of Bachelet's term, however, was a much more directly political and symbolically weighty event: the death of Augusto Pinochet. Taken ill in late November, the aging and somewhat beleaguered former strongman died in a military hospital on 10 December 2006.

---

70. Such state bodies included the Council for National Monuments and the Ministry of Public Works.

71. The museum, eventually a somewhat-rushed affair, was finally constructed in late 2009, and a heavily revised Human Rights Institute proposal made it through Congress in August of the same year. See Hite and Collins (2009).

At the time of his death, he had been processed in various human rights cases and one financial fraud case. Many more cases were pending, and charges in the two more advanced human rights investigations had been set aside for health reasons.[72] Nonetheless, his demise provoked suggestions that as an ex-president he was owed a state funeral. After some vacillation, this was not granted, and neither were public buildings allowed to display signs of mourning such as the flying of flags at half mast. Bachelet, herself a former defense minister,[73] did not attend the private funeral at the main Military Academy. The service was attended by her own defense minister, however, who was roundly booed by attendees and looked ill at ease throughout an event that felt in some peculiar sense like the last hurrah of unrepentant Pinochetismo. The "great man" was later cremated, his ashes scattered because of family fears that his burial site might be profaned.

Although the management of the death itself was tricky, the physical removal of the brooding presence who had overdetermined the justice debate for so long seemed to alleviate built-up pressure on all sides. Cases against other former repressors continued, and a certain disappointment among accountability actors that Pinochet had died unsentenced—albeit not quite untouched—was tempered by the view that the courts might actually now find it easier to proceed against others. In terms of official policy, though, Bachelet had failed to demonstrate a sure touch. The eventual mix of vacillation, second-string acknowledgement, and muted official censure risked pleasing no one.

A similar pattern emerged from Bachelet's handling of two other major irruptions during her term. The first began just weeks before Pinochet's death, when the Inter-American Court of Human Rights issued a verdict in the *Chile v. Almonacid* case.[74] The verdict, as expected, condemned Chile's continued application of the amnesty law as contrary to its international obligations. Amid growing external concern over Chile's neglect of other rights issues, such as indigenous questions and the treatment of prisoners and protesters, the verdict brought an explicit commitment that national practice would be

72. The investigative magistrate system involves a "processing" phase that, although it comes before formal charges, conveys the judge's strong presumption that the person has some responsibility for the alleged crime.

73. Further, she is the daughter of a senior air force general who, like many constitutionalist officers, was arrested immediately after the coup. He died in prison.

74. The case concerned the 1973 illegal execution of a teacher in the southern Chilean town of Rancagua.

brought into line with international law. Although repeated periodically over the ensuing months and years, the commitment was simply not fulfilled. By March 2010 the promised legislative proposal had still not materialized, while the 2008 death of Juan Bustos, the widely respected parliamentarian and jurist entrusted with its drafting, boded ill for prospects that it ever would.[75]

The sense of unforced errors and a possibly excessive readiness to defer to right-wing sensibilities was reinforced over the 2008 inauguration of a monument to Jaime Guzmán. A right-wing ideologue close to Pinochet, Guzmán had been assassinated shortly after the return to democracy (and just days after the publication of the Rettig report). Adopted ever since as a martyr for the right, proof that violence had been "on both sides," Guzmán's figure became even more attractive to the political right after Pinochet's decline, as a possible alternative founding father. Architect of the 1980 Constitution and a deeply, conservatively religious individual, Guzmán represents the right's view of the positive legacies of the dictatorship period. The right-wing Unión Demócrata Independiente (UDI) party (which he founded) accordingly commissioned a memorial to him, and invited Bachelet to officially inaugurate it upon completion. Initially minded to accept, only major public debate about the decision and its symbolism produced a late-in-the-day climbdown by Bachelet, which yet again left all sides unhappy.

Bachelet did take occasionally valiant stances over certain justice issues, insisting in early 2008 on the resignation of a serving general implicated in past HRVs, and allowing the courts an apparently freer hand than had Lagos. The abiding sense of her term, however, is one of an administration that became gradually more successful precisely when emphasizing other issues, such as social policy. Although Bachelet herself was riding high in the polls by the end of her term, the Concertación as a whole was looking increasingly jaded, as well as beset by reelection worries.[76] Against this backdrop, although Bachelet held on to the idea of the state memory museum as a lasting personal legacy, it may well come to figure less highly than once anticipated in her list of memorable achievements in office.

75. A compromise proposal presented to the Senate in June 2008, two months before Bustos's death, was rejected in March 2009 after failing to secure the necessary votes.

76. Bachelet herself was not eligible for reelection, but signs of fracture and minor corruption scandals in the Concertación conspired to make the coalition's 2010 electoral prospects a worry from the very beginning of her term. Moreover, as presidential terms had been reduced from six years to four by 2005 constitutional changes, the positioning of possible candidates began almost as soon as she had taken office.

SUMMING UP: ACCOUNTABILITY POLICY
AND CHANGE UNDER THE CONCERTACIÓN

Wilde (1999) documents an emerging pattern in the mid-1990s of leaving the courts to deal piecemeal with individual cases, since it became increasingly apparent to successive Concertación administrations that accountability was a politically unrewarding issue. The courts thus became the most significant arbiters of accountability stasis or change. Since they were lacking in accountability enthusiasm during most of the period, the practical outcome was a steady trickle of unremarkable judicial resolutions upholding the applicability of amnesty. Only occasionally did a conviction make headlines, usually due to a contemplated exception or exclusion rather than some spectacular judicial innovation.[77] Thus government policy arguably amounted to leaving accountability well alone by leaving it to the courts. It was not until court behavior itself changed in 1998 that leaving it to the courts implied accepting the possibility of much more resolute pro-accountability outcomes.

Government policy in the decade after the Pinochet case makes it difficult to accurately assess how far new judicial activism was welcomed. The Concertación's renewed executive activism in 2003 might be viewed as an attempt to wrest the initiative from the courts precisely to dampen renewed enthusiasm for accountability and ensure a return to the status quo ante. Alternatively, it might be read as a positive grasping of the opportunity to significantly reconfigure Chile's delicate truth-versus-justice equilibrium. In this reading, 1998's irruption was not so much a foreign intrusion into a stable domestic equilibrium as a sign of the times, ripe for the kind of comprehensive accountability change that previous administrations had considered impossible or ill-advised. Particularly in the most recently concluded presidential period, different parts of the state seemed to act in distinct, occasionally even contradictory, directions over accountability. Like earlier administrations, Bachelet's appeared more comfortable acting in "softer" policy areas (including, in her case, memorialization). In Bachelet's final year it also became increasingly clear that the Concertación's monopoly of post-transitional politics would be interrupted by a right-wing electoral victory. Thus an additional factor in activity during 2009 was the choice between radical pro-accountability action

---

77. Such convictions included the Letelier murders, specifically excluded from amnesty, and the *degollados* verdict, which, like other notable 1990s convictions, concerned crimes committed well after the amnestiable period.

likely to be reversed in the future—essentially a valedictory salute from the Concertación's present political generation—and continued caution, anticipating future political direction by preserving the principles of amnesty.

Explaining Post-transitional Accountability: Actors, Strategy, and Judicial Receptivity

The Chilean government has not to date been an active architect of the country's post-transitional accountability trajectory. Even the burst of executive interventionism around 2003/4 followed the established Concertación pattern of responding to irruptions while handing the justice dimension on to the courts. This pattern has made judicial response to HRV cases the major institutional determinant of justice outcomes, with executive intervention visible, if at all, in and through the courts. Chile's post-transitional accountability history has therefore been forged in the interaction between accountability actors and justice institutions: specifically, between lawyers and judges. The section that follows analyzes this interaction in some depth along three thematic axes: accountability actors, legal strategies, and judicial receptivity. These represent, as defined in chapter 3, the key protagonists and processes for understanding Chilean accountability history since 1990, and change since 1998. The tripartite structure permits a critical examination in each part of the role supposedly played by internationalized intervention in domestic change, thus allowing testing of the argument advanced in chapter 3 regarding the potentially independent and unarticulated nature of some transnational accountability activity.

ACCOUNTABILITY ACTORS

The universe of accountability actors in Chile is characterized by its emergence from an early, dense network of lawyer-led human rights organizing with a correspondingly pronounced emphasis on formal legal action. Much early legal activity was defensive rather than pro-accountability.[78] But this activity did leave behind a "paper trail" of archival and documentary evidence, as well as a portfolio of cases within the court system. This early portfolio was heavily

---

78. That is, it aimed to improve a detainee's treatment or hasten release, as lawyers rightly believed that the prosecution of perpetrators was virtually unachievable. See chapter 4.

weighted toward cases involving disappearance. HRO lawyers and legal strategists, although perhaps not particularly ingenious in developing multiple or novel "lines of attack," did prove extremely resourceful in generating cases and keeping them alive in unfavorable conditions during the dictatorship period. Careful repertoires of intervention evolved, intended primarily to keep cases out of the military courts and to postpone or avoid their definitive closure. Endless submissions of witness statements and suggested lines of inquiry to judges were designed more to combat closure than in the hopes of catalyzing any real breakthrough. Nonetheless, this habitual resort to professionally led, case-by-case legal action was perhaps the principal legacy of dictatorship-era human rights organizing in Chile.

Post-transitional Fragmentation of HROs: The Decline of Coordinated Legal Action

After transition, the conditions for a renewed legal offensive with a more explicit goal of accountability did not materialize. Accountability actors proved largely unable or unwilling to independently create such conditions in the face of official reluctance and the perpetuation of amnesty. The iconic Vicaría disappeared altogether, and so ceased to exercise its former centripetal force over other organizations. The human rights community appeared to both shrink and fragment, and remaining organizations were extensively streamlined. Many well-known human rights lawyers moved into private practice. Previous instances of lawyer cooperation[79] lapsed into inactivity and were finally dissolved. One HRO, the Comisión Chilena de Derechos Humanos (Chilean Human Rights Commission), shrank from nationwide reach to a single central office before closing down altogether. FASIC[80] and CODEPU,[81] the two HROs that did continue legal work, suffered from a significant drop in outside interest and financial support. They took over the Vicaría's active caseload when it closed, but were forced to depend on reduced in-house legal teams plus the virtually unpaid services of loosely affiliated lawyers.

Transition did not, therefore, bring an upsurge in the presentation of new cases or new types of case. The first modest accountability successes were registered in non-amnestiable cases, but the courts clearly had no intention

---

79. Examples include the Association of Human Rights Lawyers, active from 1980, and the Association of Lawyers of Political Prisoners, founded in 1987.

80. The Fundación de Ayuda Social de las Iglesias Cristianas, founded in 1975.

81. La Corporación de Promoción y Defensa de los Derechos del Pueblo, founded in 1980.

of significantly altering their overall approach. Lawyers in still-open early cases often kept them on in a personal capacity as institutional profiles declined; "human rights lawyers" therefore came to constitute the most visible public referents of the human rights community. "Holding actions" in existing cases increasingly came to dominate a rather static post-transitional accountability scene.

The most prominent organized groups still active on this scene were FASIC and CODEPU, together with the AFDD as the main, and earliest, relatives' association.[82] Before the transition, FASIC had worked principally with political prisoners. But in 1992 FASIC inherited the Vicaría's active disappearance cases and also provided the AFDD with a new home. CODEPU, which had been founded in 1980 with a more radical political profile in response to the emergence of armed opposition, took over the Vicaría's political execution caseload. Other individual lawyers continued to represent specific relatives or victims. This reduced community did retain some capacity for concerted action, joining forces to lobby against legislative proposals they considered favorable to impunity. The only major cross-sector instance that survived intact, however, was the Comisión Ética Contra la Tortura (Ethical Antitorture Commission), a grouping formed in 1980 and stretching beyond the core human rights instances to include religious leaders and trade union representatives. The group was not, however, centrally concerned with accountability, concentrating instead on lobbying for educational initiatives and the incorporation of international legislation.

There was, moreover, evidence of increasing fragmentation and even contention within the human rights community over accountability-related legal and legislative matters. Legal strategy ceased to follow the univocal institutional "line" developed by the Vicaría in former times. Alfonso Insunza, a former Vicaría lawyer, launched a legal challenge to the constitutionality of amnesty on behalf of victims including his own brother. Other lawyers criticized the initiative, fearful that such a frontal assault on the principle of amnesty so close to transition would produce a reaffirmation or even strengthening of the principle. Their fears were effectively realized when, in August 1990, the Supreme Court unanimously found amnesty not only valid

82. The AFDD was formally founded in 1975. A later organization of relatives of victims of political execution, the Agrupación de Familiares de los Ejecutados Políticos (AFEP), never reached the same public prominence or virtually iconic status, despite having a potentially much greater membership. AFEP did, however, adhere along with the AFDD and CODEPU to the 1996 Spanish complaint against Pinochet.

but "of compulsory application."[83] This failure of early efforts at maximalism accelerated the decline in cooperative working and day-to-day contacts. Accountability was a goal not shared by all, and even those who shared it did not have a single, concerted strategy with which to achieve it.

The Accountability Actor Field in the 1990s

The "historic" human rights community, with its core group of lawyers,[84] has been strongly associated with past HRV issues and largely segregated from newer human rights issue groups in post-transitional Chile. Accountability was treated as the virtually exclusive preserve of this historic group plus the Communist Party (PC). Outlawed during the dictatorship, the PC suffered swingeing repression, losing virtually two entire Central Committees. PC interest in the issue is thus as intensely personal as it is politically legitimate: many of the most active members of the AFDD are also linked to the PC. The institutional protagonism of the PC in the accountability field has, however, helped to perpetuate a certain public stigma attached to justice demands, and some other members of the human rights community perceive the PC's protagonism as divisive. This is particularly true of the post-1998 period, during which the PC adopted independent initiatives and hardened its already inflexible stance with regard to government initiatives on justice.

One government initiative already discussed, the Mesa, provoked serious ruptures between accountability actors in Chile. The PC and others condemned the initiative a priori as a betrayal of the justice cause.[85] Following hard on the heels of Pinochet's detention in Britain, some saw it as simply a diversionary ploy to promote his return.[86] Only one of the surviving "historic"

---

83. Supreme Court resolution of 24 August 1990, "Recurso de inaplicabilidad," in Rol. 27-460. See also Hilbink (2003, 80).

84. A number of newer or younger lawyers associated with accountability issues emerged during the 1990s, mostly linked to CODEPU or the PC. After 2002, a second new group associated with the state Programa began to be more visible. This group seems set to inherit the historical mantle, although it seems doubtful that past HRV cases will persist very long into their careers.

85. "It was argued . . . that the very existence of the Mesa sent a strong signal to the judicial branch identifying dialogue as a political alternative that would inhibit the action of justice" (Elizabeth Lira in *Mensaje,* July 2001; author's translation).

86. Opinions differ about the aims and even origins of the Mesa, regarded variously as a preexisting commitment or a post-arrest pretext to bring Pinochet home. Of the actual Mesa participants interviewed, only Héctor Salazar expressed the latter view, and in a more moderate form. Although he acknowledged earlier efforts on the government side, he was adamant that it had taken the arrest to spur the armed forces to a definitive realization that there was sufficient "unfinished business" to drive them to the discussion table. Héctor Salazar, interview 17 October 2002.

HROs supported it (FASIC),[87] and relatives' groups subsequently withdrew representation of their cases from lawyers who took part. The AFDD virtually severed its historic ties with FASIC. Pamela Pereira, a long-time AFDD member who took part in the Mesa in her professional capacity as a lawyer, effectively became estranged from the AFDD after identifying so strongly with the Mesa's aims that it was alleged she had pressured judges to make rulings that would "facilitate" continued military participation (*El Mostrador,* 16 October 2000). She was removed as a prosecuting lawyer in the Caravana case, and virtually abandoned the human rights scene in favor of her alternative career as secretary of the Socialist Party.[88] Many interviewees described how this and similar fractures that followed the Mesa drove a wedge not only between the government and accountability actors, but also between members of the human rights community who were either less or more hardline about accountability and the permissibility of dialogue.[89] According to Mireya García, these breaches prevented actors from taking full advantage of new accountability opportunities that opened up.[90]

The Caravana Case: An Instance of Domestic Collaboration?

The Caravana case appears at first sight to constitute a noteworthy counter-example of collaborative networking. A working group of seven or eight lawyers of decidedly distinct ideological and institutional affinities eventually conducted the case, winning notable legal victories. Most of those who were involved, however, regard the collaborative experience as exceptional. They also acknowledge tensions and rifts with other domestic accountability actors: many more would-be participants were excluded than were included. The group itself came into being only because each lawyer had already sponsored a separate complaint and could thereby claim a role in the prosecution "by right." Collaboration, though real and significant, was thus post hoc. Coordination occurred mainly to ensure that separate approaches did not imperil the case, and did not preclude rivalries over who should take a leadership

87. Two lawyers associated with FASIC (one previously, one actually) took part in the Mesa. Officially, however, both participated in a personal capacity rather than as representatives of the HRO.

88. She continued to act in the Prats case, however, and would reappear in 2008 in a decidedly institutional role as government "fixer" trying to rescue the aborted Human Rights Institute proposal.

89. Notably, of the four lawyers who did finally take part, only two, Pamela Pereira and Héctor Salazar, were actively participating in accountability efforts through cases. Nelson Caucoto, Chile's single most active accountability case lawyer, withdrew early on.

90. Mireya García, interview 18 November 2002.

role.[91] Additionally, the peculiar progress of the case, interrupted as it was by Pinochet's period of UK detention, brought enforced collision with other accountability actors, including the lawyers behind the Spanish case.

The Caravana case had come into being as the second of the January 1998 complaints submitted against Pinochet. The file opened by Judge Guzmán under Rol. (Case) 2182–98 came to cover a variety of incidents, periods, and victims, the common thread being that each accused Pinochet and others of serious criminal offenses. Of a dozen complaints submitted between January and mid-October,[92] the most promising were one from January and another from June, both related to the Caravana killings of late 1973. Caravana emerged as the most viable episode because it was a reasonably well-established incident that had even seen some prior judicial activity. The previous complaints, initiated in 1985 thanks to the sheer tenacity of relatives, now came to serve several very important purposes. First, they provided initial investigative material for Guzmán. Second, the mere fact that they had existed meant that the crimes, although almost twenty-five years old, had not "prescribed"— lapsed for lack of timely judicial action. Third, another fortuitous technicality, the cases had been suspended by military courts through premature, and thus reversible, application of the amnesty law.

Once it became clear that Guzmán was concentrating on Caravana, lawyers and relatives from the first two complaints came together to form an identifiable group. The contact was made easier by existing political and personal contacts: both main lawyers had PC connections and some relatives were already organized into regional groupings. The group expanded somewhat as initial success awoke new interest. By mid to late 1998, the lawyers' group consisted of seven members. Eduardo Contreras represented the PC, who, in addition to having lodged the first, unrelated, January complaint, had members among the Caravana victims. Boris Paredes, Hugo Gutiérrez, and Hiram Villagra represented relatives who had submitted individual or group complaints. Alfonso Insunza was representing the daughter of one victim

91. "We all wanted to go down in history as the one who got Pinochet arrested" (prosecuting lawyer, interview last quarter of 2002).

92. These figures are based on examination of CODEPU archives. For most of the post-1998 period there has been no single, reliable public-access data available for tracking case progress. Distinct organizations published their own electronic tallies at various times on http://www.codepu.cl/, http://www.fasic.org/, and http://www.memoriayjusticia.cl/, but few are consistently updated. The most comprehensive record is a summary kept by the Programa since 2003, available only on a discretionary basis. The Universidad Diego Portales launched a project in late 2009 to make trial statistics publicly available in 2010.

because of a personal connection. Juan Bustos, a lawyer and Socialist Party (PS) parliamentarian who had previously taken part in the Letelier prosecution, represented the PS (Caravana had been an operation to wipe out PS members in regional government positions). Carmen Hertz, as the widow of a victim, had a very personal and direct reason to participate; however, since she was working for the government Programa at the time, she preferred initially to be represented by Pamela Pereira.[93]

The group's considerable legal and political achievements include the previously unthinkable: having Pinochet first stripped of senatorial immunity then processed for a crime. The subsequent suspension of proceedings against Pinochet, however, reduced both public and professional interest. Although the case remained the subject of active investigation in regard to other perpetrators, few lawyers from the original team even participated in hearings held in late 2002.[94] A similar dynamic would continue to affect this and other cases: legal strategy and team approaches became difficult to sustain as many cases dragged on for a full decade after 1998.[95] Successful coordination was also made more difficult in the immediate post-1998 period by the predictable corollary of apparent success: a growing number both of cases and of lawyers interested in representing them.

Domestic Networking Among Present-Day Accountability Actors

In sum, the Mesa did not create so much as expose and exacerbate existing tensions within the Chilean human rights community. The cohesion maintained even among politically diverse organizations during the time of the Vicaría dwindled after transition. Relations between the two major HROs who continued legal work became particularly strained in the post-1998 period, with ideological differences exacerbated by demarcation disputes over new cases.[96] The AFDD suffered its own internal divisions: the death in 1999 of its respected long-time president, Sola Sierra, accentuated a tendency

---

93. When Pereira was removed after the Mesa dispute, Hertz took on direct representation of her own case. An eighth lawyer, Juan Subercaseaux, played a strong supporting and research role from early stages.

94. Eduardo Contreras, interview 3 December 2002.

95. An eventual 2008 Caravana guilty verdict against Pinochet's personal envoy Arellano Stark was something of a Pyrrhic victory: the former general had become so frail in the course of the intervening decade that he was spared prison, released instead into the "custody" of his family.

96. FASIC lawyers complained that new cases submitted by CODEPU overlapped with their own active cases, alleging deliberate poaching. CODEPU in turn complained of a proprietorial attitude from FASIC lawyers. Interview data, October and November 2002.

to divide into pro- and anti-PC factions, with the pro-PC faction dominant after 2003.

Lawyers, like HROs, tended over time to maintain only sporadic, case-by-case collaboration within small "affinity groups," clusters of individuals linked by personal ties or shared ideology. The Caravana case produced a limited and temporary reversal of this tendency. The proliferation of new actors (see below), however, effectively multiplied the number of affinity groups, further reducing the cohesiveness of accountability demands.[97] The post-1998 expansion of the accountability-actor universe increased the likelihood of distinct or even inimical goals for legal action. Some new actors had a preference for extralegal accountability actions, such as direct action. Others adopted an essentially instrumental approach to accountability actions, seen as one possible method of bringing political pressure or establishing particular historical readings of certain events.

International Networking: A Deliberate Actor Strategy?

At the international level, the Pinochet case in Spain is often cited as an instance of transnational accountability networks in action. On closer examination, however, the domestic "ends" of these putative networks are extremely difficult to detect. The fact that the Spanish case invoked universal jurisdiction principles does not in itself make it anything more than a domestic case about other-country events.[98] Most Chilean HROs and lawyers report more, and denser, international contact and collaboration during the dictatorship period than in the build-up to the 1998 arrest. Any notion that concerted action between lawyers, HROs, or relatives' groups inside and outside Chile was behind the arrest appears particularly unwarranted. Although most Chilean accountability actors had previously known of the existence of the Spanish cases, groups had not collaborated horizontally within Chile over it and most reported skepticism as to its eventual success right up until the absolutely unexpected developments of October 1998.[99]

The PC, who brought the first domestic claim against Pinochet, had previously supplied witnesses for the Spanish proceedings. Both they and the AFDD (who adhered to the Chilean case in March 1998), however, report their domestic legal initiatives as motivated by internal political developments.

97. Although simple numerical proliferation need not produce fragmentation, in this particular instance both can be observed.

98. See comments by Zalaquett reported in Brett (2009, 13).

99. Interview data, September 2002 to March 2003.

Indeed, any suggestion of deliberate sequencing (bringing an "international" case followed by national cases) founders when it is considered that the cases rapidly came to clash rather than reinforce or complement one another. The very existence of the Caravana complaints was used by both Pinochet's supporters and the Chilean government to try and persuade Spanish judicial authorities to relinquish their claim. The Spanish lawyers accordingly pressured Chilean accountability actors, particularly the Caravana lawyers, to abandon their domestic claims.[100]

The evidence does not support a strong interpretation of the "boomerang" thesis, which would suggest that Chilean accountability actors cooperated systematically with outside groups, having the Spanish case brought on their behalf in order to unblock unyielding domestic avenues. First, domestic actors did perceive national avenues, particularly the judicial, to be offering improved prospects starting around 1996 or 1997.[101] Second, domestic actors instigated a set of cases in Chile after the Spanish investigation was under way. This was not done in concert with the Spanish case lawyers, but by groups who, though aware of the Spanish case, judged it either unlikely to succeed or simply of no direct relevance for their own domestic strategy decisions.

As to the effects, as distinct from the origins, of the Pinochet arrest, all Chilean accountability actors interviewed believed the Spanish case had proved an indirect stimulus to domestic accountability progress in Chile. Nonetheless, none identified it as the single or sole cause of such progress.[102] Nor did they view transnational legal activity as a possible or desirable strategic alternative to domestic accountability. Those who expressed any opinion unanimously felt that the best possible outcome had been the eventual return of the issue to the domestic sphere. Nor were any actors interviewed actively contemplating similar actions or future transnational activity as a priority. Chilean actors' involvement with other-country venues has generally been driven by particular geographical circumstance rather than motivated by

---

100. Hiram Villagra, interview 13 November 2002.

101. Hugo Gutiérrez, interview 14 November 2002; and Eduardo Contreras, interview 3 December 2002. Sebastian Brett recognized the currency of this perception even though he himself did not share it (interview 15 October 2002). See also Correa Sutil (1999).

102. The sole possible exception is Roberto Garretón, who had earlier testified to the British Law Lords as to the unlikelihood of Pinochet's ever being tried in Chile: "Between 1990 and 1998 there was no attempt to discuss human rights or to change the Constitution. The official line was: 'Chile is reconciled; we're living in a democracy, the [political] right is democratic and no one cares about human rights any more.' Then Pinochet gets arrested, and the next day we discover that people *do* still care about human rights and the 'democratic right' is nowhere to be seen. We discovered all of that in October 1998" (interview 10 January 2003).

"venue shopping."[103] That is, internationalization has been a function of the "international" nature of Chilean repression (Wilde 1999, 489) rather than a deliberate strategy aimed at bypassing domestic venues.

Diversification of Actors, Goals, and Types of Claim

Domestic HROs and lawyers reported temporarily increased but not sustained interest from outside groups after the Pinochet case, consisting more often of requests for information than offers of collaboration.[104] Neither domestic nor international networking seem presently to be strong features of the Chilean accountability scene. Domestically, unprecedented accountability success post-1998 seems to have been as much a source of conflict as a product of or stimulus to cooperation. The period has seen disputes over strategy, terrain, and credentials between established accountability actors. At the same time, new actors have been drawn into the accountability field. These include relatives and survivors attracted by improved prospects of success. They also include groups such as the PC "switching" previous political activity into the judicial system since the courts seem to be offering, at the present time, better possibilities for justice than other channels. Increased demand has thus been generated, in the form of hundreds of criminal and civil HRV-related complaints entering the judicial system from 1998.[105] Lawyers, for their part, were drawn (back) into accountability work by the desire to be part of a historic moment and to participate in success. Thus increased demand came from an increasingly wide range of claim-bringers after the late 1990s.

New relatives' groups emerged, occasionally aligned more closely to the political right than the left.[106] But perhaps the most notable change after 1998 was the emergence of organized survivors' groups, for the first time systematically pursuing civil or criminal recourse over torture, imprisonment, and exile. Some of these groups were formed explicitly to take advantage of a perceived opening of domestic judicial space after the Pinochet case, while

103. Thus members of the Letelier family were involved in U.S. legal actions because the crime was committed in the United States. The Prats case was investigated in Argentina for similar reasons. A civil case over Caravana took place in the United States in 2003 because, although the crime was committed in Chile, both the perpetrator and the victim's family were resident in the U.S.

104. Interview data, September 2002 to March 2003.

105. See table 2 for overall case statistics to February 2010. The post-1998 rise is not as steep as often believed, in part because over a hundred historical cases still existed in the system at the time, and in part because many new complaints were accumulated to existing investigations or merged.

106. A group of around eight families from the northern city of Iquique made news when it approached the UDI in 2003 for discussions over possible reparations.

preexisting groups were also spurred to consider legal action. One specific judicial action also had a significant, if unintended, effect on claim-bringing. In June 1999, Guzmán divided the already unwieldy Pinochet investigation into a more manageable collection of twenty episodes, each representing particular detention centers or repressive agencies. Intended as nothing more than a simple administrative measure, it caused groups to coalesce around the episodes, pooling information and exchanging ideas.[107] This represented a significant shift in the approach to accountability. Previous investigations had usually been carried out in isolation. Although relatives' groups had always provided a potential meeting space for individual claim-bringers, cases would typically be in different courts and at different stages. The opportunities for practical strategic collaboration were correspondingly few, and the conduct of a case was almost completely at the discretion of its lawyer. Once investigations were grouped into episodes, however, judges began to "streamline" hearings, stipulating, for example, that a maximum of two or three lawyers would be allowed to speak at any one hearing. Lawyers therefore also had to agree on lines of argument and take turns appearing. One HRO began to promote a group approach from the start for torture cases, inviting individual survivors to form support structures before submitting a single case on behalf of the entire cohort.[108]

Although these new developments promoted agglutination rather than strictly individualized new action, the expansion of the legal actor field beyond relatives to include survivors makes the Chilean accountability scene on balance more fragmented than in the past. New affinity groups, rather than relying solely on the traditional group of historic lawyers—which previously imposed a certain legal continuity—proved more ready to "shop around" for representation. Some even decided to ask group members with legal training to act as in-house case lawyers. This sometimes negatively affected the quality of representation, as nonspecialists took on roles for which they did not have the requisite skills or experience.[109]

107. Examples include a group of former prisoners of the same detention center, Villa Grimaldi, who supported one another in advancing old, and bringing new, criminal complaints. Criminal complaints, though usually individual, can be made or adhered to by more than one person, particularly when each has a direct link with the events concerned.

108. As of late 2009, CODEPU acted for around 160 people grouped into ten torture cases, filed between 2000 and 2004.

109. In 2003, for example, one regional former prisoners' group insisted on submitting claims to the Inter-American Commission, against the advice of a long-standing HRO, whose representa-

Groups can want different things from the legal process. Some are focused on the imprisonment of individual perpetrators. Others have more "systemic" goals, such as to reaffirm the institutional nature, and massive scale, of repression through the accumulation of individual guilty verdicts. Groups such as the "119" have pursued a mixture of legal and political activities, forming and re-forming with an essentially anti-systemic identity whose strongest consistent goal seems to be denunciation of Concertación policies.[110] Another post-1998 group, the National Association of Former Political Prisoners (Agrupación Nacional de Ex-Presos Políticos, ANEPP) began sponsoring civil claims en masse to embarrass the government into negotiating reparations: legal action as a form of political lobbying.[111] These groups are neither homogenous nor universally successful. In particular, the adoption of civil claims seems to bring in its wake particular tensions absent from the bringing of criminal complaints. The association with financial gain is at times felt to discredit the accountability movement, and the fact that lawyers usually charge for this type of claim is an additional source of suspicion.[112]

A decade after the new wave of complaints were first brought, certain patterns and trends are visible. Criminal cases are usually seen as more urgent and more significant than civil cases, with civil cases brought by former exiles who continue to live outside Chile particularly susceptible to criticism as frivolous or self-serving. Within the universe of criminal cases, an informal hierarchy has grown up in which both judges and complainants give priority to death and disappearance cases.[113] Groups that began as united have tended to fracture, often along party affiliation lines, as cases have dragged on for almost a decade. Some disagreements have been directly about how to conduct legal action, while others have involved purely personal tensions. Disaffection with the slowness and remote nature of the legal process has also

---

tives repeatedly informed them that the cases would have to first pass through all possible domestic stages.

110. The group was formed by relatives and colleagues of 119 MIR activists killed in faked "confrontations" with the security forces. Various offshoots now exist, one of which has switched its focus to memorialization activities. See Hite and Collins (2009).

111. Former group member and lawyer Victor Rosas, interview 14 January 2003.

112. Criminal complaints can have a compensation claim appended (though they do not necessarily have to). Lawyers usually ask for a plaintiff contribution toward costs when standalone civil claims are brought, as external donors will not usually fund them and proceedings are entirely written, increasing the costs of notarizing depositions and other documents.

113. Survivor groups involved in torture cases have been known to accept and even urge lawyers and judges to spend more time and energy on cases of fatal violence than on their own complaints. Interview data and meetings with Tejas Verdes survivor group, late 2008.

led some groups, or factions within them, to cast around for new activities. A renaissance of memorialization activity since 2000 can often be traced to groups formed around legal action.[114] Some groups that have continued to engage with the legal process have had to replace lawyers subject to the exigencies of earning a living, while almost all have also lost group members due to life-cycle issues including aging and deaths. Those groups that took on extra activities such as memorialization or political campaigning had perhaps more success in renewing themselves intergenerationally, but groups whose sole activity is legal action based on a direct survivor identity are obviously at a disadvantage in this regard. The experience of the legal process itself has been traumatic for some (see below), while for others it has broken down a certain mystique that formerly inspired a rather reverential attitude.[115]

Additional Actors: State Agencies and Politicians

Increased use of the judicial system has drawn previously peripheral or dormant actors into a more prominent accountability role in recent years,[116] which can cause conflicts. The CDE has been drawn into occasionally contradictory positions with executive policy as well as with the Programa, another state agency. When the CDE adhered to the Caravana prosecution in 2000, it argued in favor of stripping Pinochet's immunity at the same time that government figures were allegedly trying to have the case closed altogether. Moreover, its growing pro-prosecution role did not prevent the CDE from defending the state against civil claims. In the Sandoval case, the Supreme Court was asked to rule simultaneously on a criminal action, prosecuted by the CDE as a *querellante* (complainant), and a civil action for the same offense that was nonetheless being *defended* by the CDE. The first, abortive, attempt to resolve this tension came when the CDE briefly embraced its new anti-accountability position on amnesty, effectively abdicating the role of prosecutor. The second, slightly more successful tactic adopted was for the CDE to quietly fade into the background, taking a less active role in all types of cases. The almost simultaneous rise of Programa lawyer participation in certain

114. The focus on repressive centers triggered by Guzmán's early subdivision of cases is clearly visible in the "map" of later campaigns for the recovery of sites.

115. Lawyers have had to battle tendencies among more established groups to "parcel out" routine judges' requests for specific testimony according to who is available, rather than who actually witnessed the event in question.

116. Not strictly "accountability actors" as defined in this book (agents, mostly from civil society, who consciously pursue justice claims), these additional actors have nonetheless been drawn into the renewed justice debate after 1998 as protagonists or interlocutors.

cases led to particular care by both agencies to avoid treading on each other's toes. In particular, both have instructions to avoid the evident absurdity of state-employed lawyers appearing for opposing sides in the same case.[117]

The Programa, mentioned above, became an intriguing outpost of progressive accountability action within the state apparatus over the early 2000s. Successive reorganizations provided it with the space to carve out its own accountability role, but the choice to do so rested finally on the composition of its payroll and its peculiar relationship with the Ministry of the Interior (where it is located). By the mid-2000s the Programa had transformed itself from a worthy but essentially secondary institution housing records and tracing remains, to one in the front line of accountability. This change was visible in an influx of lawyers such as Carmen Hertz, Boris Paredes, and Hugo Montero, known for outspoken anti-impunity views and unlikely to accept a post in any state institution half-hearted about this cause. By the later part of the decade the Programa, with work in the areas of memorials and archives as well as legal cases, was the most active single entity overseeing and pursuing cases. Judges largely tolerated its participation "alongside" (often replacing) private human rights lawyers' activity, and its legal staff was an intriguing mix of old Vicaría hands and younger lawyers. The Programa has become increasingly self-conscious of its own peculiar position within the state apparatus, walking a fine line between wishing to promote its work and not wanting to draw undue attention to its stretching of the limits of its original mandate.

As far as politicians' views are concerned, particular party "lines" within the Concertación had previously been of little import since the legislature was relatively inactive on accountability. Lagos's 2003 human rights proposal, however, gave a new lease of life to the Human Rights Commissions (parliamentary subcommittees) of both chambers. The lower house commission came under the influence of a small but vociferous group of Socialist Party deputies who rejected various government proposals as unduly lenient.[118] Individual Socialist Party politicians were also drawn into the spotlight by very personal connections. Carolina Tohá and Juan Pablo Letelier, children of high-profile victims of dictatorship repression, were both members of parliament at the time, and Tohá, particularly, affiliated herself in public with some of the more radical demands made by HROs. Michelle Bachelet trod

117. Interviews with CDE lawyers, 2003/4; and Programa lawyers, 2007/8.
118. *El Mostrador*, 2 April 2004.

a decidedly more cautious line (befitting her position as then minister of defense[119]) regarding a case over her father's death in 1974.[120] The relevant parliamentary commission subsequently had to negotiate sensitive bills, including the Valech commission secrecy law and the unresolved post-2006 Almonacid "interpretive law." Concertación representatives on the commissions have generally proved reluctant to underwrite particularly unpopular official compromises with the right, finally voting down the first, 2008 version of the Human Rights Institute proposal because AFDD members feared its possibly restrictive impact on the Programa.[121]

In sum, the post-1998 period has given rise to recognizably new types of actors and claims as well as drawing existing actors such as the CDE, the Programa, and politicians into an intensified justice debate. New survivors' groups may also represent a tendency toward "re-politicization" of the theme of victimhood. During the dictatorship period, relatives, particularly, had hidden or denied political affiliations that might be prejudicial to legal outcomes. Some survivors consider that an image had been constructed of the "absent," "passive," or "innocent" victim as somehow more deserving of empathy. Direct claims by survivors—as distinct from those made by relatives on behalf of victims—sometimes reflect an expressed desire to reassert political identities and demands.[122]

A link between modest post-1998 accountability success and "demand inflation" can perhaps be traced in the multiplication of claim-bringers, as well as in the fact that those new groups that do adopt court-focused accountability goals often pursue civil claims in addition to or alongside criminal complaints. More radical demand inflation is visible in the emergence of groups such as "HIJOS Chile," part of a region-wide network of children and grandchildren of victims of repression. HIJOS and a related group known as the FUNA undertake denunciatory direct actions, including public "outings" of known repressors. These groups are at one and the same time an example

---

119. She served in this post until late 2004, when she was replaced in order to campaign as a Concertación presidential candidate.

120. The action was brought by former air force colleagues who, like Bachelet and others, were convicted of treason for opposing the coup. The Bachelet family did not directly participate in the complaint.

121. The proposal, spun off from the memory museum idea that originally accompanied it, went through severe modification in the drafting stage. The institute, which was to absorb the existing Programa, appeared to lose the faculty to adhere to legal cases, which has been key to Programa accountability interventions.

122. Conversations with members of various survivors' groups, March and September 2003.

of new organizing styles applied to historic themes and a "throwback" to the oppositional, confrontational style of the 1980s.[123]

Thus it can be seen that an increase in actor numbers does not necessarily lead to more coordinated activity. Over time, it may also produce a move away from exclusive reliance on the legal realm. The courts are the present medium for, and perhaps the proximate cause of, much of the flurry of new activity. But they are not necessarily the ultimate or most suitable medium for all the new goals and unresolved claims that have come to light. The issue is particularly pertinent since some new groups are clear that they are in fact using the courts principally for non-judicial goals (such as the bringing of pressure on politicians for reparations or other policy change). The tactic of forcing the present government to respond, politically or financially, by making it the defendant in civil cases, however, appears to have backfired. The state, via the CDE, felt impelled to defend its corner, and state coffers, by making new, and retrograde, contentions. In particular, by arguing that exile had been a fully legal act it upheld by implication the legitimacy of the whole body of law laid down by the military regime.[124]

Over time the government has nevertheless shown some readiness to readdress truth and reparation aspects of the new scenario, with initiatives such as the Mesa of 1999–2000, legislative proposals in 2003, the 2004 torture commission report, and subsequent reparations. On the whole, however, accountability actors seemed to remain committed to making maximum possible headway in the courts. Many expressed greater faith in present judicial rather than political receptivity to accountability claims, a tendency that is only likely to be accentuated now that political alternation has produced a right-wing presidency.[125]

LEGAL STRATEGIES

The fact that Chile's human rights response was legally shaped from the very beginning has been both an asset and a liability for subsequent accountability

123. HIJOS shares organizational and communicational characteristics with modern anti-globalization movements, but its highly critical and confrontational approach to the state could equally belong to regime opponents, or indeed traditional relatives' groups, during the dictatorship.

124. The CDE responded in May 2001 to a civil suit for exile brought in late 2000, stating that Decree Law 81—under which exile was carried out—was legal because done by the "competent authority" of the day.

125. "The judicial branch has done what the political class has failed to do in Chile . . . The most significant advances have been won through the courts" (Hugo Gutiérrez, interview 14 November 2002).

prospects. On the plus side of the balance sheet, it has given Chile a rich seam of casework on which to draw in the present, more propitious accountability context. Cases that were brought and never resolved, or only temporarily suspended, can be reopened in the present day. Here the continuity of the Chilean judicial system during and after transition works to the advantage of latter-day accountability, avoiding problems (such as prescription) that have dogged accountability efforts in El Salvador and elsewhere. Chile's tradition of continuous legal action over HRVs also means that it boasts an array of organizations and lawyers conversant with the use of the domestic courts for such purposes. Where initial investigations existed lawyers could, and did, use their right to contribute to court files, turning these into a veritable repository of established truths.[126]

The accumulation of personal knowledge about interrelated cases, victims, and perpetrators is perhaps the greatest asset of historical human rights lawyers, "legal capital" providing a solid base on which to build in the more permissive post-1998 context. The very nature of Chile's repressive history—targeted, systematic, ordered—also helps to make the truth not only accessible but, often, provable. On the negative side, legal outcomes in the dictatorship period were rarely favorable. Pursuing a case at all might well mean foregoing improved future prospects: dictatorship-era judicial resolutions, however inadequate, could be definitive.[127] Locating, accounting for, and transferring old cases has proved a time-consuming obstacle for lawyers and courts alike in the present day. Lawyers have resorted to disguised resubmission of old cases to prevent delays, and recognize that both they and the new judges have occasionally been driven to overlook the existence of an inconvenient, because unfavorable, prior resolution.

The surviving universe of unresolved cases is skewed toward disappearance, although it is in other senses quite disparate. Legal actions in the dictatorship era were for the most part spatially and temporally dispersed according to the date of commission, type of claim, residence of the claim-bringer, or location

126. The 1991 Letelier (re-)investigation was regarded at the time as the main and perhaps only opportunity to put the entire regime on trial, and lawyers therefore probed as widely as possible. According to Hiram Villagra, "It's no coincidence that [lawyers] from Letelier appear later in the Pinochet prosecution [Caravana]: Letelier opened doors. The main outlines, the raw data, are all there in the Letelier file: Cóndor, Prats, Berríos, all the cases that are coming to fruition today" (interview 13 November 2002).

127. Cases that were closed by the premature application of amnesty have recently been successfully reopened. Cases that were definitively closed on some other pretext, however, or where unduly lenient sentences were imposed, pose greater obstacles.

of the offense. Although it offered certain potential for venue shopping,[128] this spread of cases contributed to a piecemeal approach. Combined with the extremely negative prevailing opportunity structure, with courts very ready to reject or close cases, the result was a strategic reliance on "holding measures": maintenance in the hope of improved future conditions. Those improved conditions did not arrive with transition, as many had hoped they would, and Chilean lawyers perhaps proved slow to push for, instead of simply awaiting, judicial change. The case-by-case strategy previously imposed was largely preserved, and there has been little discernible use of "leading case" strategy—attempts to prompt judicial innovation or movement by sustained litigation over a particular juridical principle.[129]

Human Rights Organizing Patterns and Legal Strategy
Inherited from Transition

Most human rights lawyers and HROs in Chile chose from early days to work within the dictatorship's imposed legality, exploiting its weaknesses rather than denouncing its fundamental illegitimacy. Later, much energy was invested in contests over jurisdiction between civil and military courts.[130] HROs and their lawyers settled into a reactive, rather than proactive, legal rhythm, to which some attribute a certain atrophying of the legal imagination when it came to later use of the courts. The habit of meticulous legal action with a primarily defensive intent proved difficult to break. One interviewee, the legal director of a major HRO between 1990 and 1996, suggested that the legal community held back unduly at transition due to a combination of this habitual modesty of ambition with an unrealistic expectation that the Concertación would do more politically to end impunity.[131] Various interviewees questioned themselves, in retrospect, as to why the first post-transitional criminal complaint against Pinochet took almost a decade to

128. Lawyers did, and still do, go to great lengths to design a submission so as to maximize the chances of it being seen by a court or magistrate they believe to be sympathetic.

129. This strategy has been used to greater effect in other rights-related issues, such as environmental protection or disabled access, by some NGOs in association with the Universidad Diego Portales's law clinic.

130. Lawyers were in a double bind since cases were routinely transferred to the extremely hostile military court at any suggestion of security force involvement. Thus a lawyer who worked a case too assiduously, providing evidence about a police or military perpetrator, could inadvertently trigger its transfer and closure. For analogous reasons, lawyers did not always risk challenging military jurisdiction: once challenged, military judges would often not only deny the requested transfer to civilian courts but also find a pretext to permanently close the case.

131. Adil Brkovic, interview 23 January 2003.

materialize.[132] The extremely controlled parameters of transition provide a large part of the answer, with judicial structures largely unchanged in form, function, or incumbency, and amnesty, as we have seen, roundly reaffirmed.

If accountability actors were correct in believing conditions particularly unfavorable for innovation between 1990 and 1992, however, some acknowledge that they took few active steps to build alternatives.[133] The modest successes claimed for the early 1990s are almost all negative. HROs, lawyers, and relatives' groups campaigned against successive government proposals aimed at expediting or resolving the "human rights question." Although successful in that the proposals were abandoned, these were essentially reactive strategies. The initiatives were coming from within the government, as they had come from the regime in former times, and the human rights community seemed in danger of simply transferring its habit of reactive criticism from one set of authorities to the next. Such criticism necessarily divided the historic human rights community, as some senior members of the Vicaría's legal team had gone on to become architects of official transitional justice policy. The human rights community thus subdivided first over the question of whether accountability should even remain a goal in democracy. The visible pro-accountability remnant was in turn divided as to how accountability should subsequently be understood and pursued.

The accountability field also lacked new impetus. Although Rettig documented many deaths and disappearances, it did not provide substantial revelations about any case. The amnesty law, moreover, covered an estimated 80 percent of the incidents documented. There was accordingly no new wave of cases,[134] nor were there immediate changes to the legal conditions surrounding them. The question of political prisoners was largely resolved by executive discretion, with lawyers left out of the loop. Such was the official desire to negotiate and compromise rather than litigate or legislate that, although programs of reparation, return, medical, and other assistance were offered,

132. "The time to bring a complaint against Pinochet would have been right after Rettig" (Adil Brkovic, interview 23 January 2003). There had in fact been one previous attempt by two Communist Party lawyers, whose complaint went to a military court, where it was almost immediately closed. Eduardo Contreras, interview 3 December 2002.

133. "The problem [in Chile] is that lawyers, human rights initiatives, have been lacking in theoretical grounding, right from the beginning. It's all been so parochial" (Adil Brkovic, interview 23 January 2003). Other lawyers interviewed compared Chile unfavorably with Argentina, insisting the latter had produced more eminent jurists. Interview data.

134. The courts, however, did respond to information received directly from Rettig about some victims.

there were no serious proposals or even demands for the erasing of political prisoners' criminal records.[135] This virtually unquestioning acceptance of the legal and constitutional edifice inherited from the dictatorship period is one of the most striking comparative features of the Chilean transition. Louis Bickford comments on it as an aspect of Chilean "socialization,"[136] probably instrumental in a certain pessimism demonstrated by 1990s accountability actors. The lawyer behind one eventually successful 1998 Pinochet complaint describes it thus: "We were told by some of the best human rights lawyers, people I absolutely respect, that we had absolutely no chance; that we were pushing against a locked and bolted door. Even after [the] London [arrest], they said 'If they send him home you'll lose.' After we got the *desafuero*, everyone realized that at some point after 1990 that door had been silently unbolted and unlocked from the inside—but no one's really sure, even now, why that happened or who made it happen."[137]

The Impact of the Legal System and Legal Procedures on Strategy

Accountability prospects were and are shaped by aspects of Chilean legal structure and judicial procedure. What follows, although not a comprehensive survey, highlights aspects of the pre-reform justice system that are of particular relevance for accountability.[138] Under Chile's soon-to-be-superseded investigating magistrate system, criminal complaints (*querellas* or *denuncias*)[139] are submitted to a judge, who personally conducts any subsequent investigation, determines guilt, and decides on sentencing. Lawyers have traditionally therefore set great store by so-called *alegatos de pasillo* (corridor litigation)—efforts to informally influence judges' thinking on particular case verdicts and over general juridical principles.[140] Proceedings are also

135. Famously, one high-level PS functionary remains ineligible to run for elected office due to a criminal record earned when imprisoned, as a student leader, for publicly calling Pinochet a "dictator."

136. Louis Bickford, unpublished report, 1998, 6n25; on file with author. A revised version was later published; see Bickford (2000).

137. Eduardo Contreras, interview 3 December 2002.

138. More detailed accounts of this system, and the transformations it has recently undergone, can be found in Duce (2004) or Duce and Riego (2002).

139. The *querella* is a move by an interested party to initiate criminal proceedings. The *denuncia*, a simpler procedure for notifying an alleged crime, can have various sources, including the police.

140. Interviews with Héctor Salazar, 17 October 2002; and Sergio Concha, 30 January 2003. Judges, for their part, deny that these efforts influence judicial outcomes. Alberto Chaigneau, interview 6 January 2003.

written (not oral), based on a case file built up by the judge. This serves to reduce the "theatrical" element of accountability cases (Osiel 2000a), as there is no public interrogation of the accused before witnesses or a jury.[141] It also indirectly serves to boost the public and media profile of human rights lawyers above that of their clients: the only widely reported parts of the process tend to be the final *alegatos* at which lawyers present their concluding oral arguments.[142]

A particularly significant characteristic of the Chilean penal system is that it allows direct victims[143] of a crime to initiate and participate in criminal proceedings. This relatively rare faculty was virtually indispensable for the early initiation of HRV proceedings, since the justice system almost never acted ex officio in accountability cases before 1990. The involvement of direct victims or their relatives is prioritized: private individuals who fit neither category can only make a claim if they supply *fianza* (surety).[144] HROs and similar bodies are not allowed to bring cases in their own right, again placing the onus on survivors or victims' relatives.[145] This fact introduces a very particular dynamic to the three-way relationship among the justice system, lawyers, and their clients. In the early days, Alejandro González found himself touched and somewhat daunted by the faith relatives placed in the ability of lawyers, and by extension the legal system, to provide them with an answer.[146] By 1998 and thereafter, although organized relatives' groups had remained staunch in their demands for accountability, not every victim's family felt the same way. One of the special judges assigned after the Mesa recounted the experience of reopening a case and being confronted by the man's only surviving relative,

141. In Argentina, this dynamic has been identified by survivors as a traumatic but valued aspect of the "truth trial" model: perpetrators are forced to answer in open court for their actions and can be publicly confronted by survivors and other witnesses. In Chile, by contrast, survivors are likely to be summoned to private confrontations with the accused only if testimonies directly conflict. Anecdotal evidence suggests that this very different possibility is often experienced as a disincentive. Conversations with individual claim-bringers, Santiago, first quarter of 2003.

142. *Alegatos* are open to the public and in the Letelier case were, exceptionally, televised. A decade later, Pinochet's senatorial immunity hearings for Caravana case were likewise widely reported. Some newspapers even reproduced *alegatos* verbatim alongside personal profiles of the lawyers who had made them.

143. This term is used here in its general sense, rather than the particular usage adopted elsewhere in this book.

144. A sum representing security against libel, intended to dissuade false or frivolous claim-making.

145. The PC's January 1998 criminal complaint against Pinochet, for instance, was initiated through the person of then secretary general Gladys Marín. Her status as the widow of one victim exempted her from *fianza*.

146. Alejandro González, interview 14 January 2003.

insisting that she should "leave well alone." "What am I to do? Tell him that, after years of willfully refusing his uncle justice, the state now insists he have it, whether he wants it or not?"[147]

Simply stated, the issue is of ownership of cases. Where it is the state that wants to (re-)initiate prosecutions, the choices are perhaps clearer: the state has always reserved the right to impose punishment on behalf of the public good, rather than by exclusive reference to the victim of a crime. For lawyers, however, the dilemmas are more complex. A culture has grown up around human rights lawyering in Chile that sets great store by the notion of representing the individual relative or survivor, pursuing "only" what he or she desires from a case. This culture may be circumstantial—given the strong structural incentives to have a relative involved—or may represent a genuine ethical commitment. It is, however, occasionally self-deceiving, as well as being strategically questionable. Some of the lawyers who advanced this principle most strongly during interviews were nonetheless center stage in the unseemly tugs-of-war over post-1998 cases already discussed. One declared himself offended by the suggestion that lawyers might have actively sought new cases to bring during Pinochet's UK imprisonment.

This lawyer was unwilling to contemplate an openly instrumental approach to cases, which would "cluster" similar types of claims to make a sustained assault on particular legal obstacles. During the same conversation he nevertheless openly described his frustration at having been initially unable to find relatives willing to act over the lesser-known, southern section of the Caravana: "You practically have to drag the complaints out of these people by force."[148] The complex relationship between these lawyers and their clients is perhaps an area ripe for further exploration from a socio-legal perspective. Here, it is sufficient to note that bringing a case sets up a dynamic of codependence between relatives or survivors and lawyers. Thereafter, much of the initiative is handed to lawyers, who can make written representations, submit evidence, suggest procedures, and request charges. The system rewards active participation, and assiduous lawyers can end up practically investigating a case "for" the judge.[149]

---

147. Serving case judge, interview 2003.

148. Human rights lawyer, interview, Santiago, last quarter of 2002.

149. The Poblete-Córdoba case file, opened in 1974, graphically illustrates this tendency. The folders covering its first twenty-four years contain a sequence of copious handwritten submissions from human rights lawyer Sergio Concha, interspersed with very occasional one-line instructions from various military and civilian judges. File examined in FASIC archives, January 2003.

The influence of geographical happenstance on case outcomes has already been mentioned. Exceptions include the use of *ministros en visita* or *ministros de fuero*[150] for allegations against public figures, and, since 2001, the use of specialized judges for HRV cases. Both exceptions have loosened the association between accountability cases and particular territories.[151] Strategy implications have included the disguised resubmission of old cases to these new judges as well as, between 1998 and 2006, the careful inclusion of Pinochet in lists of accused persons in order to qualify for inclusion in Guzmán's Rol. 2182–98 investigation. Submissions were always shaped to some extent by forum preferences, but the addition of these new alternatives seems to have made reading and "rating" different courts more widespread.[152] Perceived differences between instances, however, are not stable.[153] Legal strategists must additionally consider whether attempts to repeat positive precedents in fact risk provoking reactions. This danger is magnified by another structural feature of the Chilean system: jurisprudence is not binding. Interpretations are valid only for the case in which they are delivered, and judges are free to produce contradictory rulings in similar cases. But this does mean that while interpretive shifts that favor accountability are difficult to "bind in," negative ones should be correspondingly easier to modify.

The personal preferences of judges over accountability have in recent times perhaps overtaken structural differences between courts as the principal determinant of case outcomes. Some judges are notoriously and consistently pro-amnesty, others—fewer in number—reliably pro-accountability.[154] Judicial appointments are therefore closely watched and commented on by lawyers, who treat them as a marker for political and Supreme Court authorities' attitudes toward accountability. Specialization within courts has increased the salience of specific appointment patterns: for example, judges known to favor accountability could be in effect sidelined through promotion to the civil

150. The distinction is a minor one: a judge who will need access to sources normally protected by parliamentary, military, or other special privileges (*fuero*) has to be specifically authorized.

151. *Ministros en visita* technically operate as judges of first instance in the relevant jurisdiction for the duration of the investigation. Special HRV case judges are likewise attached administratively to particular districts. Nonetheless, the outcome in practice has been to concentrate cases in the capital.

152. Sergio Concha, interview 30 January 2003.

153. Many historic lawyers report that in former times, lower courts in the capital were usually more favorable than either provincial lower courts or the Supreme Court. In more recent times, as the Supreme Court has vacillated, it has alternated with the Santiago Court of Appeal in being perceived as the more progressive on these matters. Sergio Concha, interview 30 January 2003.

154. See Casas in Brett (2009) for specifics.

bench of a higher court. Overall, this combination of lawyer protagonism and judicial discretion risks producing an uneven, excessively personalized type of justice. Cases at times appear to be resolved according to the enthusiasm and inclinations of key actors rather than the strength of evidence or gravity of the offense. Sentences for the same offense can also vary widely. In 2008 a former agent announced his intention to appeal to the regional human rights system after his sentence for complicity in a murder was almost a decade longer than those imposed on the direct perpetrators. In the same year, the Supreme Court began to use a discretionary sentencing formula known as "half prescription" to dramatically reduce final sentences for human rights crimes.[155]

Such developments are less than ideal from various viewpoints, and can even have negative implications for witness safety. If, for example, the odds of a guilty verdict come to rest too evidently on the volition of claim-bringers, an incentive is created for attempts to intimidate witnesses and survivors.[156] It is moreover unclear whether personalized justice can easily be overcome, in this issue area or more generally. Chile is currently moving toward a separation of investigative and judicial functions, in which *fiscales* (public prosecutors) have taken on many of the functions previously reserved for investigative magistrates.[157] Nonetheless, and as we will see in chapter 7 for El Salvador, without additional efforts to make justice outcomes more consistent and predictable, such changes can simply mean that the individual attitudes and receptivity of *fiscales* in turn become determinant.

Post-transitional Accountability: Overcoming Major Legal Obstacles

The major legal obstacles to accountability in the Chilean setting have traditionally been threefold: the amnesty law, *cosa juzgada,* and prescription. Only the amnesty law is specific to accountability cases. The others are general legal principles that have presented particular problems in HRV cases. Amnesty has generally proved the most daunting: the statute itself was problematic enough, but prevailing judicial interpretations of it were also excessively stringent. During the dictatorship, courts virtually without exception invoked

---

155. See Fernández and Sferrazza (2009) for details of this trend, which produced expressions of concern from international HROs and representations to the relevant UN and Inter-American system committees.

156. This has been a more prominent problem to date in Argentina, after one witness disappeared and another was briefly abducted in mysterious circumstances in late 2006.

157. The arrangements for phasing in of reforms, however, means that all cases for dictatorship-era crimes will continue to be seen under the old system.

amnesty at the mere suggestion of security agent involvement. This approach, in which neither the crime nor the perpetrators were even identified before the case was (supposedly) definitively closed, was the single biggest obstacle to accountability hopes for over two decades. After the transition, strategic assaults on amnesty were, as we have seen, both rare and unsuccessful. Loopholes in the text itself were not, perhaps, explored or exploited with the same efficiency as they were in Argentina.[158] Efforts were instead concentrated on the minority of cases where the amnesty law clearly did not apply.[159]

Amnesty did, finally, begin to change: not in the letter of the law, nor even in general principles of validity, but rather in interpretation. Courts first allowed the exploitation of exceptions, crimes to which amnesty did not apply. Second, they moved the point of application of the amnesty law: it was "lifted" from preemptive use at the beginning of an investigative process and moved toward the end. The first of these judicial changes, "exceptionalism," or the gradual removal of individual cases and categories of crime from the reach of amnesty, is best exemplified in Chile by the doctrine that kidnapping is an ongoing crime that cannot be amnestied. As regards the point of application of amnesty, the prevailing doctrine since 1998 has been that crimes must be specified, and perpetrators identified, before amnesty can properly be applied.

These changes are often, and in a sense correctly, identified with the September 1998 Poblete-Córdoba resolution,[160] which stated both principles. Neither doctrine, however, was entirely novel. Lawyers were contending that kidnapping was an ongoing crime well before transition, and the first known acceptance of this contention came in the mid-1990s.[161] The principle that full investigation should precede amnesty was the same one that Aylwin had tried to persuade the courts to adopt back in 1991. Thus the change in accountability outcomes from 1998 came about not through innovation in strategic argument but through changed judicial response to existing lines of argument. Although Aylwin's early suggestion had apparently been unsuccessful, Adil Brkovic detected a gradual realization over the 1990s, in government, judicial, and even military circles, that to continually block cases by invoking amnesty

158. In Argentina, specific exclusions affecting crimes against property and abduction of children were exploited to weaken, and finally defeat, the two laws that provided amnesty.

159. Examples include the Letelier killings and the *degollados* assassinations, both discussed above.

160. Sala Penal of the Supreme Court, resolution 12 September 1998.

161. This occurred in the Santiago Appeals Court, although it was later overruled by the Supreme Court. See Correa Sutil (1997, 151n19).

at its earliest possible point of application was unsustainable. A gradual "soft-ening" of the judicial stance on interpretation thus reflected, for Brkovic, a policy agreed among institutional actors to get investigations over with "once and for all" before allowing amnesty to again seal off cases without the appli-cation of penalties.[162] Regardless of whether this interpretation is fully correct, it illustrates one essential point: amnesty change from 1998 was perceived as essentially a judicial-institutional trend. Human rights lawyers observed and capitalized on this change, and doubtless their perseverance contributed to it, but they did not claim direct authorship. It is perhaps telling therefore that this major interpretive shift of recent times was in essence a relatively con-servative one. Leaving the principle of amnesty untouched, it ceded only the absolute minimum ground required to permit a fuller answer to be given to (some) outstanding claims.

A strategic approach to amnesty after 1998 logically involved efforts to further expand categories of exemption to include those specified by inter-national, as well as domestic, law. This exceptionalist strategy sought to grad-ually have more categories of crime declared inadmissible for amnesty: first disappearance, then illegal execution, then torture. The Poblete-Córdoba rul-ing sent favorable signals, and textual analysis of subsequent claims shows that lawyers began to more often invoke international law in efforts to capi-talize on that isolated success. The first conviction for a theoretically still-amnestiable crime (a killing, as opposed to disappearance, demonstrably committed within the 1973–78 period) finally materialized in 2002. But the courts' initial venture into exceptionalism, over disappearance, once again came under pressure from defense lawyers and the government in late 2004.[163] Although the specific principle of exemption for kidnapping was eventually upheld, amnesty itself was not definitively vitiated. Indeed, between 1998 and 2002 the kidnapping thesis provided a perverse incentive for perpetrators to confess to murder. Homicide committed between 1973 and 1978 for politi-cal reasons remained apparently automatically eligible for amnesty, and so agents rushed to prove that they had killed, rather than kidnapped, a named person, often by indicating where his or her remains were to be found.[164]

---

162. Adil Brkovic, interview 23 January 2003.

163. See above regarding the Sandoval case.

164. Ironically, one brake on this trend came when lawyers and some judges proceeded to charge the agents with more minor crimes related to the illegal disposal of remains. Secret graves had often been disturbed and bodies reburied in the late 1980s or early 1990s, attempted cover-up offenses that clearly fell outside the amnesty period.

Early lawyers' efforts to rely on international treaty law produced uncertain returns, with judges noticeably slow to embrace it as a sufficient counterargument to amnesty. Five years after the initial breakthrough, the UDP's Annual Report stated that "since Poblete-Córdova [*sic*], the [Supreme] Court has not repeated its explicit invocation of international treaties for the interpretation of amnesty norms" (UDP 2003, 195; author's translation). Lawyers nonetheless persisted, embarking on complex debates about the order of precedence of international commitments with regard to the constitution[165] and domestic secondary legislation alike. By the late 2000s progress had definitely been made, with international law an almost obligatory referent in verdicts. Specific outcomes, however, were still far from reliable. The point of contention simply shifted to whether a particular set of acts actually qualified as a war crime or crime against humanity in international law. On this point, lawyers Lidia Casas and Hiram Villagra agree that Supreme Court practice has been erratic.[166] In 2008 it was still possible, for example, to find conflicting Supreme Court opinions on matters as basic as whether Chile had or had not been in a state of "internal war" (and therefore subject to the Geneva Conventions) back in 1973. More recalcitrant judges, even where unable to hold out completely against accountability for fear of reversal on appeal, took refuge in alternative strategies such as lenient sentencing (see below). Alternatively, they invoked other obstacles such as *cosa juzgada*—the commonplace "double jeopardy" principle that no one should be tried twice for the same offense.

These alternative obstacles provide more fertile terrain for those opposed to accountability, since, in contrast to self-amnesty, they are based on generally sound legal principles that human rights organizations and lawyers are often reluctant to challenge. Paradoxically, the previous flawed, premature invocation of amnesty by the courts has been successfully used as a weapon against both *cosa juzgada* and prescription. Once doctrinal change over amnesty was detected, accountability actors could and did begin to (re-)present criminal claims over crimes committed during the period covered by the amnesty. Defendants claimed that *cosa juzgada* applied; human rights lawyers, however, successfully maintained that the earlier applications of amnesty had been so flawed as not to constitute completed criminal actions at all. Since no

165. Lawyers focused in particular on Article 5, which laid down the incorporation procedure for international treaty commitments and had been reformed in 1989 to be slightly more protective of rights.

166. Casas and Villagra as quoted in Brett (2009).

one had ever been formally accused, they argued, no present-day defendant could legitimately argue that he or she had previously been tried. The fact that a case had been initiated could, however, be used to overcome prescription problems since the opening of an investigation, even for a minimal period, turns the prescription clock back to zero.[167]

Another facet of jurisdictional determinism in Chile has been the routine handing over of HRV allegations to the military court system, which is even more retrograde than the civilian. Although the principle that cases involving civilians should be seen by civilian courts gained ground after 1998 (Couso 2002), military judges initially reacted by applying for transfers of jurisdiction, adding to the already considerable number of HRV cases they held.[168] Up until the late 2000s, when military courts apparently accepted the inevitability of new trends and ceased to oppose the transfer of cases, this constituted a major caveat to the post-1998 improvement in judicial receptivity over accountability in Chile. Military courts have their own system of appeal, and Supreme Court oversight of them is limited to exceptional recourses that do not transfer jurisdiction.[169] The preservation of this second structural obstacle to accountability is characteristic of Chilean post-transitional justice, which repeatedly stops short of definitive institutional or legislative change. The contrast with Argentina, which recently abolished its own military justice system, is equally characteristic.

After a decade of renewed accountability activity, the patterns that emerge include a continued need for patience on the part of complainants. Most cases brought or reinvigorated around 1998 have not yet been closed. Many tended to languish after the investigative stage had been completed, with special judges reluctant to see their task through as far as charging or sentencing well-known former agents. Some seized the opportunity to send "sensitive" cases up to the next level, that of *ministro de fuero*. Judges (including Alejandro Solís, who inherited a substantial portion of Guzmán's caseload upon the latter's 2005 retirement) undertook a drive to reduce the backlog by closing

---

167. Thus, for example, a crime with a fifteen-year prescription limit committed in 1980 would have to be investigated before 1995 in order to escape being "prescribed." But had a case been opened briefly in 1990, and suspended again the same year, a new fifteen-year period would have begun. Prospective complainants would therefore have until 2005 to initiate renewed action.

168. Military courts successfully acquired the Poblete-Córdoba case, for example, as late as November 1996. Precise total figures are not known, as military courts apparently did not respond to the case survey ordered by the Supreme Court in 2001. Up until the mid 2000s, lawyers nonetheless tended to estimate that the military courts held at least as many cases as the civilian system.

169. The Supreme Court explicitly renounced additional oversight during the dictatorship.

cases ready for charging and sentencing. Such apparent zeal was enough in Solis's case to earn him a reputation among defendants as a "hanging judge," when in fact it could equally be argued that "housekeeping" was his main preoccupation.

Programa lawyers, better resourced and today more numerous than their HRO counterparts, are perhaps the best placed to discern trends and patterns in the post-2003 case universe.[170] Their perception in late 2009 was that lawyers and judges alike prioritize cases of disappearance over those of proven death (illegal execution) or survived torture. Locating and identifying remains continues to be a central preoccupation with this first type of case, and lawyers need to work hard to keep up momentum after this particular milestone is reached in any given investigation. Perhaps counterintuitively, torture cases have proven relatively more difficult to prosecute despite the existence of direct testimony. Archaic legal codes have not helped, but physical evidence has been the major sticking point. State medical legal services, not designed or resourced to cope with a flood of cases of this magnitude, have simply been unequal to the tasks presented by all types of cases. The failings have been most dramatic in the misidentification of remains: a major scandal broke in 2005 when it came to light that a series of earlier handovers to relatives had been based on tests known to be inaccurate. The system has fared little better with torture cases: judges inexpert in assessing the veracity of testimony simply packed survivors off en masse to take psychological tests designed, and generally used, as crude "lie detectors" for suspects about to be sentenced. Lawyers report that overall it is "much easier to get disappearance cases sentenced than any others, especially torture"[171]—easier, too, to get judges to pay attention to the disappearance dimensions of larger episodes.[172]

Lawyers' strategy responses generally follow earlier patterns of pushing gradually against the principal obstacle of the day, "using arguments one step ahead of . . . the doctrinal position at the time."[173] Relatives' group strategy varies. AFEP, as an association of relatives of victims of execution, has been relatively disadvantaged by the continuing focus on disappearances. As disappearance cases are "turned into" executions by the discovery of remains

170. The year 2003 marks the date of the Programa's reinvigorated legal work, as well as the beginning of their active-case database. Currently represented in most cases for fatal victims, the Programa actively monitors these and many more.

171. Programa lawyer, interview last quarter 2008.

172. The first verdict in a torture case was, finally, achieved in September 2009. Sentences were however extremely low, at only three years (Academia de Guerra Aérea case, Rol. 8113-08).

173. Hiram Villagra quoted in Brett (2009).

or definitive perpetrator testimony proving date of death, AFEP has become more active. In late 2008 it was proposing a fresh assault on the courts over the issue of accuracy of identification, which would go some way toward reversing a post-2002 trend for the number of new complaints to first level and then decline. Other groups and individual relatives have been effectively kept in waiting by the lengthy case process. Some have tried to remain active, meeting lawyers regularly and submitting occasional, respectfully worded "requests for updates" in the hope of keeping judges moving forward. The bringing of subsidiary civil complaints has also emerged as one possible additional avenue. But civil claims, whether against the state or against individual defendants, present particular technical problems: although the amnesty law does not specifically prohibit them, the general civil code specifies that they should be placed within four years of an incident. Some courts have accepted that imprescriptibility granted for criminal actions should also apply to accompanying civil claims, while others have accepted claimants' contention that they were not reasonably able to exercise claims at the relevant time.[174] The issue, however, has not been resolved in any stable manner. This together with the perception that the general public is unsympathetic to apparently financially motivated claim-making has militated against a more widespread use of civil claims.

The Aims of Post-transitional Accountability Strategy

By early 2010 Chile's post-transitional legal framework as regards accountability remained largely unchanged in its procedural and structural characteristics: all change had been interpretive. In general terms accountability-actor strategy has apparently followed, rather than directed, judicial change. Accordingly it has, like judicial change, been aimed at the exceptional cases where interpretive innovation might be achieved, rather than at overturning the statute wholesale. Actors have thus continued the case-by-case, cumulative style of litigation that first emerged during the dictatorship. Case-based reinterpretations of the amnesty law nevertheless appear to be slowing, as change has approached the upper limits within which the essential shape of the still well-defended statutory principle can be maintained. Efforts to innovate in the use of international norms are hampered by a combination of the controversial subject matter with a more general lack of familiarity with international norms and structures: characteristic, according to some, of

174. Adil Brkovic, interview 23 January 2003.

lawyers and judges alike.[175] It is therefore possible that recent accountability progress will stall in the courts unless it can be underpinned and extended by the stimulation of complementary political change, including legislative change. In this context, the future of the 2006 Almonacid ruling and long-awaited interpretive statute assumes particular significance.

The Interaction of Other Goals with the Pursuit of Criminal Accountability

Criminal prosecution can be seen as wholly or partly aimed at producing a certain kind of "official" truth. Often, this means reversing a previous travesty of official truth, as in cases where victims of execution were tarnished as traitors. Claim-bringers seem particularly keen that the courts, as opposed to some administrative or executive instance, set the record straight where the courts had themselves corroborated the original lie.[176] Some may therefore hope that accountability can substitute for or even stimulate the kind of wholesale social condemnation that perpetrators of HRVs in Chile never really suffered. In this interpretation the repeated legal actions against Pinochet, contributing as they did to his political and personal decline, could be considered a success despite the lack of a final conviction.

The long history of negative accountability outcomes in post-transitional Chile contributed in the past to a part-genuine, part-strategic substitution of truth for accountability as the overt goal of legally channeled initiatives. The AFDD gave its demand to know the fate of family members perhaps the same public emphasis as its equally strong desire to see perpetrators convicted. Government initiatives from the Rettig commission onward have also prioritized this goal, in many ways less demanding than prosecution. This multivalent interest in "more truth" about the disappeared created an apparent coincidence of interests in the later 1990s between government, private actors, and even the military, who finally acknowledged that the issue of the fate of the disappeared required a fuller response. It is possible that having previously allowed this goal to dominate public discourse may have trapped

175. Francisco Cox, interview 28 October 2002. Martín Abregú contrasted the Chilean professional setting unfavorably with the more substantial training in international law presently received by Argentine law students. Interview, 7 February 2003. Matters have improved slightly, however, since reforms obliged sitting judges to take regular refresher courses in various aspects of legal practice.

176. Rosa Silva, spokesperson for the Caravana families, stated that it was not until the first *desafuero* verdict against Pinochet that she felt her father had been truly vindicated, declared innocent by the same system that had previously labeled him a traitor. Hiram Villagra, interview 13 November 2002.

the AFDD into being offered the "solution" of the Mesa. The Mesa did, after all, represent an effort to obtain what relatives had been saying they wanted: to know the fate and whereabouts of those still disappeared.

The outcome produced "demand inflation." Those who, like the AFDD, had refused to participate seized on the flawed results as confirmation of their initial reservations. They were soon demanding more vigorous measures against those who had refused to inform as well as those who had deliberately doctored the final report.[177] Thus the goal of truth can produce a natural progression to the pursuit of accountability for what has, and has not, been revealed. In this regard, the impact of investigative journalism and confessional literature on public opinion, as well as in motivating individual accountability actions, has perhaps been underestimated.[178] Truth goals can, on the other hand, come to be inimical to accountability. Where the desire to obtain the truth is particularly highly prioritized, as in the early transitional justice model, "truth-for-justice" trade-offs can result, with amnesty or individual immunity conceded as a supposedly necessary price. The desire to establish the overall picture or secure key convictions in a given case can also lead to accountability compromises. Hector Salazar acknowledges that lawyers have encouraged recent confessions from lower-ranking officers by sending out signals, small concessions such as not contesting bail for those who cooperate with investigations.[179] It is in the course of these calculated concessions, and cost-benefit analyses of particular courses of legal action, that some lawyers have fallen foul of the maximalist demands of other accountability actors (including, on occasion, their own clients).

Other types of truth revelation have reopened old controversies over the veracity of accounts of past crimes. In late 2008, the unexpected reappearance of Germán Cofré, classified in Rettig lists as "disappeared," sparked debate over the accuracy of victim registers. Eight more individuals were subsequently found to have been mistakenly included in the Rettig lists. Some actors on the political right seized the opportunity to revive old accusations about deliberate exaggeration of HRVs, for political or financial motives

177. *El Mostrador*, 3 May 2001.
178. Many Argentine accountability actors, for instance, point to the part played by a journalistic work, Horacio Verbitsky's 1995 book *El Vuelo*, in stimulating the modern accountability renaissance in that country. *El Vuelo* (The Flight) dealt with the confessions of a participant in "death flights," during which drugged prisoners were dumped into the open sea from helicopters during Argentina's Dirty War of 1976–83. Interviews with Martin Abregú, Ana Chávez, and Maria Ester Alonso, carried out on 22 October 2002, 3 March 2003, and 5 March 2003, respectively.
179. Héctor Salazar, interview 17 October 2002.

(Cofré's family had been claiming a reparations pension for his supposed disappearance). The row put the human rights community on the defensive. Relatives' groups who had been campaigning for reopening of Rettig and Valech lists in order to submit new names were given pause by the suggestion that final numbers might fall rather than rise as a result of the 2010 revision.

Resort to International Law and Regional Mechanisms

There has been a discernible increase in references to international law in accountability complaints over the decade since 1998.[180] The invocation of international norms, however, is not per se innovative. The Geneva Conventions were habitually cited by defense lawyers in the very first military tribunals in 1973 and 1974.[181] Other specific conventions and instruments were cited as they were signed or ratified by Chile. What has changed—marginally—in recent years is their reception by judges, although this is still one of the most recalcitrant aspects of accountability change. Lawyer Francisco Cox, for example, was unequivocal: "If I want to make a point, I use international law; if I want to win the case for the client, I stick to national [law]."[182] Speaking back in 2002, Cox also claimed that international treaty law had played only a marginal role in changing judges' attitudes toward human rights. Nor did any other interviewee or source cite reference to international law as a cause, rather than a symptom, of changing judicial attitudes over accountability. Only Hugo Gutiérrez defended the general principle that litigation may have produced rather than proceeded from judicial change: "Insisting and persevering with a single line of argument [is what] allows institutions to change, evolve."[183]

The use of regional or international legal mechanisms to advance individual cases seems to have been relatively limited in the Chilean setting, perhaps precisely because domestic legal channels remained theoretically available. Regime opponents, particularly exiles based overseas, made conscious and

---

180. A chronological survey of criminal complaints submitted under Rol. 2182-98 reveals that in 1998, claims solely invoking national penal codes predominate. The main citation of international law is of the Geneva Conventions. Complaints from 2003 onward, however, are more likely to invoke additional international norms, including the American Convention on Human Rights and the Convention Against Torture (lawyer interviews and author analysis of CODEPU archives).

181. Lawyers cited these protocols to argue that prisoners should be protected from capital penalties. "All the arguments being accepted today . . . have been around since right after the coup, but it's only today that the courts have embraced them" (Hugo Gutiérrez, interview 14 November 2002).

182. Francisco Cox, interview 28 October 2002.

183. Interview, 12 March 2003.

effective use of available fora for expressing international censure (see Ensalaco 2000, 98–124). But Inter-American Commission reports and Court verdicts declaring Chile's self-amnesty law illegitimate[184] have made little discernible difference in terms of juridical or political impact at the national level. Francisco Cox was unsurprised, intimating that a general judicial disdain for all things international extended to the proceedings of the Inter-American Commission and Court.[185] Felipe González, too, believed that the Chilean authorities, although careful not to disqualify such rulings in public, paid them relatively little heed.[186] Unless and until the Almonacid bill materializes, no regional case has produced subsequent explicit modification of Chilean law. Post-1998 survivors' groups showed perhaps more interest in the possibilities of regional action than did traditional HROs and lawyers, but this enthusiasm was often based on ignorance of the requirements and actual likely returns offered by such a step. Some groups took a more sophisticated view of Inter-American claim-making as an indirect mode of applying domestic political pressure, although many acknowledged that they were uncertain of its possible efficacy.[187]

JUDICIAL RECEPTIVITY

Recent judicial change over accountability in Chile, although limited, nonetheless appears at times both to have outstripped executive policy and to have moved faster than any "push" factor from domestic accountability actor pressure. Perhaps counterintuitively, accountability progress has been produced by a relatively unreconstructed judiciary. Judicial scholars Hilbink (2007), Couso (2005), and Huneeus (2010) agree that there has been no wholesale "conversion" to the cause of defending individual rights. They argue that the Chilean judiciary continues to be, on the whole, formalist in interpretation, decidedly non-activist in matters of constitutional and personal guarantees, and mildly deferential toward the political authorities of the day. Nonetheless, the Chilean courts appear to be the institutional actor that moved furthest, most decisively, and yet least explicably on accountability in the late 1990s.

---

184. See, for example, Inter-American Commission reports from 1996 and 1999, respectively: Report 34/96, Case 11.228, Meneses Reyes; Report 133/99, Case 11.725, Carmelo Soria. See also the Inter-American Court verdict, *Almonacid Arellano v. Chile*, 26 September 2006.

185. Francisco Cox, interview 28 October 2002.

186. Felipe González, interview 8 September 2003.

187. Author observation of meetings of various groups, including the Valparaíso former political prisoners' organization, 25 April 2003.

Many interviewees cited incidental judicial reform changes (including renewal of the Supreme Court, agreed in 1997) and domestic political shifts (particularly the signals sent by and after the Pinochet arrest) as the two underlying motors of judicial accountability change. Both suggestions lend themselves in different ways to the interpretation that judicial outcomes are, as Couso implies, merely tracking a change in national political will. But in each of the two major manifestations of judicial accountability change—new interpretations of disappearance and amnesty, plus the deployment of dedicated HRV case judges—the judiciary seemed finally to clash with more cautious executive policy. Nor does it seem completely satisfactory to suggest that purely exogenous influence was decisive, in the form of external political, moral, or professional pressure on Chilean judges to behave more like their fearless Spanish counterparts. Lawyer Hugo Gutiérrez, usually unsparing in his criticism of national judicial shortcomings, was nonetheless skeptical about "demonstration effect" explanations for what he perceived as fundamentally an internal process.[188] With perhaps a single exception,[189] most actors interviewed agreed that something had been afoot within the Chilean judicial setting well before Pinochet's UK arrest.

Talk of significant change should not be allowed to obscure the fact that the courts' actions have overall remained distinctly conservative (viz. the preservation of amnesty). Court actions should also be disaggregated. In the early 2000s the Supreme Court, without actually reversing landmark lower court verdicts, "took the scissors" (in the words of Felipe González) to Appeals Court rulings that directly relied on international human rights law.[190] Nor has characteristic judicial slowness been eliminated, despite the undoubted progress that followed the assignation of specially dedicated judges to human rights cases in successive tranches since April 2001. The Supreme Court took well over a year to finally suspend proceedings against Pinochet in the Caravana case; and in 2004 repeatedly delayed the Sandoval case ruling, key in clarifying new interpretations of the amnesty law.[191]

188. "I think the judicial route was working; I was confident that we were close to breaking through the wall of impunity surrounding Pinochet and other criminals. It was a slow process, and Pinochet's detention allowed for more rapid advances. But even if it hadn't happened I think we would have got to the same place, just more slowly" (Hugo Gutiérrez, interview 14 November 2002).

189. Cooper (2001, 125) quotes Fabiola Letelier as asserting, circa 2000, that "this [opening] is a result of *international* justice and *international* pressure."

190. Felipe González, interview 8 September 2003.

191. See above. The ruling finally upheld the original conviction, and in late January 2005 Contreras began serving a twelve-year sentence.

The Chilean Judicial System and Post-transitional Reform

As we have seen, the Chilean judicial branch, while not subject to such universal condemnation as its Salvadorean counterpart, has generally been characterized as a traditionalist, conservative body. A tendency to be slow in adopting or adapting to change is combined with a hierarchical, relatively disciplined "corporate" identity centered on the Supreme Court. Such a structure, while reducing the scope for individual judicial activism, can on the other hand operate to facilitate reform where the center can be recruited as an ally or instigator of change. Correa Sutil (1999) echoes the verdict of Hilbink (1999) in characterizing the post-transitional judicial branch as resistant to change. Indeed, judicial reform had represented one of the few unfulfilled projects or "pending modernizations" of the dictatorship itself (Correa Sutil 1999, 292). The neoliberal economic model inherited from the regime continued to place particular strains on an increasingly antiquated system. Thus the Concertación adeptly used the shared goal of judicial modernization for economic reasons to engineer a gradual pro-reform consensus across the political spectrum. By 1994, Justice Minister Soledad Alvear was additionally able to count on the backing of an influential civil society group, Paz Ciudadana. An almost textbook reform drafting process ensued: consensual, gradually paced, and drawing on able and enthusiastic technical support.[192]

The Impact of Judicial Reform on the Courts Since 1997

In summary, judicial reform processes begun in the mid-1990s laid the foundations for a major overhaul of the criminal justice system which would not, however, be fully implemented until 2004/5. A full account of the changes lies beyond the scope of this book,[193] but measures particularly relevant to accountability progress in the medium term included a 1997 change to Supreme Court appointment procedures, identified by many interviewees as determinant. A swath of Pinochet-era judges were retired, while an expansion of numbers

192. Paz Ciudadana was born out of concerns about crime levels, sparked by the high-profile kidnapping of a scion of Santiago's preeminent media dynasty, the Edwards family. Zalaquett aptly describes the resulting reform process as a "curious alliance of *El Mercurio*"—the Edwardses' famously right-wing broadsheet—"with Diego Portales"—the university law faculty, staffed in the main by young, liberal technocrats, which masterminded the initiative. Interview, 28 November 2002.

193. For more detailed discussions of Chilean judicial processes and recent reforms, see particularly the work of Correa Sutil, Hilbink, Prillaman, and Duce. Prillaman (2000) needs to be read in the light of certain cogent criticisms, alluded to in Hilbink (2000). Huneeus (2010) specifically considers judicial change in the light of recent accountability developments. All broadly support an emphasis on endogenous historical factors and domestic drivers.

from sixteen to twenty-one potentially diluted the influence of those remaining. The Court was additionally subdivided into specialized *salas,* including criminal and civil benches. Of these the Sala Penal (Criminal Bench), which logically sees most accountability-related issues, was perceived by interviewees as having been particularly—albeit only relatively—progressive in initial composition and subsequent judicial "line."

A second major innovation made new appointments subject to ratification by the Senate. This change was in fact criticized by most interviewees, including judges. Some felt that the Senate's built-in right-wing majority had led to the appointment of "illiberal" or anti-reform candidates, while others felt that party-political alternation or even a "lowest common denominator" approach to selection had been the result. Certainly, the most immediate visible casualty of the new system was a judge associated with a pro–human rights stance. Milton Juica, who had presided over the conviction of police officers in the *degollados* murder trial, was vetoed by the right when first proposed for a vacant seat on the Supreme Court. Juica was, nonetheless, appointed when next proposed, under Lagos's presidency. Fortuitously, the delay meant he was destined for the criminal bench, where his progressive reputation was most likely to be put to the test in cases involving accountability principles.[194]

Juica's eventual tenure on the Supreme Court overlapped with Carlos Cerda's as president of the Santiago Appeals Court.[195] This coincided with the assignment and reassignment of special judges. Cerda was influential in the latter, while it fell to Juica to reassign Juan Guzmán's extensive caseload of human rights investigations in October 2002. Awaited with some trepidation by those who had viewed it as intended to censure Guzmán's zeal, the redistribution was in the event widely read as supportive of continued investigation. Additionally the ascendancy of Cerda and Juica could itself be read as indicative of a generally liberalizing, if not specifically pro-accountability, strand in reform goals: both had been associated with positive action in HRV cases in the 1980s.

Those who consider that Chilean courts have a propensity to follow political signals might argue that, to the extent the judicial reform project secured the introduction of "Concertación-approved" judges, the subsequent actions

194. Since the Court was divided into specialist *salas,* recruitment is always specifically to the *sala* in which a vacancy arises. Judges appointed to other *salas* may, however, have occasion to rule on accountability issues when a matter is brought before a full sitting of the whole Court, as with the Pinochet *desafuero* rulings of 2000 and 2004.

195. The presidency of the Appeals Court rotates by internal election every twelve months.

of those judges represented the administration's accountability policy. Correa Bulo, for instance, a Supreme Court judge strongly identified with the progressive redefinition of kidnapping as a permanent crime, was routinely identified by the media as "the Concertación's man" on the Court.[196] On the other hand, executive preferences were demonstrably not reliably or stably pro- accountability. Judge Guzmán was repeatedly censured over minor matters, appearing to fall into both political and professional disfavor just as his Caravana investigations against Pinochet reached a delicate stage. Political intervention in the definitive 2002 Supreme Court vote was decidedly anti-prosecution. Couso (2005) contends that accountability shifts simply reflect a perennial tendency of the Chilean judiciary to defer or accommodate to perceived sociopolitical change, a contention supported by Elizabeth Lira.[197] This image of the Chilean judge as sunflower, drawn by the inexorable shift of political fortune, would, of course, explain the apparent capitulation to specific interventions restraining the outcome of the Caravana case. It does not, however, sufficiently explain why the judiciary has at times seemed unduly zealous over post-1998 accountability, to the point of visibly exceeding the executive's wishes (UDP 2003, 138).

Judicial Shifts on Accountability Since 1998

Major practical manifestations of changed judicial-branch receptivity over accountability claims in Chile[198] to date consist of the interpretive shifts over disappearance and amnesty already discussed; one significant administrative action, in the assigning of specialized case judges to investigate HRVs; and the symbolically significant action of stripping Pinochet of parliamentary immunity to allow criminal charges to be brought against him. The shift over disappearance contained in the Poblete-Córdoba verdict is generally remembered as the first Supreme Court–level acceptance of one major set of exceptions to amnesty, finding that the portion of an ongoing crime that had been committed after 1978 was subject to criminal prosecution and penalties in the usual way.[199] The second major change in interpretive practice, requiring full

196. See, for example, *El Mostrador,* 12 November 2000.

197. Elizabeth Lira, interview August 2001. Also as quoted in Brett (2009).

198. It should be noted from the outset that change has been restricted to the civilian courts. The military justice system has proved impervious to change, and progress has only been achieved via the successful transfer of cases into the civilian court system.

199. This thesis is not unique to Chile, as is sometimes erroneously implied: it is the basic understanding informing the 1994 Inter-American Convention on the Forced Disappearance of Persons.

investigation to precede amnesty, led to the reopening of many prematurely suspended investigations.

The most significant administrative action taken by the judicial branch was the naming of specialist judges in April 2001 (see above). The Supreme Court had already, in January and February 2001, named two new *ministros en visita* to investigate specific incidents mentioned in the Mesa's results. They had also, in this early period, assigned another such incident to Guzmán.[200] The April action, however, went considerably beyond the victims named in the Mesa report. Nine judges were named exclusively, and fifty-one preferentially, to investigate a total of 114 cases of disappearance. The Supreme Court periodically renewed these appointments over the next fifteen months. In May 2002 the Santiago Appeals Court took similar action of its own, naming six judges for HRV cases in its particular jurisdiction.

Back in 1993, it had seemed likely that Contreras and Espinoza would be not just the first but the only high-level former military officers to be charged with HRV crimes in Chile. A decade later, charges were pending against almost 400 of their former colleagues.[201] By late September 2004 approximately 300 victims of disappearance and 450 of political execution had cases in the courts, although no more than a dozen of these had reached the sentencing stage.[202] By February 2010 the figures were 302 open cases representing over 1,000 victims, with 782 agents indicted or already sentenced (see table 1a).[203] This accumulation of cases against many key repressive figures constitutes the definitive breakthrough in a formerly moribund accountability scenario. Nonetheless, the most dramatic, and certainly the most commented, acts of the judicial branch over accountability in the recent period were those relating to Pinochet himself (see table 2).

In 2000, and again in 2004, national tribunals suspended Pinochet's parliamentary immunity from prosecution, opening the way for criminal charges and implying, at the very least, that there was a case to answer. In the first instance the Santiago Appeals Court and then the Supreme Court ruled, in June and

---

200. Guzmán already had the required *ministro en visita* status due to his ongoing investigations into Caravana and related crimes.

201. Figure from address by Nelson Caucoto to the IPS/FLACSO conference "El caso Pinochet," Santiago, 14 November 2002.

202. Figures supplied by CODEPU, 6 October 2004.

203. Programa de Derechos Humanos del Ministerio del Interior. It should be noted that, as cases are accumulated by episode, the total number of open cases can go down even though more crimes and agents are being investigated. In general, the trend over the decade is toward more activity and a rise in the number of agents charged and sentenced.

Table 1a Human Rights Prosecutions in the Chilean Courts Since 2000

Case Universe	Cases for death and disappearance: 302 Cases for torture, illegal burial, or conspiracy: 32 Total open investigations for HRVs: 334
	Known victims of death and disappearance: 3,186* Victims covered by the 297 ongoing cases: 1,038
	Percentage of known victims With open cases: 32.5% With cases already resolved: 6% With no case, either open or concluded: 61.5%
Agents (Perpetrators)	Former regime agents indicted, charged, or sentenced in HRV cases: 782
	Average rise in agents charged year on year: 14%
	Ranks affected: The vast majority are former security force personnel (armed forces and police), at all levels from general to rank and file.
	The figures nonetheless include 53 civilian agents
Sentencing	Former regime agents sentenced: 286
	Number of agents at each stage of sentencing: First instance: 35 Second instance (appeal): 87 Confirmed by Supreme Court: 206 The sum of these totals exceeds 286 because some agents have multiple sentences, which are at different stages
	Total sentences emitted: 499 Many agents are subject to more than one sentence
	Number of full acquittals: 4**
Pending Charges and Ongoing Investigations	Formal investigations and indictments (*procesamientos* and *acusaciones*) currently pending: 3,043
	Number of former agents affected: 557
	Additional acquittals or case suspensions presently under challenge: 45
Prison Sentences Actually Being Served	Former agents with confirmed sentences: 206
	Currently serving jail time: 60
	Conceded benefits (parole/ reduced sentence): 146
	Note: The total of 60 is the highest in the region, not excepting Argentina, where a larger number of detainees masks extensive use of preventive detention. Only two former agents are currently serving final sentences in Argentina (see CELS Argentina, http://www.cels.org.ar/).

*Official numbers for deaths and disappearances remain at 3,195. This total should, however, be revised downward, as here, to reflect errors discovered in 2008 and 2009 in official registers.
**Eight more sentences were dissolved by application of prescription at appeals stage

Table 1b   Situation of Emblematic Individuals

	Confirmed Sentences	Sentences at Appeal Stage	Pending Charges or Investigations	Longest Single Sentence	Army Rank
Manuel Contreras, former head of DINA secret police	17	19	61	15 years	General

Current confirmed sentence total 161 years, plus one sentence already served (Letelier assassination). Appeals stage sentences would bring total to over 300 years. Subject to extradition to Argentina if ever released.

	Confirmed Sentences	Sentences at Appeal Stage	Pending Charges or Investigations	Longest Single Sentence	Army Rank
Miguel Krassnoff, high-level DINA operative	12	10	45	10 years, 1 day	Brigadier
Marcelo Moren Brito, DINA operative; commander of Villa Grimaldi torture center	14	10	50	11 years	Colonel
Alvaro Corbalán, operations director of the CNI	4	0	2	Life	Major
Hugo Salas Wenzel, last pre-transition director of the CNI	1	0	1	Life	Major-general

Life sentence for twelve Operación Albania murders or kidnappings. This was the first HRV sentence against a general.

	Confirmed Sentences	Sentences at Appeal Stage	Pending Charges or Investigations	Longest Single Sentence	Army Rank
Sergio Arellano Stark, Pinochet's personal envoy in the 1973 "Caravan of Death" episode	1	0	1 (7 more Caravana episodes)	6 years	General

Sentenced for four Caravana murders; processed for 45 more, and for 57 kidnappings. Sentence and further charges suspended in 2008 for health reasons

NOTE: The data shown represent the situation as of November 2009. All quantitative data are valid from 2000, the date from which reliable comparable statistics began to be collected. All ranks given are on retirement. Since around 2006, serving armed forces personnel charged in HRV cases have been automatically retired from active service.

SOURCE: Observatorio de ddhh, Universidad Diego Portales, Santiago, Chile; based on figures supplied by the Human Rights Programme of the Chilean Ministry of the Interior, except where otherwise stipulated.

Table 2   Major Criminal Investigations Against Augusto Pinochet, 1998–2006

Case	Pinochet's Immunity Removed by Appeals Court	Pinochet's Immunity Removed by Supreme Court	Pinochet Processed*	Status at Pinochet's Death
Caravana	June 2000	August 2000	Yes	Charging suspended for medical reasons
Calle Conferencia	Requested Oct 2000	Refused Aug 2003	No	Case suspended**
Operación Cóndor	May 2004	August 2004	Yes	House arrest Charging suspended for medical reasons
Prats	Dec 2004	Refused Mar 2005	No	Case suspended**
Riggs (tax fraud and financial crimes)	Sep 2004	Oct 2005	Yes	Charges pending
Operación Colombo	Jul 2005 Apr 2006***	Sep 2005 Apr 2006	Pending	Processing pending
Villa Grimaldi	Jan 2006	Sep 2006	Yes	Charges pending

*A pre-charging status that carries a strong presumption of involvement
**These cases continued against other suspects
***Additional charges

August 2000 respectively, that Pinochet could face charges for complicity in the Caravana murders, although subsequent medical tests initially ruled out further action. In the second instance, the Appeals Court ruled in June 2004 that there were grounds to proceed against Pinochet in the Cóndor investigation. Charges were duly brought in mid-December 2004, and Pinochet was placed under house arrest on 5 January 2005. The impact of this repeated stripping of Pinochet's parliamentary immunity by the courts was to prove more symbolic than practical: the Court's 2004 change of heart as to Pinochet's medical fitness reopened the possibility of sentencing, only to be preempted by his demise.

Nonetheless, for the man who had virtually *been* the law for over a decade and a half to be brought low by national—rather than third-country—tribunals was certainly a most unwelcome blow and probably a great surprise.

Judicial shifts over accountability since 1998 are both too radical and occasionally too unpredictable to be responding to a single new set of political (policy) signals. The upholding of the Poblete-Córdoba ruling, described by Hugo Gutiérrez as the Supreme Court's "best ever" performance on accountability to date, "finally cut the umbilical cord between amnesty and impunity"[204] at a time when executive interest in the issue was markedly absent. The courts also manifested apparently independent enthusiasm in the naming of special judges. Although the initial assignment was made in response to a formal request from the government, the Supreme Court went well beyond its original remit in spurring a reexamination of all pending cases. The Santiago Appeals Court's own round of additional special nominations in 2002 contained an implicit critique of political will. Although the official record states that the round was triggered by a request from the government Programa, Carlos Cerda hinted that the request had come at his own instigation, to counteract behind-the-scenes pressure for a "go-slow" from an executive reluctant to see more large-scale, visible case controversy so soon after the Mesa.[205] The October 2002 re-working of Guzmán's caseload also seems consonant with a view of the courts as a relatively zealous, albeit recently converted, actor moving accountability ahead more surely than the executive. Well-regarded, competent judicial figures were once again assigned to high-profile cases, instructed to proceed with "all possible celerity" and submit monthly progress reports.[206]

A retreat from these apparent heights of pro-accountability enthusiasm is discernible in recent drawing back from the brink over amnesty interpretation, as well as in 2008 tendencies toward lenient sentencing.[207] Both actions are, of course, susceptible to explanation by political intervention. What could explain, though, the period of apparent "excess" when accountability actors, often to their great surprise, found the courts the best repositories for their hopes for justice? Why did the Appeals Court choose in 2004 to reverse

204. Interview, 14 November 2002.

205. Carlos Cerda, interview 23 October 2002.

206. "Acuerdo del Pleno de la Corte Suprema, nueva distribución de causas en Jueces Especiales," dated 14 October 2002, available at http://www.fasic.org/juri/jueces.htm, last accessed 4 March 2009.

207. In one example, the Supreme Court reduced first-instance sentences of eighteen years for the murder of fifteen peasant farmers to noncustodial sentences of five years' parole (Supreme Court Sala Penal verdict, Liquiñe case, 25 September 2008).

its stance on Pinochet's continued immunity, precisely the subject on which political authorities had seemed most immutable?

Is There a "Garzón Effect"?

It has been suggested that Chilean judges' detectably bolder stance around 1998 was principally due to activity elsewhere—namely, in Spain. International approbation supposedly came to constitute positive reinforcement for pro-accountability behavior, with British and (particularly) Spanish judges setting a "good example" to their traditionally more cautious Chilean colleagues. This "Garzón effect"[208] supposedly convinced Chilean judges that decisive progress on accountability could be rewarded, while its continued glaring absence might fatally compromise Chile's international standing. Most domestic commentators certainly consider that the UK arrest and its aftermath increased the determination of the Chilean judicial system to show that it could deal with Pinochet and other outstanding accountability issues "in-house."[209] That the eventual outcome of cases already in train may have been affected is, then, easy to imagine if difficult to prove. The extent of subsequent judicial movement, however, suggests a domestic rather than solely externally driven agenda. A minimal commitment not to artificially extinguish the already-open Caravana investigation against Pinochet would probably have been sufficient to pacify international—certainly diplomatic—pressure. The acceptance of hundreds of similar claims, the continuation of the Caravana investigation against other suspects even after Pinochet was removed from it, and the opening of other avenues for a now-substantial accountability case universe combine to suggest more than a simple "going through the motions" on the part of the judicial branch.

If domestic judicial change on accountability has thus preceded and at times outstripped both executive leadership and international causality, what, then, lies behind the shift? Couso (2005) insists that a wholesale "rights conversion" is not the cause. His own explanation—the effects of criminal code revision, particularly the incorporation of international standards into national law—is somewhat unsatisfactory, given the rather skeptical approach to such standards made manifest even in pro-accountability rulings. Judge Carlos Cerda adduces two endogenous explanations for recent

208. Roht-Arriaza ascribes the term, now in wide currency, to Roberto Garretón. See Roht-Arriaza (2003, 196) and Roht-Arriaza and Garretón quoted in Brett (2009).

209. Rosemarie Bornand, executive secretary of the Programa; and Jorge Correa Sutil, remarks to the conference "The Pinochet Effect: Ten Years On," Santiago, October 2008.

court behavior: the influence of particular personalities and a desire on the part of the courts to pay off a perceived "debt to society."[210]

Supreme Court activity on accountability has not fully mapped either 1997 reforms or perceived judicial ideology. A "liberal" or "conservative" label did not prove a straightforward predictor of a judge's subsequent accountability attitude.[211] Nor can judicial movement on accountability be adequately explained by reference only to the Supreme Court. Post-1998 change has been visible at all levels of the court system, including among the dedicated human rights case judges. Some, such as judge Mario Carozza, were relatively new judicial figures. Others, including Guzmán himself, special judge Raquel Lermanda, and even the anonymous first-instance judge in the Poblete-Córdoba case,[212] are figures previously considered conservative who have been "converted" by their experiences of investigation. Just as personalities can shape political trends, it appears there is likewise room for cumulative individual change to shape legal outcomes even in Chile's relatively corporatist, disciplined judicial structure.

The Limits of Judicial Accountability Change

Hilbink (2007) and Huneeus (2010) are right to argue that a certain amount of progress on accountability has not heralded a full-scale Chilean rights revolution.[213] Accountability change, though undeniable and significant, has very real limits, some operational, some attitudinal. Others are essentially speculative, insofar as certain court actions can be interpreted as being closer to the preferences of the executive and other restraining influences than may at first appear to be the case. Moreover, post-1998 changes are potentially reversible because they do not reflect any change in law. Political alternation, or simple internal changes in the "balance of power" among judges, could quite easily change outcomes. For example, some senior judges have made it

---

210. Cerda suggested that judges belatedly recognize, at least in private, that their signal failure to protect rights in the past may have contributed to present low levels of public confidence in the justice system. Interview, 7 November 2002. Supreme Court judge Milton Juica made a similar point in a December 2008 public presentation of a report on justice system transparency. See also Huneeus (2010).

211. Two of the three judges who finally halted the 2002 Pinochet prosecution had previously voted for it. One of them had previously been considered that Court's most dependably pro-accountability judge.

212. Case lawyer Sergio Concha remains convinced that a chance personal encounter with the judge, a former fellow student, played a major part in producing this landmark ruling. Sergio Concha, interview 30 January 2003.

213. See also HRW (1998) and CODEPU (2003b).

clear that they privately regard the ongoing-crime thesis of kidnapping to be a legal absurdity, whereas fundamental aspects of amnesty, such as its constitutionality, remain unchallenged.

It is at least possible to read court actions on accountability as essentially contingent, having less to do with the particular issue at hand than with a desire to assert autonomy vis-à-vis other branches of government or the "political class" as a whole.[214] Conversely, some find a suspicious coincidence between judicial outcomes and perceived executive or even military wishes, despite the apparently more radical initial posture of the courts. Thus the Supreme Court, in its 2002 reassignment of Guzmán's cases, instructed judges to "put particular emphasis" on the location of remains. In the prevailing legal climate this constituted an explicitly non-accountability goal, since its logical result would be the declaration of unlawful death and, ultimately, the invocation of amnesty. This made the location of remains essentially a truth objective. The Court's pursuit of this enterprise thus chimed with the apparent thrust of Concertación policy from Rettig through the Mesa and Valech commission: to privilege truth even when actually facing renewed justice demands. In a similar vein, the Court's simultaneous call for swiftness, although consonant with accountability claimants' long-standing desire for justice, most obviously echoed the preoccupations of the army. Military authorities have repeatedly called for a swift end to judicial "uncertainty" and the "parade" of former officers through the courts, claiming a deleterious effect on institutional morale.[215] It is difficult not to detect the influence of this reiterated desire on the Supreme Court's early 2005 attempt to impose a time limit on outstanding cases.[216] A simple desire for swiftness could as easily represent a pro- as an anti-accountability line, but in combination with the emerging recent pattern of lenient sentences it suggests the latter. The increasing exposure of divergent views within the judicial branch over accountability also suggests a more neutral reason why the traditionally centralizing Supreme Court might wish to see an end to the matter.

In sum, there is little sign that the Chilean courts in general, or even the Supreme Court in particular, have a firm design or policy of their own over

214. The period of greatest apparent distance between judicial and executive preferences over accountability in 2003/4 coincided with a series of financial and other scandals in which the courts showed little compunction in indicting high-level political figures of both left and right.

215. Public statements by then Army Commander in Chief Cheyre in September 2004, which were interpreted as disguised attempts to lobby for a full-stop law.

216. See above.

accountability. As with executive policy and the changeable, sometimes contradictory actions of different government agents, the Supreme Court seems to be rather at sea, navigating on the tide of events. It has produced erratic sequences of outcomes that defy easy extrapolation of a particular agenda. If there is, indeed, a "bottom line" for the Supreme Court, this would appear to be a determination to defend its perception of the dignity of the judicial branch per se. Judicial reforms proposed and actual since 1996 have created an atmosphere of alternate negotiation, more or less grudging cooperation, and occasional defensive suspicion between the two branches. Actions over accountability have followed the same general pattern: occasional boldness followed by cautious retreat, with occasional rumors of executive intervention.

Executive intervention appeared to peak during the Lagos presidency, despite his repeated insistence on the formula of "letting the courts decide." That discourse allowed the government to shift both the burden of decision and the potential costs of unpopular outcomes onto the courts. Subsequent events suggest that the Supreme Court resolved to no longer be seen as following political dictates. The Court's second *desafuero* decision against Pinochet in 2004 can be read directly as a rebuke to Pinochet's brazenness, or alternatively as a signal to the government that any future attempts to "save" Pinochet would have to be made without court collusion. The courts were no longer available to give unequivocally political solutions a judicial gloss, and future political solutions would have to be named as such, rather than carrying a judicial imprimatur. The mutual displacement of responsibilities has largely persisted, with the executive's continued failure to give new legislative shape to amnesty constituting a virtual abdication of responsibility. Accountability has perhaps become a classic site of "judicialization" of politics in its simplest sense. Minority social positions over a sensitive social issue are played out on the legal stage, with judges thrust into an unaccustomedly prominent role for which they are not prepared and with which they are not entirely comfortable.

Conclusions

This chapter has shown that, despite the early existence of a well-organized, legally channeled human rights movement, there was very little accountability change in Chile for a significant portion of the post-transitional period.

Successive democratic governments appeared unwilling to address outstanding justice demands, even as the real and imagined constraints of Chile's highly controlled democratic transition were diluted over time. Newly opened political channels were unresponsive, while judicial channels continued to respond negatively. Even so, small core groups of lawyers managed to keep claims alive. This continuity of accountability pressure, with the concomitant accumulation of cases and legal know-how, eventually proved a useful launching pad for renewed accountability pressure in the more favorable circumstances prevailing since 1998.

An unprecedented degree of domestic legal activity and interest surrounded the October 1998 arrest and subsequent overseas detention of Pinochet. But other factors—such as the strategy choices of the domestic accountability lobby, changing civil-military relations, and judicial renewal—each made a distinctive contribution to a renewed domestic appetite for the bringing of criminal complaints. Indeed, judges, rather than domestic accountability actors, seem to have played the key role in the transformation of the Chilean accountability scenario since 1998. It has been argued here that it took a perceptible change in receptivity from a relatively unreformed judiciary to produce significant breakthroughs. In and after 1998, judges reversed previous stances on a range of legal obstacles to criminal accountability. Nonetheless, this shift remains partial and reversible. Most notably, Chile's self-amnesty law remains textually intact, and accountability progress has relied on reinterpretation of and exceptions to it.

If the constellation of actor, strategy, and judicial aspects of accountability in Chile has been reconfigured into a setting more favorable to accountability claims, the limits placed on recent accountability change have to do with the strength of countervailing forces. These include certain transitional arrangements that have persisted into the modern period, with the amnesty statute constituting the most obvious example. Political—legislative and executive—attitudes in Chile to accountability breakthroughs have also been ambivalent. The executive appeared at times relieved to let the courts assume the burden of controversial decision-making, and at other times ready to intervene to slow the pace of judicialization. A deluge of legal onslaughts on the status, fortune, and person of Pinochet appeared to be particularly unwelcome for the government of the day. These nonetheless seemed to acquire unstoppable momentum in late 2004, when the political right and the military were finally moved to distance themselves from the person and legacy of the former dictator. The political reverberations of Chile's judicialized re-irruption of accountability thus included, at the very least, a previously unimaginable sidelining of Pinochet, exploding the myth of his invulnerability.[217]

High levels of judicial activity have provoked attempts to relocate justice issues to the political arena. Early political responses attempted to steer judicial outcomes while wresting the initiative back from the courts. One early example, the Mesa, could be read as replicating the Rettig commission's dynamic of a "truth for justice" trade-off. Human rights legislative proposals in 2003 were open to similar interpretations, particularly in aspects related to incentives for new information about the disappeared. Indications to date, however, are that the judiciary is reluctant to entirely relinquish its hold over the issue—even while it continues to operate within the strict confines of a previous "legislated" solution, the self-amnesty law, which democratic authorities have not yet seen fit to challenge or replace.

In sum, it has been argued in this chapter that the particular structure of Chile's universe of accountability actors, including the predominance of lawyers and the access of other actors to legal expertise, proved central to post-transitional accountability breakthroughs in and after 1998. Legally framed pressure from these actors had existed since and even before transition, however, suggesting that domestic actor pressure provides a necessary but insufficient explanation for changed outcomes. Nor was parallel international activity the only or, it is argued here, the key determinant of change. A wave of new domestic initiatives in and after January 1998 were triggered not by external events so much as by a particular national conjuncture. Further, these measures were also predicated on strategic perceptions of a prior, and favorable, shift in domestic judicial conditions. It is accordingly argued that the Chilean trajectory is comprehensible as an internally driven process, and that judicial change in and since 1998 proved key to translating legally framed actor pressure into positive accountability outcomes.

---

217. Immediately after his UK arrest, and after a rumor of his sudden death during medical treatment had been dispelled, one national newspaper had run the oversized headline "Pinochet: Inmortal." Patricia Verdugo, interview 18 November 2002.

6

The Counterinsurgency War (1980–1992)

El Salvador was ruled for much of the twentieth century by an oligarchy that, according to James Dunkerley, "has a good claim to be one of the . . . most pugnacious and reactionary in the world."[1] Left-wing guerrilla groups emerged in the late 1970s in response to this exclusionary tradition; the regime under which massive HRVs were carried out in El Salvador was a right-wing civilian-military alliance engaged in a counterinsurgency civil war against these groups. Government forces confronted the leftist insurgent group Frente Farabundo Martí para la Liberación Nacional (FMLN) for just over a decade until a series of UN-sponsored peace accords in 1991 and 1992.

El Salvador's conflict quickly became a proxy war. The United States, driven by cold war anticommunism and the desire to avoid a repeat of the 1979 Nicaraguan revolution, became the "mentor and military, economic and political mainstay" of the Salvadorean regime (Zamora 2001, 65), pouring extensive military and economic aid into the country with the aim of preventing a guerrilla victory (Call 2003). A mixture of military stalemate and changing international attitudes finally helped send both sides to the negotiating table. The United States eventually joined the UN and other Central American governments in calling for a political rather than military settlement to the war.

---

1. Dunkerley (1982, 7). See also Stanley (1996).

Patterns of HRVs

Political violence during El Salvador's civil war is notable for its sheer scale as well as for the difficulties it presents in reaching an accurate final death toll.[2] Many victims were from rural communities where institutional reach, never comprehensive, had been disrupted further by the war. Military tactics such as the massacre of civilians and forced displacement of entire villages blurred the boundary between combat deaths and HRVs. Right-wing death squads, closely linked to state security forces, were also used to disguise official involvement in repression. Both state and death squad agents made use of extreme exemplary violence, such as extrajudicial executions accompanied by severe mutilation. By comparison with the Southern Cone, El Salvador therefore suffered a higher absolute and relative[3] incidence of fatal violence, with proportionately less reliance on an infrastructure of repression involving clandestine detention centers and the like. El Salvador also saw much more significant political violence from the left. The official Salvadorean truth commission report[4] documented such FMLN practices as kidnappings, bombing campaigns, and assassinations.

Fatal violence was at its height between 1978 and 1983, becoming less frequent and more selective between 1983 and 1987.[5] According to the truth commission, a "marked decrease" in death squad activity was attributed to public denunciation of the practice by the U.S. government (UN 1993, 31) as well as to the 1984 election of José Napoleón Duarte as president. Duarte had been supported by the United States precisely as a moderate alternative who would "tone down" HRVs. Deaths and displacement, however, remained high, with aerial bombardments used to dislodge the FMLN from whole expanses of territory (34). The years 1987 to 1989 saw the first signs of progress in peace talks. Attacks nonetheless escalated in the run-up to the 1989 presidential elections, won by Alfredo Cristiani of the right-wing ARENA

---

2. Call (2002, 386) suggests seventy-five thousand war-related deaths, mostly of noncombatants. Stanley (1996, 1) suggests fifty thousand.

3. Fatal violence was higher in El Salvador relative to the full total of serious HRVs and also per head of population. See Stanley (1996, 3).

4. Published in 1993 as UN document S/25500. Page references cited here are from the official English edition, titled "From Madness to Hope" (UN, 1993).

5. Call (2002) and UN (1993). Before the FMLN's formal emergence in 1980, right-wing violence was targeted at the five leftist groups that were its precursors, as well as at supposedly "subversive" popular organizations.

party. In the final two years of the war, although both sides had virtually acknowledged that a military victory was not possible, violence continued as combatants attempted to secure the upper hand for eventual negotiation of a cease-fire.

EXTERNAL INTERVENTION AND HRVS

The key external actor in the Salvadorean war was undoubtedly the U.S. government. Although winning the counterinsurgency war was the prime U.S. concern, human rights atrocities soon sparked controversy within the United States. Much private lobbying pressure, whatever its source, was directed at the U.S. government, a result both of the limited space available within El Salvador for human rights mobilization and the perception that the United States was largely running, and certainly bankrolling, the war. Official U.S. intervention in defense of human rights, however, was of questionable sincerity. Pressure over particular notorious incidents, the "big case approach," often provoked only superficial responses from Salvadorean authorities (Popkin 2000, viii, 50–79; Stanley 1996, 257). The other main thrust of U.S. policy was largely ineffectual intervention in the criminal justice system.[6]

The U.S. Congress displayed more sensitivity to human rights concerns than did the executive, attempting in 1981 to make further aid conditional on improvements in the human rights situation. Monitoring depended on U.S. State Department data, however, and suspicions arose that the certification requirement had simply led to inaccurate and ideologically biased official reporting.[7] External pressure, governmental and private, did have some ameliorative impact on HRVs over the course of the conflict (Stanley 1996, 253). Nonetheless, political and military logic generally seemed to prevail. Even the United States's eventual embracing of a pro-negotiation policy, decisive in forcing a reluctant Salvadorean army into line, owed more to perceptions of a military stalemate than to human rights concerns.

---

6. See chapter 7 and Popkin (2000, 57–73).

7. See "Report of the Secretary of State's Panel on El Salvador" (U.S. Secretary of State's Panel on El Salvador 1993, 2–3, 29–35). The report absolves the State Department of outright lying, but candidly admits that certification "had little effect on the situation on the ground" (34).

Human Rights Organizing and Legal Strategies During the War

A few HROs emerged in El Salvador in the late 1970s, with the formation of the nongovernmental Comité de Derechos Humanos de El Salvador (CDHES);[8] Socorro Jurídico;[9] and COMADRES, the first relatives' organization.[10] Salvadorean HROs, however, tended to be less numerous and organizationally weaker than their Chilean counterparts, not least because they operated in such an unpropitious and hostile situation. In-country human rights organizing lacked clear institutional channels or interlocutors. Domestic leverage over the army was virtually nil: civilian politicians had either no capacity or no real desire to limit counterinsurgency techniques. Neither were the courts prepared to exert control over military strategy, defend rights, or produce accountability.[11] What is more, the courts never had been—something that helps to explain why legal strategies were neither the instinctive recourse nor a learned preference for the HROs that did emerge.[12]

Human rights organizing became an urgent and yet dangerous undertaking. The Catholic Church, which had served as an umbrella for human rights organizing in other countries, itself became a direct target. The highly symbolic 1980 killing of outspoken archbishop Oscar Romero was followed months later by the rape and murder of four U.S. churchwomen, sending a grim message about the extent of impunity and the absence of institutional protection. HROs were also targeted: the offices of the CDHES were dynamited in September 1980, and two of its functionaries abducted and killed the following month. Two more staff members, including the institution's president, would be killed before the war ended. Mirna Perla, a sometime lower

8. CDHES was founded in 1978 by university law students. In documents from the conflict period it is usually referred to as the Comisión no-Gubernamental (nongovernmental commission), in order to distinguish it from an official body of the same name that functioned for a few years after 1982.

9. Socorro Jurídico, an early HRO with a legal cast, was set up by the Jesuit order. After 1982 it was distanced from Catholic Church structures, in part because of its de facto links with the left.

10. The Comité de Madres Oscar Arnulfo Romero (COMADRES) began in 1975 as an informal network of mothers whose children had disappeared into military or police custody after street demonstrations. Then-archbishop Oscar Romero gave the group personal encouragement and a meeting space in its early years, leading them to later adopt his name. Alicia García, interview 5 August 2003.

11. See Popkin (2000, viii) on the "irrelevance of law in El Salvador's wartime reality."

12. Ernesto Chacón of the CDHES suggests that legal strategies had been tried but abandoned during the 1970s. Collusion between judges and security forces had meant that those who denounced HRVs were themselves targeted. This very real disincentive to in-country legal action persisted into the war period. Interview, 14 August 2003.

court judge who later joined the CDHES, recalled the frustrations and real danger of operating in those times: "The only things we could do were direct actions, like occupying the cathedral, or international *denuncias.* . . . There was very little legal response. . . . Pastor Ridruejo[13] used to come, we would do general documentation for him—but there never seemed to be time to give attention to one single case and follow it up. And it wasn't safe: people from CDHES and Socorro Jurídico were in hiding. We gave emergency responses in the immediacy of the moment—press conferences, whatever."[14]

Although many organizations were founded by lawyers and had legal pretensions,[15] legally focused domestic activity seemed more likely to provoke than to effectively combat fatal violence. Functionaries were not exempt: judges of all political persuasions were assassinated during the war, some by the FMLN, others by the military and the right. Mirna Perla's own husband, Herbert Anaya, another former judge turned human rights activist, was assassinated in October 1987. The killing forced her, like many other HRO activists and lawyers, into exile. Thus a notable contrast with Chile is the virtual absence of a community of human rights lawyers taking early leadership roles.

HROs did play a role in channeling information to international organizations, including the UN's Human Rights Committee,[16] and to U.S. civil society groups. Popkin asserts that most major HRV incidents did eventually become known inside the country, although the information was usually at the level of rumor or hearsay. Hard facts—such as evidence that might satisfy legal standards—could rarely be accumulated.[17] This unavoidable imprecision contributed, both before and after the peace accords, to impunity. The lack of precise data also enabled domestic and U.S. authorities to dispute the

13. Pastor Ridruejo was the UN Human Rights Commission's special representative for El Salvador between 1981 and 1992.

14. Former HRO activist Mirna Perla, interview 24 July 2003. Currently a Supreme Court judge, Perla had been a lower court magistrate between 1980 and 1987 before resigning to work for the CDHES. She later continued human rights work from exile, returning to her domestic judicial career in 1995.

15. Including Socorro Jurídico and Tutela Legal, which were both originally Church organizations.

16. The committee appointed a special relator for El Salvador in 1981, and myriad reports and UN General Assembly resolutions followed. It is unclear what real contemporaneous impact this may have had on HRV patterns, although this early monitoring did inform subsequent UN protagonism in the peace process.

17. Thus HRO records in El Salvador usually cannot match the kind of meticulous documentation amassed by Chilean groups—who were, additionally, more able to use the courts to generate a paper trail.

veracity of each specific incident.[18] Such step-by-step refutation undermined the conquering of legal or institutional space at every stage, and helped to politicize the issue of information. This politicization was exacerbated when, with U.S. internal tension over Central America policy at its height, the U.S. Congress grew distrustful of State Department data and turned to Salvadorean HROs for information.

The credibility of domestic HRO data certainly suffered as a result of such intense contestation.[19] Some domestic groups, in their understandable determination to keep HRVs on the agenda, were also perhaps too ready to deny signs of progress, attributing every violent incident or unexplained death to continued military or death squad activity.[20] Additionally, the active links between some domestic HROs and the guerrilla forces, routinely exaggerated by the authorities to discredit organizations, nonetheless had some grounding in fact.[21] These connections left some HROs vulnerable to a change in political priorities after the war, when the FMLN's energies were redirected to the task of building a mainstream political party. In the shorter term they also introduced a potential contradiction of aims between the human rights movement and the guerrilla forces. Since accountability was never a viable alternative, human rights progress meant reducing the commission of HRVs. Thus a principal aim of HROs had to be to end the war, while the principal aim of the FMLN was to win it.

The Judiciary During the War

In many senses, human rights impunity in El Salvador was not specific exceptionalism but part of a wider pattern. Even prewar, the judiciary was "highly politicized, corrupt and unprofessional" (Call 2003, 831). The war, of course, hardly improved matters. Wartime accountability was highly selective: high profile cases were resolved or not according to the preferences of military

18. Reports of rural massacres, including El Mozote and Rio Sumpúl, went unacknowledged for months or even years by U.S. embassy sources, who adduced the "impossibility" of traveling to remote or guerrilla-controlled areas.

19. See U.S. Secretary of State's Panel on El Salvador (1993, 35–38).

20. Conversation with former international HRO representative, mid-2003.

21. One HRO lawyer, confirming the links, recalled being told by his immediate boss, a cleric, "That desk you're sitting at is just one more trench in the revolutionary war." Interview, San Salvador, third quarter of 2003.

and civilian authorities. This usually meant impunity, except where the per-petrators were the FMLN.[22]

Judicial treatment of detainees was also highly flawed. A series of legisla-tive decrees suspended constitutional guarantees and rendered extrajudicial confessions admissible in court.[23] Since the criminal justice system boasted little in the way of evidence-gathering capacity, torture was routinely used to obtain confessions. It was generally accepted that the outcome of a judi-cial process owed little or nothing to the known facts. Some judges made it known that leniency toward accused guerrillas could be bought, while oth-ers were intimidated in the opposite direction by threats and assassination attempts.[24] In short, "in the 1980s it was dangerous to be a judge in El Salva-dor," particularly an assiduous or conscientious one.[25]

After 1984, the Supreme Court began to appear more loyal to military and far-right interests than to the government. Duarte's incoming administra-tion at least attempted human rights improvements, and succumbed to U.S. pressure for criminal justice system reform.[26] The Supreme Court, however, resisted reforms that would have redistributed its own highly concentrated powers. In December 1985 it reinstated attorney general Francisco Guerrero, whom the legislature had voted to dismiss for his poor performance in inves-tigating human rights cases, including the Romero assassination.[27] In 1988, the Supreme Court dismissed charges against military officers accused of par-

22. FMLN crimes that prompted unusually vigorous justice system activity included the Zona Rosa case, over the 1985 murder of four U.S. marines; plus the Pickett and Dawson case, over two U.S. airmen shot down and later executed by the FMLN. Popkin, however, notes that undoubted bias in the criminal justice system was not always able to overcome genuine incompetence: the virtual lack of investigative capacity across the board meant many FMLN atrocities went unpun-ished (2000, 179).

23. Decrees 507 of December 1980, 943 of January 1982, and 50 of February 1984. See LCHR (1987, 39–42).

24. Call (2003, 831–32). See also LCHR (1987).

25. UN (1993, 270). According to Supreme Court figures, twenty-eight judges were killed in war-related violence during the 1980s. According to Mirna Perla, "Because the Supreme Court knew all about the [state-perpetrated] violence, . . . [lower] judges didn't dare investigate. A judge who stood up against impunity would be killed" (interview, 24 July 2003).

26. In July 1984 Duarte signed an agreement with the official U.S. funding agency, US-AID, for judicial system reforms. In August he created the "Cestoni commission," which would suppos-edly dedicate itself to a year-long investigation of emblematic human rights cases, including the Romero assassination. That commission was followed in 1985 by the more permanent Comisión de Investigación de Hechos Delictivos (CIHD). See, however, Call (2003) and LCHR (1987, 1989) for criticism of the intentions behind, and performance of, these measures.

27. Guerrero, a member of the right-wing ARENA party and close associate of one of the case's chief suspects, had the investigation suspended within months of taking office.

ticipation in a peasant massacre. Supreme Court president Mauricio Gutiérrez Castro rightly became personally notorious as architect of this extreme
line. The truth commission singled him out for special criticism, citing as
only one example the El Mozote case, where he "interfered unduly and preju-
dicially, for biased political reasons, in the ongoing judicial proceedings" (UN
1993, 121).

Emblematic HRV Episodes

Archbishop Oscar Romero, indefatigable defender of the poor and denouncer
of repression, was assassinated on 24 March 1980. The domestic investigation
dragged on for over a decade, even though it was widely rumored that Major
Roberto d'Aubuisson, a right-wing extremist who went on to found ARENA,
had been responsible. From 1984, President Duarte fought his political battles
with ARENA through the case, periodically bringing it back into the public
eye. Amnesty was nevertheless eventually applied to close the domestic investigation, but not before the truth commission report had reiterated the allegations against d'Aubuisson—by then deceased (UN 1993, 127–31).

On 2 December 1980 four U.S. churchwomen were raped and murdered
by National Guardsmen. This incident did more than perhaps any other to
"inflame the debate over El Salvador in the United States,"[28] not least because
unsympathetic U.S. officials implied that the women may have been gun-
toting guerrilla sympathizers who had run a roadblock (UN 1993, 218n63).
Pressure from the women's families and U.S. advocacy organization the
Lawyers' Committee for Human Rights (LCHR; now Human Rights First)
contributed to an eventual domestic trial. In 1984 the triggermen were given
thirty-year sentences, though responsibility higher up the chain of command
was not addressed. Ironically, the official pretence that the men acted alone
was used to keep them in prison: their repeated applications for amnesty after
1993 were turned down on the grounds that their crime was "not political"
(*New York Times*, 3 April 1998).

In December 1981 between five hundred[29] and eight hundred[30] civilians
were massacred during an army operation in the northern village of El

---

28. U.S. Secretary of State's Panel on El Salvador (1993, 51).

29. This figure comes from the truth commission. See UN (1993, 114).

30. This figure comes from Argentinian forensic anthropologists involved in ongoing exhumations. See EAAF (2001, 49).

Mozote. The atrocity was not officially recognized until exhumations began in 1992. Authorities continued to insist that only guerrilla combatants had been killed, even as the remains of young children began to be unearthed. The incident became a symbol of the habitual lack of progress in cases not involving high-profile victims: judicial proceedings did not even begin until 1990 and official measures never progressed beyond exhumations.[31]

One final emblematic incident, the Jesuit assassination of 1989, influenced the peace process itself, and has played a key role in the accountability history of El Salvador ever since. On 16 November 1989, during an FMLN assault on the capital, a military unit entered the campus of the Central American University (UCA) and murdered six Jesuit priests, their housekeeper, and her teenage daughter. Salvador expert Terry Karl has described the killing and resultant international outcry as "one of the major catalysts that brought about the peace agreement."[32] The incident eventually produced what was to be the last semblance of judicial accountability before the 1993 amnesty law successfully institutionalized domestic impunity.

The twists and turns of the domestic investigation included the destruction of evidence by a specially convened "Military Honor Commission," and removal of the only known eyewitness to the United States, where she was sequestered by the FBI and later retracted her testimony.[33] Outcomes included the first-ever conviction and sentencing of a Salvadorean soldier of officer rank for human rights atrocities. The way this outcome was brought about, however, demonstrated that the perennial inefficiencies, flaws, biases, and exceptionalism of the judicial process had not been resolved. Although absolute impunity could not be sustained, the authorities did their utmost to limit repercussions.

Case judge Ricardo Zamora, handpicked to lead the investigation, was, tellingly, the same judge who had performed "satisfactorily"—that is, with due regard for the usual proprieties and his own safety—in the meandering and now-stalled Romero investigation. Although Zamora performed rather more credibly in the Jesuit case, his investigation was significantly and deliberately hampered by military and civilian authorities. Two state prosecutors resigned

---

31. See Binford (2001, 205).

32. Karl's comments came after the verdict in a U.S. civil case over the Romero killing, 3 September 2003.

33. For details see UN (1993), Doggett (1993), Whitfield (1998), and Carranza (2001), although most accounts struggle to resolve the contradictory and incomplete accounts offered by various protagonists.

publicly in January 1991 as a protest against "government interference." U.S. congressman Joe Moakley, dispatched by the U.S. legislature to carry out an independent inquiry, intervened regularly and often, and in characteristically colorful style. He repeatedly denounced in public first his own and then the Salvadorean government for deliberate obstruction.

Despite proceeding in an atmosphere of intimidation and violence,[34] the investigation did finally reach the public hearing stage in September 1991, although international observers were extremely unimpressed by trial procedure and evidentiary standards.[35] The jury, supposedly selected by a lottery process, was nonetheless chaired by a Supreme Court employee.[36] Even presiding Judge Zamora described the scene, in retrospect, as "a zoo."[37] The final verdict defied logical analysis. One defendant was found guilty only of the murder of the teenage girl, while others were found not guilty of crimes to which they had specifically confessed (Doggett 1993, 313–28). The sentences passed, thirty years for murder, seemed at least respectable. The final peace accords, signed in Chapultepec just seven days previously, however, made it extremely likely that amnesty would follow and the sentences would therefore never have to be served. The relatively harsh sentencing was mainly designed to placate U.S. officials and other external observers who wanted to see some semblance of justice in this particular case. El Salvador's pre–peace accord accountability record is well represented by this apparent engineering of judicial responses primarily for outside consumption, a pattern evident time and time again in cases like those described above.

The Transition Process (1989–1993)

In January 1992, the FMLN and government signed a final peace accord ending twelve years of civil war. Notably, the peace emerged from a "strategic

34. Zamora plus the former state prosecutors, subsequently retained privately by the Jesuit congregation to act in a prosecutorial role, received repeated death threats, and all three left the country immediately after the verdict. Their caution was vindicated a month later, when the head of the state prosecuting team—who had repeatedly warned his staff not to be "too zealous" over the case—was shot.

35. See particularly an observer's report by Robert Goldman for LCHR, published as appendix C in Doggett (1993, 313–28).

36. Prosecuting lawyer Sidney Blanco discovered this fact after the case, and by chance. On a last administrative errand to the Court before fleeing the country, he was attended by the same person who had presided over the jury.

37. Ricardo Zamora, interview 31 July 2003.

stalemate" (Call 2003, 831), and international actors—the United States and the UN—drove the process. Whereas Southern Cone transitions had seen electoral replacement of authoritarians under an explicit democratization agenda, in Central America the transition agenda was instead overdetermined by the need to end armed conflict. Peace accords, rather than elections, represented the definitive transitional moment. Democratization was both a secondary goal and a significant challenge, due to the extreme weakness of previously established democratic patterns.[38] Transition consisted essentially of the renunciation of military force by actors who nonetheless continued to dominate the subsequent political landscape.[39] The only former actor definitively obliged to exit the political scene, according to the terms of El Salvador's negotiated peace, was the armed forces. Among the most explicit commitments in the final peace accords were the restructuring of the security forces and the creation of a new civilian police force, although the details of implementation were delegated to a specially created multiparty commission.

THE ROLE OF THE UN

If the United States had driven El Salvador's war, the UN drove its peace, serving as mediator, verifier, and institution-builder through and beyond the negotiation process. This level and length of UN involvement was unprecedented for the organization, beginning before the peace accords and proceeding through to the certification of compliance, as well as capacity-building interventions in contested areas like security services reform.[40] But the UN's role in establishing a protected space for a truth commission (see below) was undoubtedly its single major contribution to transition-era accountability. It seemed clear that only international protection could make a truth-telling exercise possible, given the charged post-conflict atmosphere. This very same "outsider" status, however, was one of the principal arguments later used by

38. Elected governments were not entirely absent in the war period, during which a succession of civilian-military regimes maintained a façade of formal electoral democracy. Zamora (2001, 63) nonetheless concludes that "transition efforts had absolutely nothing to build on by way of democratic culture, given [Central America's] long experience of authoritarian military regimes" (author's translation).

39. Thus the Salvador accords transformed the FMLN into a political party; the first post-accord elections, in 1994, were won by ARENA, the same party that had held power during the last years of the war.

40. The United Nations Observer Mission in El Salvador (ONUSAL) was set up in May 1991. ONUSAL was replaced in April 1995 by the scaled-down United Nations Mission in El Salvador (MINUSAL), and a year later by an even smaller verification office.

furious opponents to rebut the truth commission's findings. More generally, UN protagonism has itself been blamed for supplanting domestic HROs in the latter stages of the conflict. Popkin suggests that the unprecedented direct involvement of the UN in all stages of the peace process may have weakened or sidelined the Salvadorean HRO community, which certainly remained at the margins of official transitional justice initiatives. Thus, where links with Salvadorean counterpart institutions or civil society remained underdeveloped, the UN may have substituted for rather than stimulating national processes of accounting and reconstruction (Popkin 2000, 160–70).

Transitional Truth, Justice, and Reconciliation Measures

The role of domestic HROs in making the full horror of the Salvadorean conflict known to the outside world was certainly instrumental in driving the UN and certain "friendly countries" to intervene in favor of peace negotiations. Nonetheless, military logic rather than human rights considerations finally drove both sides to the negotiating table.[41] Accordingly, the human rights community was neither central to the peace process itself nor able to influence its outcomes. The two—or perhaps three[42]—main parties to negotiations were pursuing their own political and institutional interests, which at least in the case of the direct combatants included protection from future legal reprisals.[43]

Thus Sieder rightly observes that transitional justice in El Salvador was a "party-dominated process," in which human rights issues "all but disappeared from the political agenda" (2001, 183, 188). Nonetheless, the series of peace agreements in 1991 and 1992[44] did mandate an "Ad-Hoc Commission" to purge military officers involved in HRVs, plus a UN-supervised truth commission that could make binding recommendations for institutional reform.

---

41. In particular, the FMLN offensive on the capital in late 1989 gave the lie to official claims that the war was all but over. The massacre on the UCA campus under cover of the offensive also helped swing U.S. and other international opinion against continued support of a "military solution."

42. The military had its own representatives in the peace negotiations, and at times seemed at loggerheads with the government over both the latter's readiness to concede a cease-fire and the inclusion of military downsizing in the negotiating agenda.

43. The FMLN, claimed one HRO source, "didn't consult anyone, they just sold human rights on the bargaining table alongside everything else" (interview, first quarter of 2003).

44. Chronologically, the San José Agreement of 27 April 1991, the New York accords of 25 September 1991, and the final Chapultepec accords of 16 January 1992.

Essentially preventative justice measures, including military restructuring, were also achieved in the aftermath of the transition, although reparations for HRVs were virtually nonexistent.

Transitional Justice

The relatively little-known Ad Hoc Commission, instituted in mid-1992, arguably represented El Salvador's most novel contribution to transitional justice.[45] A mechanism to purge the security forces, it was agreed to as a last-minute compromise on the basis of which the FMLN abandoned its insistence on incorporation into the army after the war (Samayoa 2002, 568–72; Kritz 1995, 3:386). The panel, made up of three Salvadorean civilians, was charged with reviewing the human rights records of military officers and making recommendations for dismissal. After four months of intense activity the Ad Hoc commissioners handed a list of 103 names to the president and the UN in September 1992.[46]

The confidential list featured most of the military high command, including Defense Minister René Emilio Ponce. The government was extremely reluctant to implement such a sweeping purge, and between January and March 1993 the issue became a thermometer for civilian-military relations and the stability of the peace process itself. President Cristiani procrastinated until the publication of the official truth commission report in March redoubled the pressure on those who, like Ponce, were named in both reports. U.S. intervention, including a freeze on military aid, finally forced reluctant capitulation in June 1993. Nevertheless the outgoing high command, like all other supposedly "purged" officers, were awarded honorable discharges and full pensions.

TRANSITIONAL TRUTH

El Salvador's UN-sponsored truth commission operated between July and December 1992 and published its report, titled "From Madness to Hope: The

45. Zamora and Holiday (2007) describe it as "the first (and only) example of a Latin American military subjecting itself to a civilian review panel."

46. The zeal of the commissioners—handpicked by the government—came as a surprise to many. According to Thomas Buergenthal (1995, 304), one of the truth commissioners, "The government and the military only agreed to the establishment of the Ad Hoc Commission because they were convinced that it would not dare to discharge its responsibilities honestly." Quoted in Kritz (1995, 304).

12-Year War in El Salvador," in March 1993. The commission's final mandate was to examine "serious acts of violence" committed by state or rebel forces between 1980 and 1991.[47] It had uniquely broad powers to name perpetrators and make binding recommendations. The UN's involvement countered some of the disadvantages of the commission's short time frame—only six months—and the fact that all commissioners and staff were non-nationals, a measure designed to reduce intimidation and enhance claims to objectivity. The commission received twenty-two thousand complaints, and so was forced to select "representative" cases for investigation and publication (UN 1993, 19). Witness testimony was published anonymously. Evidence was graded at three levels of reliability, and perpetrators were named only at the two higher levels. The commission's hard-hitting final report assigned responsibility for over 80 percent of proven atrocities to the armed forces, and 5 percent to the FMLN. Thirty-three "paradigmatic" cases were analyzed in detail, with over forty military officers and several FMLN leaders named as responsible for the incidents described. The report recommended the removal of the military officers, plus a ten-year ban from public office for them and their FMLN counterparts.[48]

The naming of perpetrators, undoubtedly controversial for a non-judicial instance like the commission, was addressed head on by the report. It revealed that political authorities had initially supported naming, seen as a way of exculpating institutions by emphasizing individual criminality; the government had only changed its tune once the full extent of naming and shaming by the commission became apparent.[49]

The report was exceptionally scathing about the judicial system as a whole, diagnosing a "glaring inability . . . either to investigate crimes or to enforce the law" (UN 1993, 178). Supreme Court president Gutiérrez Castro was singled out for criticism and the Supreme Court was called on to resign en masse. Unfortunately, such vehemence also undermined accountability prospects by

---

47. UN (1993, 18). On the matter of classifying non-state combatant actions as "HRVs" the commissioners took the view that international humanitarian law governing internal conflict was applicable to the FMLN, and that they had incurred additional obligations for territories they had laid claim to and effectively controlled during the war (21–22).

48. The commission, however, did not have the power to make this particular recommendation binding (UN 1993, 176).

49. UN (1993, 13–14). The report gives the impression that such pressures were resisted. The name of General Mauricio Vargas was allegedly removed, however, to permit his appointment as government delegate to the UN for peace accord implementation (judicial and additional source, interviewed in San Salvador, second quarter of 2003).

stating that "El Salvador has no system for the administration of justice which meets the minimum requirements of objectivity and impartiality" (178).

REACTIONS TO THE TRUTH COMMISSION REPORT

The government, which had prior access to the report in January 1993, made strenuous but ultimately fruitless attempts to have publication delayed or names removed. The armed forces were more outspoken. Despite the fact that he had already "resigned,"[50] General Ponce, defense minister, appeared on television on 23 March 1993, flanked by the rest of the high command. He read a statement rejecting the report as "unfair, incomplete, illegal, unethical, biased and insolent," and accused the commission of having exceeded its mandate, "defrauded the hope and faith of Salvadoreans," and "marginalized the rule of law" (Doggett 1993, 264). Ponce and his vice-minister, Juan Orlando Zepeda, had already attempted to sue a domestic HRO for publishing the same information it had submitted to the truth commission. As to the Supreme Court, Gutiérrez Castro famously riposted that "only God" could remove him (266). He and his cohort accordingly ignored the exhortation to resign, and were not replaced until the first scheduled round of post-accord judicial appointments in 1994.

Accordingly, although the report's tone was strong, its actual impact on institutions and civil society was relatively limited. Its revelations did not lead to trials, disappointing those who had pinned perhaps unrealistic hopes on the commission's ability to deliver justice.[51] Many recommendations were not fulfilled, and institutional reforms carried out post-transition were more likely to be those stipulated in the peace accords than those recommended by the truth commission (Sieder 2001, 183; Popkin 2000, 161). For their part, HROs report a loss of dynamism and confidence related to the commission's mode of operation.[52] Well-resourced and externally staffed, it effectively bypassed national organizations. Additionally, HROs—which had high expectations that the commission would instigate prosecutions, and encouraged rural communities to cooperate with it on that basis—subsequently

50. This occurred on 12 March 1993, amid the Ad Hoc Commission controversy.

51. Popkin (2000) and Mirna Perla, interview 24 July 2003.

52. Interviews with Roxana Marroquín and Claudia Interiano, Centro para la Promoción de los Derechos Humanos "Madeleine Lagedec" (henceforth "Centro Madeleine Lagedec"), 20 June 2003.

found their hopes dashed and their credibility vitiated by the general amnesty that immediately followed the report's publication (see below).[53]

THE BUILDUP TO AMNESTY

In the run-up to publication of the truth commission report, key actors, including the Catholic Church, seemed to anticipate or even promote amnesty, with rumors rife of "horse-trading" between the government and the FMLN. In early 1993, ARENA politician and future president Calderón Sol told *El Diario de Hoy* that "we need a general amnesty broad enough to cover all acts and reach to all Salvadoreans." The paper commented that "speculation that the FMLN will also be accused . . . [means that] an amnesty for all concerned would suit them too."[54] Public debate was clearly tending toward a politically pacted, preemptive amnesty that would soften the blow of the truth commission's naming policy.[55]

No HROs are on record as opposing the widespread presumption that some form of amnesty would be used to underpin the final peace settlement. The CDHES, for its part, opposed not the principle but only the timing of amnesty, suggesting it be postponed until after 1994 elections (*CDHES Resumen Noticioso*, 23 February–8 March 1993). It does seem, however, that many of those who accepted the principle of further amnesty did not expect it to be as indiscriminate as was eventually the case. HROs had possibly been misled by the less drastic terms of the previous amnesty, the Ley de Reconciliación Nacional of January 1992. That statute had served mainly to allow political "normalization" of the FMLN, and had refused to grant amnesty for incidents that the pending truth commission report might choose to highlight. Thus, even during the same period when it seemed to accept that there was to be further amnesty, the CDHES was urging survivors to corroborate their truth commission testimony "in preparation for its submission to judicial authorities." Indeed, when the eventual 1993 statute attempted to abolish

---

53. Mirna Perla, interview 24 July 2003.

54. *El Diario de Hoy*, 12 January 1993. Reproduced in *CDHES Resumen Noticioso*, 8–10 January 1993; author's translation.

55. It suited the FMLN to appear more reluctant. Salvador Samayoa, of its Political Commission, claimed: "It is possible that . . . recommendations of amnesty will emerge. . . . If that happens, we would find ourselves obliged to go along with whatever the broader society considers to be best for the future of the country" (quoted in *CDHES Resumen Noticioso*, 23 February–8 March 1993; author's translation).

all kinds of liability for every crime, the CDHES launched an unsuccessful challenge to the law's constitutionality (see below).

The 1993 Amnesty Law

The final chapter in El Salvador's foreshortened transitional justice narrative was a major amnesty law virtually coterminous with publication of the truth commission report. On 20 March 1993, just five days after the damning report had been released, the Legislative Assembly approved the Ley de Amnistía General para la Consolidación de la Paz, Legislative Decree no. 486. Article 4e of the statute extinguished civil as well as criminal liability, making it the broadest such law in the region. The law also, uniquely, amnestied some types of judicial malpractice. The statute was put to immediate effect. On 31 March, the capital's First Criminal Appeals Court (Cámara Primera de lo Penal, Primera Sección Centro) amnestied and ordered the release of the only perpetrators actually convicted for the Jesuit killings.[56]

Some FMLN sources make much in retrospect of the fact that they were not officially part of the legislature that voted in the sweeping 1993 text.[57] They also draw attention to earlier FMLN demands for prosecutions in emblematic cases, including Romero and the Jesuits. There seems, however, to have been a certain element of grandstanding about these demands, ritually countered by the government with lists of FMLN crimes. In the final analysis, both sides had agreed to let the UN decide what was to be investigated and how (Popkin 2000, 89–95). Moreover, although the possibility of accountability had not been textually ruled out by the peace accords, it had been clear since the beginning of negotiations that amnesty was highly likely to figure in any eventual settlement. The left, which had been the main beneficiary of previous amnesties,[58] was far from ill-disposed toward the principle. Indeed, the

56. The truth commission report had effectively given its blessing to this outcome, calling it "unfair" that the two men should be in prison "when the people responsible for planning the murders and the person who gave the order . . . remain at liberty" (UN 1993, 54). An obvious alternative interpretation, that the planners should also be prosecuted, was never seriously entertained.

57. The FMLN's political views were, however, represented indirectly by members of Convergencia Democrática, former leaders of an FMLN-allied political grouping who had returned to the country in the early 1990s to participate in electoral politics. Convergencia Democrática representatives voted against the law.

58. An October 1987 amnesty aborted the trial of FMLN militants for killing four U.S. marines, and the January 1992 Ley de Reconciliación Nacional, discussed above, allowed FMLN leaders to return to the country. Although Article 6 of the law exempted cases to be dealt with by the truth

recollection of one FMLN negotiator is that the guerrilla forces, rather than the military, first raised the issue during final peace negotiations.[59] The FMLN appeared to regard amnesty as a necessary precaution to counter the threat of prosecution for breaches of humanitarian law, as well as a necessary step for its conversion into a legalized political party.[60] Thus, although the law was roundly denounced by some sectors, there was no realistic prospect of challenging it. The UN's hands were also tied. Their own truth commission report had chosen to avoid direct comment even though amnesty was being openly mooted, close to the report's completion date, in direct response to its anticipated findings.[61] Accordingly, the UN secretary general went only so far as to criticize "undue haste" in the promulgation of the law.[62]

THE FIRST DOMESTIC CHALLENGE TO AMNESTY

An early attempt by the CDHES to challenge the amnesty law was rejected by the Supreme Court on 20 May 1993. The court avoided addressing the substance of the recourse, which had alleged fundamental flaws in the statute's incorporation, publication, and compatibility with fundamental constitutional rights. The verdict, delivered with unaccustomed swiftness, claimed that amnesty should be regarded as "a purely political question" outside the court's purview. It nonetheless ventured the opinion that amnesty should be treated as "an annulment, with retroactive effects, of a penal norm,"[63] thus implying that amnesty abolished not only the penalty for a crime but also the very crime itself.[64] The 1993 law accordingly proved remarkably success-

---

commission, it authorized the Legislative Assembly to subsequently take "such steps as it esteemed convenient" to resolve those cases. See PDDH (2002, 99–101).

59. Ana Guadalupe Martínez, interview 24 August 2003.

60. Interviews with retired general Mauricio Vargas and with former FMLN commander Ana Guadalupe Martínez, 15 July 2003 and 24 August 2003, respectively. Both pointed out that given the prevailing political balance at transition, the left could expect to be disproportionately penalized by any nationally driven prosecution efforts.

61. See, for example, *El Diario de Hoy*, 12 January 1993; and *CDHES Boletín*, March 1993.

62. May 1993 "Report of the Secretary-General on the UN Observer Mission in El Salvador," UN Document S/25812, 2, cited in Doggett (1993, 274).

63. Ruling of the Constitutional Chamber of the Supreme Court of Justice in Unconstitutionality Proceeding no. 10-93, dated 23 May 1993. Excerpts as translated by Méndez in IEJES (1993). A fuller translation of the decision appears in Kritz (1995, 3:549–55).

64. This outlandish position far exceeds that taken by, for instance, the Chilean judiciary even in its most intransigent period. Chilean judges had instead generally abstained from specifying what crime had been committed, on the grounds that there would be no possibility of applying criminal sanctions for it.

ful, then and since, in quashing even private accountability action. Few if any previous legal cases existed, and none survived. Many HROs were additionally disheartened, accepting at face value the claim of the law to extinguish all possibility of accountability claims.[65]

Conclusions

In sum, the period from 1989 to 1993 saw immense change in El Salvador, with a unique, externally supported peace process that was remarkably successful in creating a lasting ceasefire. The human rights "cause" unquestionably benefited, as evidenced by a radical reduction in atrocities. Accountability, however, began to look like something of a lost cause. The UN operated in effect as a pro-peace, rather than a pro-accountability, actor, sponsoring a strong, albeit incomplete, truth initiative but remaining silent over subsequent amnesty. Domestic HROs, although utilized to convince communities to testify, were not entrusted with real input into the truth commission and were thus kept at a distance from the most significant transitional justice measure of the entire peace process.

Both the civilian right and the newly civilianized FMLN had reasons for actively preferring amnesty to accountability. Accountability thus remained a minority interest in political circles, and seemed an increasingly unrealistic aspiration. The pre-transition norm of de facto impunity was merely replaced by a legally guaranteed and institutionalized version in the form of extremely broad amnesty. Amnesty was officially presented as both a necessary price for peace and a precondition for the drawing of a thick line, demarcating a "before" and "after" in Salvadorean public and institutional life. Lacking independent capacity for protagonism, civil society did not generate strong pressure over past HRVs. Indeed, Popkin (2000, 161) observes that "one is struck by the lack of visible societal demand for further truth and justice."

65. See chapter 7.

7

CHANGING TO STAY THE SAME:
POST-TRANSITIONAL JUSTICE IN EL SALVADOR

This chapter examines the principal features of El Salvador's post-transitional accountability trajectory. The first section deals in turn with two chronological periods: 1994–97, and 1998 onward. Each represents a recognizable phase in the accountability trajectory of El Salvador after the peace accords. During the first phase accountability actors were scarce and there were few challenges to the edifice of impunity. In and after 1998, limited domestic and external accountability initiatives emerged, although, to date, political and judicial responses have been absent or decidedly negative. The second section of the chapter deals in turn with accountability actors and legal strategies in post-transitional accountability, offering where relevant more detailed analysis of the events outlined in the first section.

Judicial system protagonism in El Salvador has not been sufficient to warrant a dedicated thematic section: changed judicial receptivity over accountability, which proved so significant in Chile, has been virtually undetectable in El Salvador. Moreover, Salvadorean courts were effectively sidelined as accountability players when 1990s judicial reforms reassigned investigative powers and discretionality over criminal prosecution to other parts of the justice system. Substantive court action over accountability in the recent period has been restricted to a Supreme Court decision upholding the principle of amnesty. Only in the external field are there some signs of renewed efforts to challenge persistent impunity in El Salvador, in the form of third-country cases plus a handful of domestically impulsed attempts to activate regional mechanisms.

Accountability Milestones

IMPUNITY PRESERVED: 1994–1997

This period has been described as a phase of re-design and re-creation of El Salvador's state apparatus, in an effort to make transition real through a drive for democratization.[1] The FMLN made its debut as a legitimate political party in the postwar polls. But ARENA, the right-wing party voted into power before the peace accords, retained its hold on the presidency and legislature.[2] Some of the major institutional changes agreed to in the peace accords began to take shape, under the watchful eye of the UN. Reduction of military strength went forward, with the dissolution of entire divisions, including the notorious Atlacatl Battalion implicated in the El Mozote and Jesuit massacres. A new national civilian police force, the Policía Nacional Civil (PNC), was introduced.[3]

The UN's role shifted away from peacekeeping and mediation functions and toward technical assistance and capacity building.[4] The UN mission, ONUSAL, took a particularly close interest in the evolution of the new human rights ombudsperson's office, the Procuraduría para la Defensa de los Derechos Humanos (PDDH), which had been created by constitutional reforms in April 1991. Given a broad remit, the PDDH was nonetheless restricted to an essentially denunciatory and advisory role. It could investigate and report on complaints against state functionaries, but could not enforce its recommendations. With the appointment of Victoria de Avilés as its second *procuradora*, in 1995, the PDDH achieved public prominence and took on a more interventionist style. Greater profile, however, brought greater politicization. De Avilés's strong identification with the left undoubtedly heightened ARENA's antipathy to the institution she headed, culminating in a disastrous

1. Cañas and Dada (1999, 70). The authors are, however, less sanguine about the genuine acceptance of these changes by actors used to "the old system of unwritten, undemocratic rules" (71).

2. ARENA retained presidential power in every national election between 1994 and 2009, although its legislative majority at times depended on alliances with other right-wing parties. In 2003 the FMLN became the single largest party in the Legislative Assembly, but did not have an independent legislative majority. See below. In 2009, FMLN candidate Mauricio Funess won the presidency.

3. There were, however, criticisms that military intelligence functionaries earmarked for dismissal had been secretly transferred to the new PNC. See LCHR (1995, 33–34).

4. Although, according to Popkin (2000, 253), this did not happen quickly or comprehensively enough. See also LCHR (1995, 111–12).

replacement appointment that amounted to sabotage.[5] Even during the de Avilés period, however, the PDDH took relatively little action over the historical HRV question. Its agenda was driven by complaints from the public, often over labor rights issues or allegations of official corruption.

It was widely agreed, and had been spelled out in both the peace accords and the truth commission report, that El Salvador's justice system was in dire need of overhaul. Little was achieved, however, until the Supreme Court led by Mauricio Gutiérrez Castro, which had presided over much of the conflict period, was replaced. But replacement was not a foregone conclusion: Gutiérrez Castro stood for reelection in March 1994, exerting pressure on professional bar associations and even the newly formed National Judicial Council (Consejo Nacional de la Magistratura) to return him for another term. In the event, no members of the previous Court were returned and a new supreme tribunal was inaugurated in July 1994.

In sum, during the period from 1994 to 1997 the issue of accountability was submerged, with the political agenda instead dominated by weighty matters of institutional reform. Implementation and verification initiatives were focused on essentially forward-looking structural and capacity-building issues. The downsizing of the military and construction of a new, albeit doubtless imperfect, civilian police force removed the major perpetrating institutions from the public spotlight in fairly short order. It began to seem as if institutional refoundation in El Salvador was to be predicated on the drawing of a thick line establishing radical discontinuity. This *borrón y cuenta nueva* (clean slate) approach to the past was not only supported wholeheartedly by ARENA (a party strongly linked with past violence), but also underwritten by the FMLN.

1998 AND AFTER: LIMITED INITIATIVES
WITH LITTLE DOMESTIC RESPONSE

Some interviewees identified a slightly more favorable political climate for truth (as distinct from accountability) actions at local level after 1997, with newly elected FMLN mayors readier than their ARENA predecessors to at least permit public commemorations of dates related to the war.[6] HROs began to harbor hopes that eventual political replacement, via an outright

5. Remarks by Fredrik Uggla to the conference "El Salvador 11 Years After the Peace Accords," St. Antony's College, Oxford, 12 May 2003.

6. Armando Pérez Salazar, interview 16 July 2003; Camelia Cartagena, interview 15 August 2003.

triumph for the FMLN at the national level, might allow the reopening of the stalled accountability debate. In March 2003, the FMLN recorded its best ever result in legislative elections, becoming the largest single party in the national assembly. Eugenio Chicas, FMLN representative in the Central American Parliament, insisted that the FMLN had an active accountability agenda that would become apparent after the 2004 presidential elections.[7] In the event, however, ARENA retained the presidency and the FMLN showed no sign of changing its arms-length attitude toward accountability. March 2009 saw El Salvador's first political alternation since transition, with FMLN moderate Mauricio Funes taking the presidency from ARENA. The direct effect on accountability prospects is nevertheless likely to be limited, for reasons described below.

El Salvador's continued postwar economic difficulties, compounded by severe earthquake damage in 2001, have also generated a sociopolitical agenda in which accountability for past HRVs has struggled to find a place. Levels of "common" crime and gang violence rose sharply and public security became a predominant political and social concern,[8] with a concomitant rise in sympathy for tough law-and-order approaches. Attitudes toward human rights and human rights defenders were conditioned by these new concerns, with interventions framed in the language of rights criticized as apologia for the perpetrators of present-day violence. Organizations such as the PDDH became associated with an anti-victim stance. Association with the actively unpopular defense of prisoners' rights discredited their pro-accountability position.[9]

Some limited domestic accountability pressure was visible in the late 1990s, but it was not consistent and met with very little institutional response. Efforts also appear to have been isolated one from another, with a distinct absence of coordinated, strategic litigation. Although HRO Tutela Legal brought a fresh challenge in 1998 to the constitutionality of the 1993 amnesty law, they did so without establishing contact with or even identifying the bringers of a similar

---

7. Eugenio Chicas, interview 17 July 2003.

8. According to Call (2003), both crime and the fear of it rose sharply between 1992 and 1999. See also Hume (2008).

9. The PDDH was criticized in mainstream press, including *El Diario de Hoy*, 19 August 2003, for declaring that proposed anti-gang laws violated international human rights standards. The attacks continued in subsequent editions, with full-page paid adverts castigating "groups who monopolize the pseudo-promotion of human rights" and "defend left-wing assassins and delinquents." *El Diario de Hoy*, 26 August 2003, and 20 August 2003; author's translation.

claim in 1997.[10] Efforts by four groups of relatives in 2003 to trigger investigations over past disappearances were stimulated not by a strategic accountability plan but by the chance discovery of unidentified remains during 1999 building work on the site of former National Police headquarters.[11] In 2006, Tutela Legal's efforts to have the Romero case reopened were undermined by the Church hierarchy. The lawyer behind the efforts—David Morales, a former PDDH deputy whose keen anti-impunity activity is discussed below—was eventually forced out of the organization altogether by conservative archbishop Saenz Lacalle.

Newer initiatives display a trend toward activity directed outside the country. The period from 2006 to 2008 saw a cluster of missing children cases submitted to the Inter-American Commission and Court, and the opening of a third-country case in Spain. Nationally, the prevailing pattern of isolated and usually unsuccessful interventions with a specific, contingent trigger, however, suggests that new accountability claims in and over El Salvador neither respond to nor have yet produced any substantial change in domestic institutional receptivity. There has been no positive judicial precedent analogous to that provided in Chile in 1998, nor any "floodgates" moment comparable with Pinochet's UK arrest. HROs did perceive limited signals of improved judicial conditions after 2000: the entry of figures like Mirna Perla and Victoria de Avilés to the Supreme Court, and of former Jesuit case lawyer Sidney Blanco to a lower court, was regarded as a positive sign.[12] Judicial reform and replacement has not, however, so far been allowed to significantly change accountability outcomes. The generation of significant numbers of individual accountability cases has been blocked by a combination of low demand and efficient gatekeeping. After mid-1990s judicial reforms the Fiscalía (attorney general's office) now holds a monopoly on prosecution.[13] Direct access to the courts can now only be obtained via special recourse or direct challenges to the principle of amnesty. Accordingly, the Supreme Court was forced to issue a ruling in 2000 in response to two such challenges, filed in 1997 and 1998, respectively.

10. The two challenges were amalgamated by the courts, who gave a single ruling in 2000. See below.

11. Mauricio Gaborit, S.J., interview 13 August 2003. The remains were later declared to be animal rather than human.

12. Interview data.

13. This body has also consistently blocked post-transitional justice claims; see below.

THE CRIMINAL JUSTICE SYSTEM AND THE 1993 AMNESTY LAW

The Supreme Court's September 2000 ruling upheld the basic constitutionality of the amnesty statute,[14] although it did theoretically allow increased room for variation in what individual judges could do about amnesty. The verdict acknowledged for the first time the existence of a technical loophole with regard to crimes that, first, could be argued to violate fundamental constitutional rights; and, second, had been committed by public employees within a certain time period late in the conflict. The loophole arises from Article 244 of the Salvadorean Constitution, which states that "any violation, infraction or alteration of constitutional dispositions will be especially penalized by law; and civil or criminal responsibilities incurred by public functionaries, whether military or civilian, to that end will not be eligible for amnesty, commutation or pardon within the duration of the presidential period in which they were committed."[15] The first part of the article could be used to argue that, where a judge accepted that such grave infractions had been committed, the duty to "especially penalize" would preclude the application of amnesty. The second part potentially contradicted Article 1 of the 1993 amnesty law, which had amnestied crimes committed right up to 1 January 1992. This meant that incumbent President Cristiani—elected in 1989—was attempting to introduce amnesty for crimes committed within his own presidential period, in contravention of the constitution's specific prohibition. The Supreme Court's 2000 ruling acknowledged this contradiction, but stopped short of resolving it. Instead it passed the buck to lower courts, declaring that individual judges would have to decide whether amnesty should be applied to any future cases brought before them involving "infractions of constitutional rights" (not defined) or[16] crimes committed by "public functionaries" between 1989 and 1 January 1992.

The ruling is less generous than it might appear, since the time period eliminates many of the most notorious massive HRVs of the war period, and since courts have subsequently ruled that even the Jesuit massacre of 1989 did not constitute a "violation of constitutional dispositions." But the ruling's possible

14. Ruling of the Sala Constitucional of the Supreme Court of Justice, dated 26 September 2000; on file with author.

15. Author's translation.

16. Since the exception remains hypothetical, it is as yet unclear whether judges would require both exclusionary conditions to be present or—as logic would dictate—only one of them.

application was subsequently limited as much by a lack of test cases as by any demonstrable unwillingness of lower court judges to reverse the tradition of impunity. The dearth of cases is related partly to a lack of demand from private claimants (see below), but more particularly to structural considerations, including the virtual roadblock the Fiscalía presents to potential accountability claims. In this system, cases can only come before a first-instance judge at the say-so of the Fiscalía. The chances of cases reaching the courts are accordingly slim. ARENA's continued domination of the Legislative Assembly[17] allowed it to control the appointment of the *fiscal* (attorney general), at the head of this newly powerful criminal justice institution. Postwar appointees have to date proved implacably hostile to accountability.

Tantalizingly, in the only test case that did initially reach the lower courts, a judge intimated that amnesty should not apply to the multiple Jesuit murders of 1989.[18] Nonetheless, the effects of judicial reforms on accountability remained unpromising for both the bringing and the likely outcome of cases. The location of prosecutorial discretion with the Fiscalía was one obstacle, although the attitude of the Fiscalía to accountability is at least theoretically malleable. The direct impact of legal code changes on existing accountability convictions, however, was equally discouraging. Drafts for a new Código Penal (Penal Code) and a new Código Procesal Penal (Penal Procedural Code) were first submitted to the legislature in 1994 (see FESPAD 2003). Approved in 1996 and 1997, they finally took effect in early 1998. An article designed to reduce pretrial delays was almost immediately invoked to free three of the five former guardsmen convicted of the 1980 murder of U.S. churchwomen. None had served much more than half of his thirty-year sentence.[19]

The PDDH is perhaps the only official body that might be expected to look favorably on accountability claims, given its remit in the protection of individual rights. Indeed, after the departure of de Avilés from the PDDH in 1998, her temporary replacement (and former deputy) made the PDDH's first strong public declaration regarding past HRVs. He called on the authorities to trace children disappeared during the war, and insisted that perpetrators would be

---

17. The party continued to hold sway, either alone or in informal alliance with smaller center and rightist parties. Even after March 2003 ARENA still effectively dominated the legislative agenda, since the FMLN's largest-single-party status did not give it an absolute majority.

18. This case shows that it is possible, with sufficient resources, for accountability actors to persevere beyond initial stonewalling by the Fiscalía. The immediate outcome was negative, however, since the same judge invoked prescription to find that the case should not proceed.

19. Article 48 of the new Penal Code assigns credits, reducing the length of final sentence to be served, for each day of pretrial detention over and above a specified limit.

ineligible for amnesty. Again, however, government reaction was swift and negative. A new *procurador* was swiftly appointed: Eduardo Peñate Polanco, a former judge who had himself previously been censured by the PDDH for professional misconduct. Peñate was overtaken by allegations of corruption in 2000, but his replacement also lasted only one year of the stipulated three. The whole episode greatly reduced the institution's domestic and international prestige and capacity. In 2001, the PDDH came under the leadership of Beatrice de Carrillo, and one of her first actions was to appoint the extremely capable David Morales as her deputy. Morales, a former PDDH employee who resigned during the Polanco era, immediately drafted official reports deploring continued government inaction over the Romero and Jesuit assassinations.[20] Morales increased the number of young human rights lawyers[21] and former public prosecutors on the PDDH staff, and his own enthusiasm for reversing previous neglect of the accountability agenda plainly exceeded even that of some HROs.[22] De Carrillo's period at the helm, however, also coincided with the virulent electoral-era diatribes against the institution described above. This, combined with its continuing lack of enforcement powers, meant that ever more strongly worded denunciations of past impunity tended to be applauded by the small human rights community inside and outside El Salvador while being widely ignored in official circles. Former Supreme Court employee Oscar Luna replaced de Carrillo in 2007, a move that has not to date been accompanied by any particular innovation over the issue of past impunity.

ACCOUNTABILITY AND REGIONAL HUMAN RIGHTS INSTANCES

The Inter-American Commission on Human Rights (IACHR) issued two major reports at the end of the 1990s criticizing the failure of the Salvadorean state to provide justice in emblematic HRV cases. On 22 December 1999, a long-awaited Commission report on the Jesuit murders found the

20. Respectively, "Informe sobre la Impunidad en el asesinato de Monseñor Oscar Romero en ocasión del XXII aniversario de su ejecución arbitraria," PDDH, 20 March 2002; and "Informe de la Señora Procuradora para la Defensa de los Derechos Humanos, sobre la impunidad respecto de las ejecuciones arbitrarias de Ignacio Ellacuría S.J. [. . .] y Celina Mariceth Ramos," PDDH, 30 October 2002. Both published in PDDH (2002).

21. Included among these lawyers, for a time, was Gustavo Piñeda, formerly of Socorro Jurídico and the CDHES and a veteran of MINUGUA, the UN's late-1990s mission to Guatemala.

22. Gustavo Piñeda, interview 6 June 2003; David Morales, interview 18 August 2003. The PDDH's annual report expressed the usual "preoccupation" over continuing impunity, recounting recent government attempts to reaffirm the amnesty law before the Inter-American Commission.

Salvadorean state to be in active violation of the right to life and obligations to investigate and punish certain human rights crimes. It recommended further investigation and the prosecution of the material and intellectual authors.[23] A similar report over the Romero assassination was released in March 2000.[24] Initial reactions from state authorities were revealingly dismissive. Then-president Francisco Flores Pérez described the Commission's reports as "not binding, only advisory." His attorney general displayed a similar disdain.[25] The Fiscalía firmly rejected subsequent legal submissions in the Jesuit case that cite the Commission's reports. Predictably only the PDDH appeared to pay positive attention, citing the reports in later denunciations of official negligence (PDDH 2002).

Although it was accordingly difficult to discern any immediate impact of the Commission's reports on accountability outcomes, Jesuit case lawyer José Roberto Burgos considered the reports' impact on judges, particularly, to be far from negligible. Judges were, he pointed out, given a relatively good grounding in international law during and after the 1994 reforms. He believed the Commission's findings might well contribute to more progressive judicial attitudes to accountability if the hurdle of the Fiscalía were ever to be surmounted.[26] Accountability actors also viewed with optimism the 2004 appointment of Salvadorean human rights lawyer Florentín Meléndez to the Commission.[27] Coverage of the appointment in the extremely right-wing mainstream press was reasonably sympathetic, with a certain air of national pride temporarily replacing the usual hostility to the Commission's track record of criticizing Salvadorean authorities.

The early and mid-2000s also saw the first ever elevation of a Salvadorean case from the Commission to the Inter-American Court since the Court's contentious jurisdiction was accepted by El Salvador in 1995. The Serrano case, a claim for denial of access to justice by the mother of two young girls who disappeared in 1982, went before the Court in June 2003. In March 2005

23. IACHR report no. 136/99 in case 10.488, 22 December 1999, in response to a complaint submitted by Americas Watch in November 1989. Available at http://www.cidh.org/annualrep/99span/De%20Fondo/El%20Salvador10.488.htm, last accessed 4 March 2009.

24. IACHR report no. 37/00 in case 11.481, 13 April 2000. The report is in response to a complaint submitted by Tutela Legal and Romero's brother in September 1993. Available at http://www.cidh.org/annualrep/99span/De%20Fondo/ElSalvador11481.htm, last accessed 4 March 2009.

25. See Amnesty International 2001 Annual Report, section on El Salvador. AI reference POL 10/001/2001, available from http://www.amnesty.org/.

26. José Roberto Burgos, interview 12 June 2003.

27. Meléndez finished his first term as president of the Commission, and was reelected in 2008 for another three-year term as a Commission member.

the Court found in favor of the petitioner, ordering the Salvadorean state to offer specific and symbolic reparations, including the payment of costs, designation of a national day of commemoration for children disappeared during the war, and medical and psychological assistance for the family. The verdict, however, for the most part accepted the state's contention that the Court had no competence over alleged crimes occurring before 1995.[28]

In late 2007 the Salvadorean government requested a special audience with the Inter-American Commission, a move that betrayed at least some preoccupation over recent regional trends toward challenging impunity. In the year of the fifteenth anniversary of the peace accords, the government insisted on the supposed links between continued amnesty and continuing peace, describing the Salvadorean transition as "still fragile." Witnesses, including former FMLN peace negotiator Salvador Samayoa, were called on to support the government's insistence that the Salvadorean amnesty had been a consensual arrangement between the main political factions of the day.

ATTEMPTS TO REACTIVATE THE JESUIT CASE

On 27 March 2000 the Instituto de Derechos Humanos de la Universidad Centroamericana (IDHUCA)[29] submitted a new criminal complaint to the Fiscalía over the 1989 Jesuit assassinations. The timing of the attempt had to do with fears about imminent prescription.[30] The complaint was brought in the name of José María Tojeira, S.J., rector of the UCA, on behalf of the Jesuit congregation and the victims' families. It did not attempt to revisit the issue of those convicted and amnestied in 1993. Rather, it took up the neglected issue of superior orders, accusing named military commanders and even Cristiani, the president of the day, of "intellectual authorship" of the murders. The submission echoed the claims against the constitutionality of the 1993 amnesty law that were then before the courts, arguing that both the Salvadorean Constitution and the American Convention on Human Rights left the domestic amnesty law without effect. It also invoked the failure of the

28. The Salvadorean government made this stipulation when it first accepted the Court's contentious jurisdiction. The Serrano ruling therefore based its findings on the "portion" of continuing violations, such as the denial of justice, that it considered had carried forward into the post-1995 period. The verdict, and other case documentation, is available at http://www.corteidh.or.cr/pais. cfm?id_Pais=17, last accessed 4 March 2009.

29. IDHUCA, not strictly an HRO but rather an academic offshoot, was founded in 1982 as the Human Rights Institute of the Jesuit-run Central American University.

30. Case lawyer Pedro Cruz, interview 27 June 2003.

state to comply with the recommendations of the 1999 Inter-American Commission report on the case.[31]

The Fiscalía's immediate response was to abstain from answering the petition pending the Supreme Court's ruling on the constitutionality of amnesty. The text of the Fiscalía's initial communiqué nonetheless betrayed clear evidence of intent, describing amnesty as a "juridico-political act; in essence a superior law."[32] In December 2000 the Fiscalía made an outright effort to close the case. First, it erroneously referred the request for new investigations to the (now-defunct) court where the original case had been heard. Next, although sending the documentation to the "correct" court, it recommended immediate permanent closure (*sobreseimiento definitivo*) rather than investigation, claiming that the relevant prescription period[33] had lapsed. The judge accepted the contention that the crimes had prescribed, although she intimated that had the case proceeded she might not have applied amnesty.[34]

In late January 2001 a San Salvador appeals court ruled that there was no case to answer. In October 2001 a final appeal was submitted to the Supreme Court, which delayed its ruling for over two years. In the meantime, the PDDH issued a 2002 report denouncing egregious legal errors on the part of the relevant authorities and holding *fiscal* Belisario Artiga personally responsible for what it called "an illicit act . . . in flagrant violation of human rights."[35] Nonetheless, on 7 January 2004 the Constitutional Bench (Sala de lo Constitucional) of the Supreme Court finally rejected the plaintiffs' appeal, ruling that no fundamental constitutional rights had been violated by the murders or by subsequent justice system (in)action.[36] IDHUCA's response included a

31. See "Denuncia penal presentada por José María Tojeira, rector de la UCA, ante la Fiscalía General de la República de El Salvador," dated 20 March 2000. Available at http://www.uca.edu.sv/publica/idhuca/jesuitas.html, last accessed 4 March 2009.

32. See "Respuesta de la Fiscalía General de la República de El Salvador ante la denuncia penal presentada por José María Tojeira, rector de la UCA," dated 12 April 2000, available at http://www.uca.edu.sv/publica/idhuca/jesuitas.html, last accessed 4 March 2009; author's translation.

33. The prescription period for murder being ten years.

34. "Acta Audiencia Inicial del Juzgado 30 de Paz de San Salvador," case no. 431-1-00, dated 15 December 2000; on file with author.

35. Author's translation from "Informe de la Señora Procuradora para la Defensa de los Derechos Humanos, sobre la impunidad respecto de las ejecuciones arbitrarias de Ignacio Ellacuría S.J. [. . .] y Celina Mariceth Ramos," PDDH, dated 30 October 2002. Published in PDDH (2002) and available at http://www.uca.edu.sv/publica/idhuca/jesuitas.html, last accessed 4 March 2009.

36. A four-to-one majority made the ruling, with former PDDH head Victoria de Avilés casting the dissenting vote.

threat to take the case to regional or international mechanisms.[37] UCA rector José María Tojeira acknowledged that in the aftermath of the Pinochet case, groups in Spain had approached the congregation about taking action there. The Jesuit congregation and IDHUCA, however, were reluctant, preferring to push for a new domestic case that might open up national channels for cases without overseas connections.[38] When a case was finally opened in Spain in 2008 (see below), a statement from the congregation professed "respect" for the initiative, but clearly restated its own preference for domestic channels or regional actions aimed at activating domestic compliance with existing international treaty obligations.[39]

"TRANSNATIONAL" CASES REGARDING EL SALVADOR

U.S. relatives and advocacy organizations have to date brought four civil cases under U.S. domestic legislation over HRVs committed in El Salvador. These cases, pursued in U.S. courts, did not originate with domestic organizations in El Salvador. Indeed, they met with an initially cautious or even negative reception from Salvadorean HROs as well as—more predictably— from domestic authorities. The first civil claim was lodged in Florida in May 1999 under the Torture Victim Protection Act (TVPA).[40] Relatives of the four U.S. churchwomen raped and murdered in 1980 brought the claim, against U.S. residents and retired Salvadorean generals Eugenio Vides Casanova and José García. The case, known as *Ford v. García,* concluded with a jury trial in October 2000. The verdict demonstrated the fragility of claims pursued overseas, presenting a powerful counter-case to the argument that justice is "more possible" at a distance from the biases or pressures assumed to operate in situ. The jury had little or no prior knowledge of the historical and political context of El Salvador, and also repeatedly requested technical guidance

---

37. "El IDHUCA ante la notificación de la Sala de lo Constitucional rechazando la petición de amparo en el caso Jesuitas," dated 7 January 2004, available at http://www.uca.edu.sv/publica/ idhuca/jesuitas.html, last accessed 4 March 2009.

38. Initial plans for a case in Spain hinged on the fact that five of the six murdered priests were Spanish.

39. Statement "Postura institucional ante la presentación en España de una querella . . . ," dated 13 November 2008, available at http://www.uca.edu/sv/publica/idhuca/documentos/comunicado131108.pdf, last accessed 2 November 2009.

40. A domestic law allowing U.S. citizens to sue foreign torturers in U.S. courts, the TVPA extended the powers of the 1789 Alien Tort Claims Act (ATCA), which had granted such powers only to noncitizens. See chapter 3 and Ratner and Stephens (1996).

over issues such as command responsibility.[41] After three weeks of trial, the defendants were found not liable.

A May 2002 appeal was rejected, but in the interim a second civil claim had been prepared against the same generals. *Romagoza et al. v. García* resulted in a multimillion dollar award against the two defendants, and also led directly to a criminal investigation being launched against García in 2009 for immigration fraud.[42] This, like all subsequent claims, was sponsored by the Center for Justice and Accountability, a U.S. organization set up in 1998 to provide legal representation to survivors of torture. In 2003 it was the turn of former army captain Alvaro Saravia, sued for his part in the assassination of Archbishop Oscar Romero.[43] Saravia did not appear at the September 2004 hearing, and was found liable in absentia. In contrast to the earlier cases, efforts were made to broaden the range of witnesses and to coordinate more closely with Salvadorean HROs (see below). The impasse over command responsibility was broken in 2005 when Nicolas Carranza, a former Salvadorean vice-minister of defense and one-time police chief, was found liable for torture and extrajudicial killings committed under his command.

In November 2008 the CJA took part for the first time in a criminal rather than civil case over El Salvador: together with the Spanish Association for Human Rights (Asociación Pro-Derechos Humanos de España) (APDHE), a domestic HRO, they impulsed the Jesuit case complaint in Spain (mentioned above). The initiative involves lawyers and advisers with experience of previous CJA cases in the United States, and of cases in Spain over Guatemala. In this sense it represents an example of emerging transnational networks, although it can also be read as the formation of an internationally mobile "professional class" of human rights lawyers, whose vertical links with national groups remain contingent and essentially cyclical.

Explaining Post-transitional Accountability

As we have seen in chapter 6, human rights responses in El Salvador's wartime reality, where they survived at all, largely steered clear of a domestic judicial

---

41. Crucial since it was being argued that the defendants, although not directly involved in the killings, had ordered, had prior knowledge of, or failed to prevent them.

42. On 6 October 2009, the U.S. Department of Homeland Security announced deportation proceedings against García and Vides Casanova. See http://www.cja.org/.

43. *Doe v. Saravia*. This claim used the closely related ATCA legislation. See chapter 3 and http://www.cja.org/.

system that promised little and delivered even less. HROs concentrated on denunciation of HRVs to outside agencies, and no cohesive, lawyer-led domestic human rights response akin to that of Chile emerged. Accordingly, only two major dimensions—actors and strategic considerations—have been central to a post-transitional accountability scene characterized to date by relatively sparse activity.

ACCOUNTABILITY ACTORS

Since the Salvadorean human rights community was historically not characterized by a legal agenda, accountability actors as such were and remain relatively scarce. Indeed, much of this section will examine and account for the ways that post-transitional human rights organizing, even by organizations specifically addressing wartime experiences and HRV legacies, has predominantly adopted alternative, non-accountability, agendas and repertoires of action. The particular experience of the truth commission process had ambivalent effects on the Salvadorean human rights community. On the one hand, possibly unrealistic expectations of justice were raised, only to be dashed by the failure of the truth commission report to ensure any judicial consequences.[44] On the other hand, this experience and the ensuing frustration spurred the formation of two new organizations that would in different ways become significant in keeping the issue of historical HRVs alive. The first of these, the Centro para la Promoción de Derechos Humanos "Madeleine Lagedec" (Centro Madeleine Lagedec), was founded in 1992 to encourage local communities to present testimony to the truth commission. The information finally presented included accounts of rural massacres in the Sonsonate area and of the death of French national Madeleine Lagedec.[45] The commission, however, included only two of the incidents in its "representative" final sample. In 1993, after a national fund was set up for certain categories of people affected by the conflict,[46] the group began assisting rural

44. "Internationally, the Truth Commission vindicated our [denunciatory] work ... but for the victims and for Salvadorean society, there was zero impact. A whole apparatus was set up which in the end did nothing to attack impunity" (HRO evaluation, quoted in LCHR 1995, 135).

45. Lagedec, a French nurse, was killed in March 1989 during a military assault on an FMLN field hospital. Her death later became the subject of a domestic investigation under French jurisdiction at the request of her family, who argued successfully that the 1993 amnesty law prevented any possibility of an investigation in El Salvador itself.

46. Namely, the war-wounded and relatives of some people killed in combat. The so-called Fondo de Protección was designed to benefit ex-combatants rather than civilian victims, and in any case made little impact.

families to make compensation claims. Claims were far from straightforward. Relatives had to provide extensive documentation, including death certificates. These bureaucratic requirements were prohibitive in many rural areas where literacy was low and many people did not even have birth certificates. Many war deaths had simply never been officially registered.

A second organization, Pro-Búsqueda, was likewise founded in the context of the truth commission's work and in response to a hidden problem that emerged most strongly after the conflict: that of the fate of children separated from their families by military operations. Internal displacement and the exodus of refugees had dispersed families and made it difficult to trace living relatives. Additionally, children had been adopted overseas or abducted and later adopted by soldiers, treated in effect as the spoils of war. The group was founded in the Chalatenango district, where local families who testified to the truth commission about their missing children were angry when their testimony did not lead to further action. One group of women approached the courts in Chalatenango with petitions for investigation. The lack of response led them to make their own efforts to trace the children, and Pro-Búsqueda was formalized in August 1994. The organization grew into one of the best-known and most widely networked Salvadorean HROs, tracing over two hundred missing children in its first decade. Staff member Sandra Lovo was clear that no child had ever been located via the assistance of the courts: "We have used every possible avenue, and the judicial system has always been the least receptive."[47] The organization accordingly turned to regional mechanisms in the mid-2000s, reactivating a series of war-era complaints after the favorable Serrano verdict.

THE 1993 AMNESTY LAW AND ITS IMPACT ON HROS

The executive director of the Asociación Comité de Familiares de Víctimas de Violaciones a los Derechos Humanos "Marianella García Villas" (CODEFAM)[48] claimed that the passing of the draconian amnesty statute of 1993 had "extinguished the whole human rights movement—it slammed the

---

47. The organization estimated that, as of mid-2003, less than a dozen requests for investigation were still active in the courts. Sandra Lovo, interview 9 June 2003.

48. Founded in 1981 as the Comité de Familiares de Presos, Desaparecidos, y Asesinados Politicos, its name was changed in 1983 in honor of CDHES president Marianella García, assassinated that year.

door on cases."[49] Indeed, one notable feature of the Salvadorean setting was the regularity with which the HRO personnel interviewed in 2003 advanced the view that the amnesty law of 1993 prevented them from even bringing criminal complaints over HRVs. All practicing lawyers consulted, however, were clearly of the opinion that this was not so, and that the only hope of progress lay precisely in the pursuit of complaints in order to galvanize the present system. IDHUCA lawyers, responsible for most extant accountability pressure on the domestic courts, were emphatic on the point. The obvious inference is that HRO personnel had not discussed this issue with practicing lawyers with any frequency or in any depth. When challenged on the accuracy of their view of amnesty's effects, most HRO staff readily acknowledged it to be little more than a general perception that had perhaps became something of a self-fulfilling prophecy.[50]

The only HRO to offer a more sophisticated argument for its low level of domestic accountability initiatives was CODEFAM, whose view was that the law does not prevent complaints being admitted, but does impede a judge from eventually bringing charges. They considered, however, that in the existing judicial climate a suspension or closure of an investigation would be sufficient to prevent any future judicial activity over the same incident. This fear of triggering irreversible, negative judicial verdicts contributed to a strategic decision by CODEFAM not to pursue accountability actions in the years after 1993.[51] In their view, the risks of claim-making outweighed the possible rewards except where prescription was imminent or the exhaustion of domestic avenues was a formality required in order to access regional mechanisms.[52]

ACCOUNTABILITY AS A GOAL IN THE POST-CONFLICT PERIOD

Many interviewees doubted the existence of a widespread social desire for justice-as-accountability in the post-conflict period. Although El Salvador

---

49. Armando Pérez Salazar, interview 16 July 2003.

50. "I wonder if we haven't just convinced ourselves about the amnesty law" (Camelia Cartagena, interview 15 August 2003).

51. In a sense CODEFAM's logic is akin to that of the Chilean lawyers who lodged and maintained complaints and kept them alive within the court system in the expectation of a future, more favorable accountability setting. The difference lies in CODEFAM's perception that the minimal judicial functionality that would permit case maintenance in this "waiting" period does not yet exist in El Salvador.

52. Armando Pérez Salazar, interview 16 July 2003.

is, in the words of Benjamin Cuellar of IDHUCA, "a country teeming with victims,"[53] demands for justice did not materialize. Cuellar blamed what he called the "elite" rather than "social" contract that ended the war. The bargain struck between the FMLN, ARENA, and the UN had the widely socially desired effect of ending the fighting while simultaneously giving the impression that the terms under which it had been made were the only ones possible and were immutable. Thus Cuellar believed that a diffuse fear of a return to the past, and to war, was enough to dampen justice demands in the early post-Accord years. The quest for economic survival ascended—or perhaps returned—to the top of the agenda for most people.[54] Carmen Medina, country representative of a small international development agency, considered that the absence of visible demands for accountability also owes to a more general lack of "rights consciousness."[55]

Additionally—or perhaps consequently—the HROs that survived after 1993 tended, in contrast to their Chilean counterparts, to refocus their work not on impunity but on developmental and economic issues. HROs' largely positive relationship with the new PDDH itself helped to shape their priorities away from past HRVs, since the PDDH similarly worked predominantly on "present-day" rights issues, including labor rights.[56] Many interviewees also cited a relative lack of protagonism from affected communities or relatives' organizations: "we have no Madres de la Plaza de Mayo here."[57] Echoing Camelia Cartagena's suggestion that amnesty may have led to unnecessarily self-limiting HRO behavior, Supreme Court judge and former PDDH head Victoria de Avilés referred to "the self-perpetuating idea that the courts are flawed and so can't be used. This kind of fatalism, skepticism is very convenient for certain sectors."[58] Salvadorean groups' relative lack of legal expertise and experience perhaps shows itself most clearly in this apparent reluctance to use the courts other than for narrowly administrative effects such as to pursue recovery of remains (see below).

One possible exception to this relative dearth of domestic civil society actors with a developed accountability agenda is IDHUCA, the human rights institute of the Jesuit university. IDHUCA has a strong legal emphasis and a

53. Benjamin Cuellar, interview 25 June 2003.
54. Benjamin Cuellar, interview 25 June 2003.
55. Carmen Medina, interview 10 June 2003.
56. Camelia Cartagena, interview 15 August 2003.
57. This phrase was repeated word for word by three separate interviewees.
58. Victoria de Avilés, interview 25 August 2003.

special position as part of a working university with teaching and research activities. The institute benefits from the Jesuit congregation's resource base and international connections, and the UCA as a whole maintains a relatively central position in national intellectual and cultural life via its own publishing house and production of the Central American current affairs journal *Estudios Centroamericanos*. The issue of accountability for the past has been regularly aired via each of these channels, as well as through an annual commemoration of the anniversary of the Jesuit assassinations.

IDHUCA's 1999 decision to attempt new legal action over the 1989 murders was driven by a particular confluence of long-term interest and contingency. The Jesuit congregation and the victims' families had always maintained the inadequacy of the original proceedings. Renewed challenges to the amnesty law made in 1997 and 1998 added a certain impetus, as did proceedings against Pinochet in Spain and Chile.[59] The long-delayed report of the Inter-American Commission on the case was published in 1999, offering additional weight to criticism of the authorities' handling of the original case. Personnel with specific skills and an interest in legal action became available: IDHUCA had recruited several new lawyers, including former state prosecutors, trained in the post-accords period and conversant with the principles of progressive legal practice and international human rights law. At least one of them took the post specifically to indulge an intellectual interest in the possibility of reviving the case.[60]

Separate developments within the university ensured that the final outcome was the birth of a modest new accountability agenda, rather than solely an individual case effort. A project launched by the social psychology faculty to support communities affected by the 2001 earthquake discovered that many were still suffering the aftereffects of wartime trauma. Support and self-help groups were founded, and eventually four families expressed a desire to explore the possibilities of justice action. They were referred to IDHUCA, and a series of claims for disappearance were submitted to the Fiscalía in 2003 and 2004.[61] As of 2004 IDHUCA, together with Pro-Búsqueda and Tutela Legal, were the only organizations commonly identified as involved

---

59. José María Tojeira, S.J., interview 2 June 2003. See also IDHUCA (2000): "The possibility of taking this kind of step was always 'hanging in the air'; it was just never clear whether [it should be] inside or outside the country. The impulse was strengthened by the case against Augusto Pinochet in Spain . . . as well as by the proceedings launched against him in Chile" (author's translation).

60. Pedro Cruz, interview 27 June 2003.

61. Mauricio Gaborit, S.J., interview 13 August 2003.

in accountability. Of the three, only IDHUCA had a clearly developed and resourced accountability agenda plus major legal initiatives currently before domestic courts. Tutela Legal had strong field investigations but had not pursued accountability as some felt it could or even ought.[62] The legal initiatives of other groups often had alternative, non-accountability objectives pursued via legislative rather than judicial channels. CODEFAM, for example, was working on a proposal to make the legislature address the legal status of the disappeared.

COLLABORATION AND COOPERATION AMONG HROS SINCE 1997: THE COMISIÓN PRO-MEMORIA

It has been argued here that only IDHUCA can properly be considered a full accountability actor in present-day El Salvador. Broader HRO cooperation, such as might conceivably support future revitalization of the accountability agenda, is limited. Civil society organizations have generally been weak in the postwar period.[63] HRO cooperation has been affected by differences of vision, with some war-era organizations perceived by newer groups to be territorial and lacking in enthusiasm for shared initiatives.[64] Nevertheless, some new organizations joined traditional HROs in the formation of the Comisión Pro-Memoria Histórica in 1997.[65] The group, focused on HRVs and war victims, took impunity and the amnesty law as initial agenda items and might therefore have been expected to consider legally framed action. Action over disappearances nonetheless tended to be denunciatory rather than legal, including annual commemoration of the national Week of the Disappeared and the international Day of the Disappeared. The Comisión's first and main visible achievement was a monument to victims, inaugurated in a park in the capi-

---

62. Several interviewees questioned the lack of domestic action over the Romero case, which Tutela Legal has always represented, and El Mozote, where it was involved in renewed exhumations. Then-director Maria Julia Hernández, however, was emphatic that there was "nothing to be done" domestically over Romero (interview 18 June 2003). Later efforts were undermined by the Church hierarchy.

63. Comments by Miguel Cruz, director of the Public Opinion Institute of the UCA, at the conference "Post-war Conflict and Violence," held at Liverpool University, UK, 9–10 September 2004.

64. Interview data.

65. Founder members included IDHUCA, COMADRES, Tutela Legal, CODEFAM, the Centro Madeleine Lagedec, and the Lutheran church. Pro-Búsqueda joined very soon after founding, and the PDDH sent representatives to some early meetings. Founder member Camelia Cartagena, interview 15 August 2003.

tal in December 2003, constituting a rebuke to the authorities' neglect of an outstanding truth commission recommendation that a public memorial to victims be established.[66]

Despite the successful monument venture, participant Camelia Cartagena considered that the Comisión had not lived up to its early potential: "it's been positive in as much as we've kept it going, but we haven't been able to make it effective."[67] IDHUCA's superior resources and single-institution identity seem to have brought it more independent success in channeling any pro-accountability interest or energies. In 1998 it inaugurated an annual "truth festival," an artistic, cultural, and academic event spelling out the pending challenges of unfulfilled truth commission recommendations plus truth and justice measures for victims.[68]

DOMESTIC NETWORKING AMONG PRESENT-DAY SALVADOREAN HROS

In addition to the example of coordinated action in the Comisión, some HROs participated in a 2003 national campaign in favor of the International Criminal Court. Most felt, however, that to alter the status quo over account-ability would require a higher order of concerted HRO action, seen as an unlikely prospect. Roxana Marroquín of the Centro Madeleine Lagedec, in common with other interviewees, saw the Supreme Court's 2000 ruling over amnesty as opening a very small window of opportunity, but was pessimistic about HROs' ability to provide the vigorous, concerted "push" necessary for lasting progress.[69] In mid-2003 the Centro Madeleine Lagedec was attempting to make international links with EAAF, the Argentinian forensic anthropol-ogy team working with Tutela Legal on the El Mozote exhumations. Signifi-cantly, however, contacts were being pursued directly with EAAF rather than via Tutela Legal. Pedro Cruz remarked for his part that although IDHUCA's recent case initiatives had sparked comment and approbation from individu-als in domestic HRO circles, IDHUCA had not been approached formally

66. Memorialization took on a new and more contestatory relevance later in the decade, when an ARENA mayor erected a monument to Roberto d'Aubuisson in a San Salvador square not far from the UCA. ARENA legislators subsequently tried to have d'Aubuisson, author of the 1980 Romero assassination, posthumously declared an "illustrious son of the nation." The proposal was only narrowly defeated.

67. Camelia Cartagena, interview 15 August 2003.

68. See http://www.uca.edu.sv/publica/idhuca/festival.html.

69. Roxana Marroquín of the Centro Madeleine Lagedec, interview 20 June 2003.

by any organization interested in learning from IDHUCA's experiences or otherwise assisting to activate legal channels.[70]

INTERNATIONAL NETWORKING: A DELIBERATE-ACTOR STRATEGY?

As in Chile, many of the Salvadorean organizations interviewed reported reduced levels of international connection and financial support after transition. Nor was there much sense of a domestic network woven by multiple or overlapping threads into an international setting. Instead, in keeping with the individuation observed at national level, connections with outside organizations often appeared to be essentially closed, one-to-one linkages. Even domestic groups connected with the same outside organization did not necessarily have close horizontal links, as is the case of Tutela Legal and the Centro Madeleine Lagedec in their separate relationships to EAAF. The issue of competition for ever-more scarce external funding was undoubtedly one factor in internal distancing. One additional element was a relatively high specificity or idiosyncrasy of organizational identities. Certain organizations felt more natural affinity with regional counterparts than with other domestic groups, reducing possibilities for the elaboration of shared goals or strategies at the national level. Pro-Búsqueda, for example, with limited national collaborative work, had relatively high levels of contact with Argentina, where a very different political context nonetheless gave rise to a similar problem of child abduction. Pro-Búsqueda has in turn become a regional leader or hub in this field, stimulating discussions and conferences throughout Central America, particularly with Guatemala and Nicaraguan organizations. Pro-Búsqueda is also funded by dedicated children's organizations such as UNICEF and Save the Children.[71] These links, specific to the organization's theme, differentiate and perhaps distance it slightly from other national HROs. Pro-Búsqueda's legal agenda and goals are also distinctive, addressing specialized issues such as adoption and the issuing of identity documents.

Relatives' groups such as COMADRES emerged fairly early in El Salvador's conflict, and joined regional associations such as the Federación Latinoamericana de Asociaciones de Familiares de Detenidos-Desaparecidos. But relatives' groups did not on the whole manage to convert early levels of

70. Pedro Cruz, interview 13 August 2003. Instead, IDHUCA began to collaborate and exchange directly with outside groups, including the CJA and the Washington-based Due Process of Law Foundation.

71. Data from Pro-Búsqueda (2001, 2003).

visibility into sustained protagonism. Those that survived organize only a tiny proportion of relatives, playing a fairly minor role within the human rights community itself. The work of national HROs in accountability was circumscribed by this lack of direct demand. IDHUCA was particularly affected, since it adopts a "victim-centered" philosophy that views its legal work as necessarily driven by survivor and relative protagonism.[72]

THE DOMESTIC IMPACT OF TRANSNATIONAL INITIATIVES:
THE PINOCHET CASE

Interviewees asked to describe milestones affecting national accountability in the post-1998 period did not spontaneously refer to the Pinochet case in Spain. In response to specific questioning most representatives of HROs and relatives' groups reported a positive effect on morale, but none had investigated the possibility of repeat or "copycat" actions. According to judge Francisco Eliseo Ortíz, "[The Pinochet case] was well regarded in intellectual and academic circles here, and among the [political] opposition. People in general also commented on it, although I think it was seen as something distant. I didn't hear of any direct interest in studying it closely."[73] Relatives' group COMADRES went so far as to send a congratulatory letter to Spanish Judge Garzón,[74] but saw the practical ramifications as limited. Like many other interviewees, they welcomed the theoretical prospect of a domestic equivalent but did not seem to see this as something they themselves should or could be able to effect.[75] The UCA did report two specific effects. First, Pinochet's arrest was cited as having influenced the timing of the new Jesuit case complaint submitted in 1999. Second, as mentioned, unsolicited offers came from NGOs and bar associations in Europe and the United States to take up the case overseas.

THE IMPACT OF U.S. CIVIL CLAIMS

The "transnational" cases undertaken in the United States since 1999 over El Salvador are in many ways better characterized as essentially U.S. domestic

---

72. Benjamin Cuellar, interview 25 June 2003.

73. Francisco Eliseo Ortíz, interview 22 July 2003.

74. Garzón later (in 2003) visited El Salvador at the invitation of the private Universidad Tecnológica.

75. "The military here got worried all right . . . [but] it would need something like the Pinochet case to happen right here to get things moving" (Alicia García, interview 5 August 2003).

cases that happened to concern overseas events. The first case, over the U.S. churchwomen killed in 1980, was brought by and about U.S. citizens, and its prime organizational mover was U.S. advocacy organization the Lawyers' Committee for Human Rights (LCHR) (now Human Rights First). The move was essentially the outcome of a chain of coincidence. LCHR personnel had travelled to El Salvador in 1998 to interview the guardsmen originally convicted for the killing, prompted by the men's parole applications to national authorities. Information gleaned from these interviews was combined with the chance discovery that two senior military officers involved in the killings had retired to the United States and were living in Florida.

Although the LCHR had neither a history of nor a systematic interest in transnational litigation, it had been long and deeply involved in Salvadorean affairs in general and the churchwomen's case in particular. The LCHR liaised with the Center for Constitutional Rights, another U.S. advocacy organization, which had brought similar earlier claims, including the landmark *Filartiga v. Peña-Irala* case,[76] and had also collaborated with the recently founded CJA. The initial 1999 claim accused Eugenio Vides Casanova and José García of command responsibility for the deaths of Sister Ita Ford and her three colleagues.[77] Filmmaker Gail Pellett documented the 2000 trial in a film titled *Justice and the Generals*. Interviews with jurors in Pellett's film suggested that their lasting impression from expert testimony about the brutality of El Salvador's civil war had been of an utterly chaotic situation, in which the defendants could not have been expected to exercise effective command over their subordinates. Both the initial claim and a subsequent appeal were rejected.

The second, successful, claim against the same defendants was notable for a conscious decision to involve more Salvadoreans and relatively fewer U.S. experts. Survivors, rather than relatives, made the claim, and all were Salvadorean nationals and former refugees resident in the United States for many years. The claimants felt that this could both make a human impact on the jury, reducing the "distancing" effect of faraway events, and close the command responsibility gap by connecting the defendants directly to HRVs through eyewitness testimony.[78] This second case was driven by the CJA rather

76. This case produced, in 1981, the first ever ruling by a U.S. court holding that international law applied to a state's treatment of its own citizens.

77. García had been minister of defense between 1979 and 1983. Vides Casanova, director-general of the National Guard in 1980, had later succeeded García as minister of defense.

78. Ken Hurwitz, interview 26 July 2002; Patty Blum, interview 20 November 2002.

than the LCHR, whose specific commitment had been to the churchwomen's case through their long-standing relationship with relatives. The CJA, for its part, had decided back in 1998 to make El Salvador one focus for its work, drawing up a "wanted list" of Salvadorean perpetrators believed to be resident in the United States. As described above, after the success of *Romagoza et al. v. García*, the CJA submitted a third claim, against Nicolas Carranza, and a fourth, against Alvaro Saravia. Saravia, named by the truth commission as a participant in the Romero killing, had fled El Salvador for the United States in the early 1980s. After escaping extradition he had successfully, and secretly, applied for amnesty from his U.S. base in late 1993.[79] Saravia had been living openly in California since 1993, but went underground when notified of the civil claim. For the first time, a group of witnesses[80] traveled from El Salvador to testify at the hearing, at which Saravia was found liable to the tune of US$10 million.

These cases might on the surface seem to mark the beginnings of a significant movement in Salvadorean accountability history, particularly since deliberate efforts were made after the Ford case to involve Salvadorean survivors. But the origins of the cases, like their impact, seem on closer examination to be quite tightly circumscribed within the United States. The move to seek out Salvadorean plaintiffs for the second case was itself suggested by a U.S. expert, Patty Blum. She emphasized the need to give "ownership" of the issues over to Salvadoreans.[81] Nonetheless the eventual plaintiffs were drawn from the Salvadorean refugee and immigrant community within the United States. This community constitutes a distinctive, numerous,[82] and in some senses self-contained social group. Although links to the home community are maintained through family connections, none of El Salvador's domestic

79. In fact, the courts, which had already applied amnesty to the case in March of the same year, ruled Saravia's application, made through the consulate in California, unnecessary. Romero case file, Causa 134-80, at fs. [pages] 2100–2106; viewed at San Salvador's Juzgado 4° de Instruccion (formerly Juzgado 4° Penal), August 2003.

80. This group included judge Atilio Ramírez Amaya (who had abandoned the domestic investigation after being subjected to an attempt on his life just days after taking the case), Amado Garay (a self-confessed accomplice to the crime), and Maria Julia Hernández of Tutela Legal.

81. Ken Hurwitz, interview 26 July 2002. Patty Blum adds that refugees resident in the United States had, independently, approached the CJA around the same time to inquire about the possibilities of legal action (telephone interview 20 November 2002).

82. Salvadorean government census figures from as early as 1992 stated that 2,215,000 Salvadoreans were living outside El Salvador, the majority in the United States (see http://www.uca.edu.sv/publica/idhuca/migracion.html). Patty Blum estimated between half a million and one million of the Salvadoreans resident in the United States in the mid-2000s to be former refugees.

human rights or relatives' organizations reported systematic contact with the Salvadorean community in the United States. None reported having been involved in prior discussion or consultation about the cases brought in the United States. One relatives' group reported having been approached to provide information and evidence once cases were under way, but seemed relatively uninformed and as a result suspicious about the organizational profile of the CJA.

When the cases were specifically raised in interviews in-country (in 2003), most Salvadorean interviewees had heard of them but tended to be critical about their aims or methods. The fact that civil cases inevitably proceed by claiming compensation—although awards are almost never enforced—was cited by some as a drawback and even a motive for censure: "People here said 'they're just doing it for the money.'"[83] While recognizing that a certain level of secrecy or circumspection had been necessary in order to avoid defendants being alerted, some domestic HROs expressed disquiet that they had been consulted only after the event. None seemed to view the cases as a particularly positive precedent in-country, as opposed to in the United States, and none claimed to be considering similar action. As of 2004 only Tutela Legal had worked directly with the CJA, a link developed in secrecy ahead of the 2004 *Doe v. Saravia* hearing.

For its own part, the CJA clearly gave careful subsequent consideration to the issue of domestic–third country balance. Its stated aims support the prioritization of in-country accountability, contemplating external cases only where home-country impunity seems entrenched.[84] The CJA accordingly built up closer contacts with domestic groups in El Salvador after the early cases.[85] In particular there were exchanges with and visits to IDHUCA, the Salvadorean organization perhaps best attuned to accountability goals and the one most actively considering the alternatives and possible benefits of transnational action. Resource and activity profiles, however, suggested that cooperation will necessarily remain on a case-by-case basis. Itself a relatively small domestic advocacy organization, the CJA's litigation interests

83. Alicia García, interview 5 August 2003

84. Matt Eisenbrandt of the CJA, interview 24 September 2004.

85. The CJA's network of contacts in El Salvador grew considerably during 2004 during preparations for the Romero and Carranza cases. Matt Eisenbrandt suggested that as a consequence much of the earlier skepticism among HROs had been overcome, particularly since the success of the Romero case, of great symbolic significance to grassroots groups in El Salvador. Interview, 24 September 2004.

and energies are divided over a range of geographical and thematic areas.[86] Although a transnational network may yet grow out of Salvador contacts, CJA activities did not originate from any such networking but from domestic endeavors in the United States. Clearly, the early U.S. cases did not follow the "boomerang" model, which would require them to have been initiated by activists within El Salvador attempting to circumvent blocked domestic justice avenues.

STRATEGY

With such low levels of accountability claim-making, specifically legal strategies have been correspondingly scarce in El Salvador. The fact that El Salvador's human rights response was never predominantly, nor successfully, legally framed also means that there is less domestic lawyer experience and expertise to draw on. Perhaps as important, the absence of a history of legal accountability efforts itself owed much to a sector-wide dysfunction in the administration of justice that has not yet been overcome. The relative absence of specific legal strategy on the part of HROs—as, indeed, the very fact that so many of these organizations do not have a developed or prioritized accountability agenda—can therefore be interpreted as itself a rational response to an extremely negative prevailing opportunity structure.

The emergence in the late 1980s of "hybrid" organizations such as IEJES and FESPAD,[87] with a strong judicial reform focus, could in turn be viewed as a civil society effort to enlarge the space of the "possible." These groups, essentially specialized think tanks, function as research, action, and lobbying institutions focused on justice system reform. Creating the necessary structural conditions for accountability claims to prosper can itself be an accountability strategy, albeit one that is pursued at a higher level of generality. Groups that have chosen to advocate broad judicial and justice sector reform, however, have faced an uphill struggle. In terms of more direct, self-avowed accountability activity, only IDHUCA showed signs of a recently developed domestic litigation and claim-making strategy—one that, moreover, met with little initial success.

86. These areas of interest include, as of the mid-2000s, Bosnia, China, Honduras, and East Timor. Cases have been pursued against corporations as well as individuals.

87. Respectively, the El Salvador Institute for Juridical Studies (Instituto de Estudios Jurídicos de El Salvador), founded in 1987, and the Foundation for Applied Legal Studies (Fundación de Estudios para la Aplicación del Derecho), founded in 1988.

ACCOUNTABILITY PROSPECTS AND THE LEGAL SYSTEM AT TRANSITION

El Salvador's pre-transition legal system had, like Chile's, given prosecuto-rial responsibility to investigating magistrates. Although the Fiscalía did exist, its role was limited. The courts had to depend on the security services for evidence gathering, cementing an unhealthy relationship between the mili-tary and supposedly civilian justice processes, since all security services were militarized. Although El Salvador was relatively unusual for the region in undergoing extensive judicial reform even during the war (Call 2003), U.S.-sponsored reform efforts had often attempted technical fixes without resolv-ing more fundamental problems (see LCHR 1989; Popkin 2000).

Accordingly, as we have seen, such legal action as was undertaken by HROs or their precursors in the late 1970s proved at best ineffectual and at worst dangerous. Further, legal channels did not reopen after 1992. Indeed, accountability prospects became even more remote with the 1993 introduc-tion of amnesty. Some HRO personnel migrated into political circles, further exacerbating an existing lack of legal expertise and resources. The absence of habitual legal responses during the war had also been linked to actors' low expectations of the court system. Nothing happened in the immediate aftermath of transition to alter those perceptions, despite the fact that legal system changes after the war were extensive. Some changes represented clear improvements. Criminal code reforms, particularly, made great strides in the adoption of international standards and rights-guaranteeing criminal pro-cedures (FESPAD 2003). As regards accountability, however, the evolving postwar system contained both favorable and inhibitory innovations. The introduction of the PDDH, though peripheral to direct claim-bringing, was a generally positive signal for future rights protection. Code changes, however, included pro-defendant clauses that weakened accountability prospects.[88] In particular, the principle that, in case of contradiction between old and new, the code most favorable to the defendant be invoked has been used by defen-dants to claim prescription and thus escape prosecution.

---

88. As regards the 1989 Jesuit killings, for example, the old criminal code stipulated a fifteen-year prescription period for murder. Since the new code reduces the period to ten years, defense lawyers successfully argued that the crimes had prescribed four months before IDHUCA's renewed complaint, submitted in March 2000.

THE IMPACT OF LEGAL SYSTEM CHANGES
ON ACCOUNTABILITY PROSPECTS

Reforms that have proved decidedly negative for accountability prospects include changes to the physical location, thematic specialization, and nomenclature of criminal courts in the capital. Many judicial records, particularly any trace of complaints entered but never processed into full case files, seemed to disappear into the cracks between the old structures and the new. HROs and even judges confessed ignorance of the whereabouts of any such documents and profound skepticism as to whether they would ever be traced, or produced, if requested.[89] This lack of evidence of earlier claim-making is prejudicial for overcoming prescription. There is thus a sense that structural reforms make physically manifest the government's rhetorically favored policy of "not raking up the past." In one sense, the abandonment of past claims has been the price paid for institutional innovation in the name of improving present-day rights protection.

Finally, the new judicial system hands prosecutorial discretion to the Fiscalía. Judges take only a peripheral role up until trial, at which time prosecutors rather than judges select and present evidence, bring charges, and suggest penalties. The combination of this particular change with the political continuity prevailing since transition has been to concentrate prosecutorial discretion in the hands of an individual highly unlikely to be sympathetic to accountability claims. Appointment to the post of *fiscal* general, at the head of this newly powerful institution, was made subject to the approval of a two-thirds majority in the legislature. To date this appointment has in effect remained the political gift of ARENA, in combination with other right-wing party votes. Interviewees in 2003 characterized the actual operation of the Fiscalía-driven system in accountability cases as prejudicial, identifying a mixture of bad faith and genuine lack of knowledge and capacity on the part of prosecutors.[90] Thus although interviewees recognized signs of judicial system progress, including a more plural judicial nomination system and improved judicial training, they felt that the "bottleneck" operating in the

---

89. Interview data.

90. Marlon López, interview 16 July 2003; and Armando Pérez Salazar, interview 16 July 2003. The performance of the incumbent *fiscal* across a range of issues was also roundly criticized in IDHUCA's 2002 annual report (IDHUCA 2003b).

present Fiscalía had prevented such changes being made manifest in changed accountability outcomes.

The same system considerably restricts the rights of survivors or victims to bring independent action. Since private individuals cannot bring complaints before a judge, survivors or relatives cannot ordinarily trigger the initiation of criminal proceedings. Instead, they must apply after the fact to participate in prosecutions already recommended by the Fiscalía. Although any person can denounce a crime to the Fiscalía, any subsequent decision by the Fiscalía not to proceed is virtually binding, even on judges.[91] Private individuals unhappy with a Fiscalía decision not to proceed must either persuade the Fiscalía to reconsider or seek some form of extraordinary recourse.[92] HROs and lawyers can participate, as in Chile, not in their own right but only in representation of survivors or victims.

POST-TRANSITIONAL ACCOUNTABILITY: MAJOR LEGAL OBSTACLES

Amnesty, prescription, and the absence of proof were the three legal obstacles most commonly cited by interviewees as impeding accountability progress in El Salvador. The issue of the limited wartime accumulation of proof has been discussed in chapter 6. Alicia García offered an additional, graphic illustration of its significance: "We used to hear about bodies that had been dumped. . . . We would go up there and take photos, so relatives might be able to identify them. But then we'd just bury them right there—there were so many, what else could we do? We didn't know then about evidence, forensics, all of that."[93] The absence of facilities or reliable authorities for documenting and reporting deaths left many families unable even to prove that their loved ones had existed, much less attest to the manner of their death.[94]

The 1993 amnesty law is so comprehensive, and has been so comprehensively invoked and defended, that cases able to test or push at legal boundaries have accordingly been few and far between. The self-limiting tendency of

91. It is theoretically possible, though in practice unknown, for a judge to challenge a Fiscalía decision not to prosecute. The effect, however, is to send the case back to the same Fiscalía department for a binding second opinion.

92. Such recourse might include a submission to the Supreme Court claiming infringement of constitutional rights or dispositions.

93. Alicia García, interview 5 August 2003.

94. Accordingly, in Serrano case hearings before the Inter-American Court of Human Rights, state representatives argued that the two missing girls in question might never have existed, suggesting that their mother had invented the claim to obtain compensation. See Popkin (2004).

HROs and lawyers to abstain from claim-making because of the existence of amnesty has limited case numbers even further. It is correspondingly difficult to identify a conscious-actor strategy for overcoming amnesty through litigation. There have certainly been no cumulative, case-by-case challenges such as those that preceded breakthroughs in judicial interpretation of the amnesty law in Chile.[95] There were, however, three efforts to directly challenge the law: in 1992, 1997, and 1998, as described above. Each restricted itself to primarily domestic juridical reasoning, arguing the law's incompatibility with the constitution on two main grounds: first, that the constitution guarantees certain fundamental rights, stipulates vigorous prosecution of their breach, and limits the terms and timing of any amnesty for them; and second, that it stipulates the precedence of international treaty law, which in turn outlaws amnesty for certain crimes.[96]

As discussed above, the Supreme Court's response to the 1993 petition was an erratic document that offered little in the way of measured juridical refutation. For the same reasons, it was of limited or no value to HROs as a springboard for further challenges. Response to the 1997 and 1998 petitions, given as a single judgment in 2000, did open the way for case-by-case deliberation by judges as to whether the law should apply. The discretionality was, however, only granted for certain crimes or for a restricted portion of a single presidential period, reducing to a minimum the type and number of claims that might escape amnesty if seen by a sympathetic judge. Practical progress in regard to this exclusion has been predictably slow, since to exploit or even test the loophole, cases must first pass the procedural hurdle of the Fiscalía.[97] Additionally, HROs seemed unprepared for the generation of a critical mass of test cases, such as would be needed if the loophole were to be widened by a strategy of attrition.

Prescription is a significant barrier in El Salvador since prescription periods, already relatively short, were shortened further in post-transitional reforms. Additionally, since no previous legal action was possible, was taken,

---

95. This is due in great measure, of course, to the absence of the preexisting, accumulated case universe to which Chilean groups had access, and to the success of the Fiscalía in blocking new claims.

96. Articles 244 and 144 of the Salvadorean Constitution, respectively.

97. Additionally, the few subsequent decisions extant have been inconsistent both in the definition of crimes that infringe constitutional rights, and in establishing whether the second, temporal exemption applies to all crimes conceivably committed by public functionaries or only those that were committed in an official capacity. See the Jesuit case, December 2000, and subsequent court decisions; on file with author.

or has been recorded, prescription has in most instances been uninterrupted since the crime occurred. Since HRV-related crimes were concentrated in the early 1980s, many have in fact lapsed according to national legislation.[98] Ironically, the existence of the amnesty law offers a theoretical avenue for surmounting the prescription barrier, as prescription periods can be suspended where it can be shown that earlier legal action was rendered impossible by some legal or constitutional impediment.[99] It should accordingly be possible to argue that the amnesty law itself constituted such an impediment in El Salvador. But institutional attitudes would first need to change: in 2003, for example, the Fiscalía declared that as Jesuit case relatives were at fault for not exercising their right to justice sooner, it was therefore proper that this right should lapse.[100]

Perhaps the most significant comparative point to highlight is that in El Salvador as in Chile, albeit for quite different reasons, accountability progress seems more likely to be achieved through changes in interpretation than further changes in codes or institutional structure. If Chile is an example of what can be achieved without large-scale or visible institutional or structural transformation, El Salvador is a counter-case showing how little is achieved with such changes unless accompanied by interpretative and attitudinal shifts among those charged with applying the existing normative framework to accountability. El Salvador additionally illustrates, but does not resolve, the question of where and how attitudinal change can best be effected. Domestic accountability actors appeared to be pinning substantial hopes on the possible effect of decisions from the Inter-American Court. Domestic cases were not being generated in large numbers, precisely because actors perceived that national institutional responsiveness had either not changed or had not changed favorably. If judicial or prosecutorial change needs to be driven by claim-bringing, then the work of IDHUCA seems unlikely to succeed unless other accountability actors can be persuaded to join the fray.

---

98. Though not, of course, according to international law, for those that constitute internationally recognized war crimes or crimes against humanity.

99. Article 37 of the Código Procesal Penal of 1996, which entered into force in 1998. The same article abolished prescription for internationally agreed categories of crime that cannot be prescribed, including torture and forced disappearance. It stipulated, however, that the change only applied to crimes committed after the entry into force of the new code.

100. Cited in a resolution of the Cámara 3a de lo Penal de la Primera Sección del Centro, dated 26 January 2001. Viewed at IDHUCA, July 2003.

OTHER BRAKES ON POST-TRANSITIONAL ACCOUNTABILITY

Legal obstacles proved, as we have seen, apparently immutable in postwar El Salvador, not least because the relevant institutions did not seem bound by juridical logic and appeared impervious to outside criticism.[101] Leverage for would-be claim-bringers seemed slight, on the national as on the international stage. But the number and frequency of claims was also restricted by "nonlegal" obstacles to claim-making. First, there is the lack of will among a majority of relatives or survivors. Although their participation is not technically necessary for the Fiscalía to order investigation—it can and should do so ex officio—in practice few criminal investigations advance without prompting from interested parties. Additionally, the unwillingness of relatives or survivors to generate claims did impede HRO action, since HROs cannot adhere to cases without this consent. IDHUCA representatives made it clear that from a strategic point of view they would have preferred to generate many more claims, but they are handicapped by this lack of demand.[102]

A second and related issue is that of "self-disqualification" and the long delays occasioned by the virtual absence of impetus for accountability action between 1993 and approximately 1998.[103] These delays, as well as compounding a loss of historical continuity and public profile among the groups that might drive accountability, imperiled the very possibility of legal action because of prescription. Even IDHUCA, well resourced and legally adept, took no action on the Jesuit murders between 1993 and March 2000, incurring prescription problems as a result. Case lawyer Pedro Cruz admitted that there was no real explanation for the hiatus, although his first written submissions in 2000 claimed that the congregation had been awaiting the Inter-American Commission report finally published in December 1999.[104]

THE INTERACTION OF OTHER GOALS WITH THE PURSUIT
OF CRIMINAL ACCOUNTABILITY

The complex interaction of the desire for peace with the desire for an end to HRVs and the desire for accountability has been discussed above. Additionally,

101. Antonio Cañas, interview 22 July 2003.
102. José Roberto Burgos, interview 12 June 2003; Benjamin Cuellar, interview 25 June 2003.
103. Around which time Tutela Legal submitted its challenge to the constitutionality of the 1993 amnesty law.
104. Pedro Cruz, interview 13 August 2003.

however, three other phenomena have each had a significant impact on El Salvador's accountability trajectory: first, the early establishment of human rights as a politically, rather than legally, framed problem; second, the use of legal and legislative channels for ends other than accountability; and third, the desire for acknowledgement or additional truth measures.

The adoption of political rather than legal strategies by human rights groups in wartime El Salvador was born of a seemingly accurate perception of the lack of domestic legal possibilities. It may, however, have clouded subsequent perceptions of new possibilities, the need for innovative legal strategy, or the extent of actual or possible judicial change. Additionally the political channels used, although they contributed to the UN-led peace process and truth commission, subsequently proved to be a dead end for accountability. If the utility of political channels for accountability claims in Chile was limited by transitional "pacts," their utility for the same ends in El Salvador was limited by the fact that both government and opposition entered wholeheartedly into amnesty. Pedro Cruz, for his part, found that the Jesuit case—just one example—"is always analyzed and talked about from the perspective of the war, the peace, the politics; rather than from the juridical point of view which is actually where there is a chance to move it along. . . . Organizations have found it difficult to reconstruct or reimagine themselves after the peace. There are lots more possibilities on paper than people think. . . . But organizations today have teams of other sorts of professionals—psychologists and the like—they don't have legal people."[105]

Although some HROs did go on to make use of legal channels, many did so in pursuit of administrative or other non-accountability goals. It is perhaps telling that the two organizations whose thematic focus implies systematic legal-administrative needs chose legislative lobbying, rather than rights claims in the courts, as their principal strategic approach. Thus the Centro Madeleine Lagedec's main legal preoccupations through the 1990s were procedural matters rather than accountability. The center worked to prove identity rather than pursue criminal accountability. The drive to establish and document wartime deaths often grew from the center's accompaniment programs for affected communities, some of whom made a decision to recover and commemorate their dead.

Although the work was legally framed, requests were not for criminal investigation but for exhumation. In some areas, the center built up a direct

---

105. Pedro Cruz, interview 13 August 2003.

relationship with local justices of the peace, who can order the local forensic service to exhume remains, certify death, and emit the corresponding certificate. But criminal liability is not thereby established or investigated. The center more often pursued its goals administratively and politically than by litigation. Flaws in the present administrative system mean both the Fiscalía and magistrates can disclaim responsibility for exhumations, and local forensic services are anyway extremely limited and under-resourced. The center was therefore pushing in the mid-2000s for a legislative project to regulate these matters. It reported resistance from politicians, wary that this might be a back-door attempt to reopen the issue of criminal responsibility (something that was not in fact the case).[106]

Pro-Búsqueda similarly evolved along theme-specific lines in ways that used legal system and structures only secondarily, and for purposes other than accountability. There are two main types of legal recourse involved in Pro-Búsqueda's work. The first is a tailor-made procedure to restore original identities, names, and birth documents to traced children. After 2000, this procedure was carried out via direct contact with the Procuraduría General de la República (Procuraduría),[107] bypassing the courts. The second type, a request for investigation, is oriented toward the locating of children and not the investigation or punishment of the acts by which they disappeared. According to staff member Sandra Lovo, "we have privileged the concept of 'the right to truth' rather than the right to justice, not because we want to downplay the importance of justice but because of how we interpret prevailing conditions and possibilities in this country. If we had stuck to demanding criminal justice I think we would have found many fewer than the 200-plus children we have traced so far."[108]

Pro-Búsqueda's experience is that relatives also privilege the location of children over the punishment of perpetrators. Recent Inter-American Commission submissions should also be interpreted in this light. Sandra Lovo considered that families' attitudes were shaped by a generally negative experience of the legal system, by their particular socioeconomic profile, and by the shape of the transition process. She drew a contrast with Argentina, where the issue of abducted children has been central to a recent revival of accountability activity: "The families I know here are mostly *campesinos* [peasant

---

106. Roxana Marroquín and Claudia Interiano, interviews 20 June 2003.

107. The Procuraduría is a subdivision of the Public Ministry, responsible for legal protection and defense whereas its counterpart, the Fiscalía, oversees criminal prosecutions.

108. Sandra Lovo, interview 9 June 2003.

farmers], whereas those I met in Argentina were middle-class professionals. The transition process was so different also: in Argentina [in 1999] human rights groups seemed to be recovering strength, whereas here the movement was snuffed out after the [peace] accords. Here, there has been lot of official emphasis on *olvido* [forgetting] and on forgiveness; and the FMLN has been kept quiet by the government harping on about how both sides violated human rights." Accordingly Pro-Búsqueda, like the Centro Madeleine Lagedec, seemed to place more faith in legislative than direct legal strategy.[109] In the early 2000s it invested considerable energy in pressing for the setting up of a national multisectoral commission to search for disappeared children. Although right-wing legislators rejected initial proposals in a 1999 vote, such a commission was finally established in late 2004.[110]

RESORT TO INTERNATIONAL LAW BY DOMESTIC ACCOUNTABILITY ACTORS

The restructuring of codes and training during judicial reforms means that national legal codes implemented since 1998 in El Salvador generally match or explicitly incorporate international standards,[111] while judges and prosecutors alike ought to be familiar with the relevant precepts. Additionally, Article 144 of the constitution specifically establishes a hierarchical presumption in favor of ratified international treaty law. Nonetheless, attempts to cite international law in domestic courts have met with little success. The Supreme Court's amnesty law decision of 2000 rejected a literalist interpretation of Article 144, insisting that international norms could not "become controlling parameters of the Constitution."[112]

Pedro Cruz described international law as one important source of case argument.[113] Nonetheless, IDHUCA's attempts to invoke international norms

---

109. Although a founding member of Pro-Búsqueda was the plaintiff in the Serrano case before the Inter-American Court.

110. On 7 October 2004, an executive decree established the Comisión Interinstitucional de Búsqueda de Niños y Niñas Desaparecidas a Consecuencia del Conflicto Armado en El Salvador. Relatives' groups criticized the commission for including representatives of perpetrator-linked institutions, including the Ministry of Defense and present-day police force. The cooperation of such institutions was, however, arguably necessary for the commission to have any real prospect of success. More cogently, the exclusion of civil society groups such as Pro-Búsqueda was also identified as reducing its credibility and likely effectiveness.

111. According to FESPAD (2002, 59–64).

112. Ruling of the Sala Constitucional of the Supreme Court of Justice, dated 26 September 2000; author's translation, on file with author.

113. Pedro Cruz, interview 27 June 2003.

against prescription or amnesty in domestic Jesuit case claims were rejected by both the courts and the Fiscalía. Camelia Cartagena was accordingly more skeptical, believing that international law was still not given due importance by courts or indeed by lawyers, reluctant to rely on still weakly established principles.[114] Antonio Cañas of the United Nations Development Programme had this to say about authorities and accountability actors alike: "El Salvador has been navel-gazing in recent years, paying no attention to the impact of the international scene or international developments at the national level."[115]

USE OF REGIONAL AND INTERNATIONAL MECHANISMS

El Salvador was the subject of almost unprecedented levels of international scrutiny, intervention, and attention during the 1980s and through the peace process. National HROs invested much energy in the supply of documentation to outside groups, including the UN Human Rights Committee. UN resolutions critical of continued patterns of human rights abuse became almost commonplace over the decade. Resort was also made to the Inter-American Commission. The issue of enforceability was, however, a key drawback for national groups assessing what outside instances they might most effectively target given limited resources and the urgency of change. The perception that national authorities, particularly the military, were relatively impervious to international censure but dependent on U.S. favor was crucial in the prioritization of lobbying activities directed at the United States. Even after the 1984 accession of Duarte, when the national government seemed to become more sensitive to its international reputation, U.S. policy remained determinant; the leverage exerted by regional and international institutions was accordingly secondary.

As regards use of the Inter-American system in recent times, despite a modest spike after the Serrano verdict, submission of individual cases is complicated by many of the same evidentiary and access issues that have derailed domestic justice efforts. Claimants who cannot demonstrate that they have already exhausted domestic remedies are technically (though not, in practice, invariably) unable to use the Inter-American system at all. Since access to domestic justice was and remains so narrow, many potential claimants thus find it difficult to resort to regional mechanisms. Nonetheless, as we have seen, in the late 1990s the Inter-American Commission made major critiques

114. Camelia Cartagena, interview 15 August 2003.
115. Antonio Cañas, interview 22 July 2003.

of Salvadorean state action and inaction. It also began to hand cases up to the Inter-American Court, although El Salvador's tardy acceptance of jurisdiction continues to present a serious obstacle.[116]

The breakthrough Serrano case benefited from a number of specific features that reduced its value as a precedent. It represented one of few domestic incidents where previous legal action could be proven.[117] Additionally, the prohibition on incidents occurring before 1995 was overcome by treating the case as one of disappearance.[118] The government nonetheless argued, and at least one Court judge agreed, that disappearance still did not trigger jurisdiction where it had occurred before 1995. The optimism with which the Serrano verdict was received may prove to be more than anything a symptom of the lack of progress in other channels. The attitude of the government to previous damning Commission reports veered between dismissal and robust defiance (see, inter alia, Popkin 2004). Even though Court findings theoretically carry more weight, the Serrano verdict had to be followed up with repeated exhortations before any compliance was seen.

Even when compliance can be secured, its justice dimension essentially consists of little more than a promise to reintroduce the case to the existing, demonstrably accountability-hostile, domestic investigatory system. Nonetheless, the fate of post-Serrano cases presented by Pro-Búsqueda is likely to be closely watched by those anxious to find alternative accountability routes, at least while domestic claims continue to founder under the combined weight of amnesty—theoretically reversible—and prescription, highly unlikely to be reversed. CODEFAM accordingly opined that "this case plus the [domestic] Jesuit case are our best hope for unblocking the judicial system over accountability."[119]

In sum, IDHUCA was the main and on many counts virtually the sole viable domestic accountability actor in mid-2000s El Salvador. Although not the only HRO using the legal system, it was the only one using it explicitly for accountability purposes. IDHUCA operated a "leading case" logic with

---

116. The prohibition on retrospective action over pre-accession crimes is not unique, and the Court has generally dealt with it by punishing only the ongoing aspects of earlier crimes (such as continued denial of access to justice). In its absolute determination to keep war-era crimes out of the Court's purview, the Salvadorean government, however, argues for a particularly maximalist interpretation in which no action can be taken unless the original crime on which the complaint is based itself occurred after accession.

117. Since the family had reported the disappearances on their 1993 return from forced exile.

118. The Inter-American Court accepted the same argument enshrined in the Inter-American Convention on Forced Disappearance and recently admitted by Chilean domestic courts: that disappearance constitutes an ongoing crime until the whereabouts of the victim are established.

119. Armando Pérez Salazar, interview 16 July 2003.

the Jesuit murders, hoping to open the way for the bringing of subsequent claims over incidents such as El Mozote. But IDHUCA's litigation strategy was cumulative, contemplating all possibilities, including the use of outside venues. Although deferring direct use of transnational spaces, IDHUCA established ties with the CJA and other third-country groups over incidents including the Jesuit case.[120] Transnational action over this particular incident, however, risks replicating the "big case" strategy that plagued ineffective accountability efforts during the war. The very things that make the Jesuit case an obvious candidate for transnational activity also reduce its replicability. Even if the case were reopened at the national level, it would then risk becoming one more in El Salvador's history of exceptionalist solutions.

In its attempts to break open the domestic setting, IDHUCA additionally faces higher national barriers than any of the Chilean HROs. These include a more unforgiving institutional context and the relative weakness of the HRO community. IDHUCA also has few significant national allies, with the organizations behind U.S. civil claims having as yet established only weak domestic links. If Epp (1998) is correct, and "rights revolutions" depend to a large extent on a service sector of lawyers and organizations that can provide support structures for advocacy and claim-making, IDHUCA may prove simply unequal to the task of single-handedly carving out a new accountability scenario. The 2009 alternation to an FMLN presidency is unlikely to usher in immediate policy change over an amnesty that continues to protect the historic FMLN leadership. The best hope may therefore be for a gradual transformation of institutional—prosecutorial or judicial—contexts that, as in Chile, eventually brings about almost-unnoticed crossover to a point where accountability becomes possible. The matter of effective demand would then return to the fore.

Conclusions

This chapter has shown El Salvador's post-transitional accountability scene to be radically different from Chile's, with visible domestic accountability progress virtually absent in El Salvador. Even before the post-1998

---

120. Although it endorsed this practice in terms that present it as primarily a threat to encourage domestic progress rather than as an imminent reality. See, for instance, ECA (2000a, 1111): "the international community cannot substitute for the functions of a local judicial system. . . . Cases in external courts . . . contribute relatively little to essential national processes [of change]" (author's translation).

breakthroughs in Chile, the contrast was stark. In Chile a fairly unpropitious post-transitional setting did not snuff out legal action, which had long been an established human rights response. In El Salvador, by contrast, transitional amnesty virtually extinguished legally framed accountability claims for most of the subsequent decade. There was, of course, much less of an existing legal tradition to begin with: El Salvador's radically different opportunity structure had produced a pre-transition human rights response that privileged external political lobbying over virtually unavailable, and anyway highly dysfunctional, domestic legal channels. From 1992, with peace negotiations over, legal channels might have been expected to open. Externally sponsored reforms to security and even judicial institutions, although incomplete, were certainly reasonably extensive by comparison with Chile. The means, motive, and opportunity for such change to be manifested in accountability outcomes, however, were much more restricted.

At the level of actors, the apparent evaporation of widespread justice demands after the peace accords in El Salvador was, if anything, remarkably complete. Either the premium placed on ending war was so urgent, or the prospect and promise of accountability so remote, that justice claims over HRVs were not strongly generated and did not find public echo. The actor scene is therefore relatively sparsely populated. Major political forces remained not only indifferent to accountability but actively committed to the preservation of amnesty, and no outlying, extra-parliamentary political party existed to play a role akin to that of the Chilean PC in championing the issue. The military, for its part, virtually disappeared from public political view in postwar El Salvador, but formal political continuity—in particular, the continued political strength of ARENA—was also inimical to accountability change.

This continuity directly affected the structure as well as the climate of the accountability debate: the post of *fiscal* general consistently went to incumbents hostile to accountability efforts. The PDDH, the only institutional actor sympathetic to the cause, struggled to find recognition in official circles or even strong allies among civil society organizations. Mid-2000s El Salvador thus seemed to present a stagnant domestic situation, with little potential for endogenous accountability change. It could therefore be seen as the perfect candidate for "boomerang" strategies—domestic actors going outside to indirectly cause national change—or even pure "transnationalism"—wholly external legal intervention that irrupts decisively onto the national scene, as the Pinochet arrest was said to have done in Chile. In point of fact, however, determined early efforts at internationalized legal activity over El Salvador had little discernible domestic impact, even meeting with a certain indifference from HROs and relatives' organizations.

As far as strategy is concerned, human rights organizing, much of which was practically and ideologically tied to the guerrilla forces during the war period, found it correspondingly more difficult to sustain independent momentum and a clear anti-amnesty message in the postwar period. Effective, consistent, legally framed actor pressure thus continued to be absent after transition. Indeed, accountability action has been virtually the preserve of a single institution, IDHUCA. Although the post-2000 period saw stirrings of renewed interest and regional case claims, these were restricted to rather narrow circles and did not acquire the very public notoriety of similar, and much more extensive, activities in Chile. Accountability remained a minority interest in El Salvador, even among human rights organizations. In the absence of a historic community of human rights lawyers, national HROs had little tradition or habit of legal claim-making or strategic coordination.

Structural and systemic considerations also help to explain a lack of visible movement. If it is difficult to see where the impulse for domestic accountability change could come from in present-day El Salvador, it is equally difficult to discern any signs of fertile institutional ground where new initiatives might take root. In keeping with the forward-looking emphasis and "fresh start" rhetoric embraced in government circles after the peace accords, Rubén Zamora and David Holiday (2007) suggested that the very term "accountability" was redefined over the 1990s to refer almost exclusively to issues of financial corruption and common criminality. Accordingly, the domestic accountability landscape as regards past HRVs remained virtually barren. Despite major structural changes in the justice sector, judicial adaptation was patchy and did not produce accountability shifts. The amnesty principle, when directly tested judicially, escaped virtually intact. Case-by-case judicial change, moreover, remained an untested phenomenon as claims stayed trapped in the bottleneck of the heavily politicized and unreceptive Fiscalía. Thus domestic legal, institutional, and legislative space for accountability claims is severely curtailed. The justice system remains incapable of, and apparently uninterested in, effecting accountability change in the face of significant political disincentives or social indifference.

In sum, El Salvador's post-transitional accountability trajectory seems to offer few prospects for imminent breakthrough. There is little discernible "push" effect in the shape of private domestic actor pressure, neither consistent nor broad based. Transnational cases have met with a certain amount of success on their own terms. Nonetheless, pathways connecting these cases to the domestic arena are presently few, although the actors behind them have begun to forge closer post hoc links with two domestic HROs. The "missing" factor of improved justice system receptivity, so key for Chile, is compounded by a dearth of domestic actors. The absence of accountability movement in El Salvador thus appears to be at both "supply" and "demand" ends. The prospects for recent political alternation to shift accountability outcomes will depend largely on prevailing views within the FMLN as to whether its own interests are best served by challenging or indeed by helping to preserve the existing edifice of impunity.

8

COMPARATIVE ANALYSIS AND CONCLUSIONS

This book has shown how the adoption of a new conceptual framework, that of post-transitional justice, seems to offer improved prospects for understanding current patterns of change and stasis with regard to transitional human rights settlements in Latin America. The framework has been applied to particular country cases to examine how, and under what circumstances, domestic courts have served as sites of contention where individual justice claims or wider political objectives regarding the legacy of past HRVs have been pursued at some distance from political transition. Consideration firstly of overall domestic histories led us to examine justice claims and the changing set of actors who have pursued accountability prior and subsequent to transition. A second analytical strand considered whether, how, and why actors, their strategies, and judicial receptivity changed over time. This exercise brought the national-international dynamic into focus, allowing for tracking "up and down" domestic, inter-, and supra-national vertices of accountability action. Systematic external intervention favoring domestic progress on accountability was found to be both rare and rarely successful. Domestic factors—in particular, changes in judicial institutions and practices—provided a more reliable indicator of movement or stasis on amnesty and accountability.

This chapter presents the major conclusions for each country setting before proceeding to draw thematic and theoretical conclusions. It is argued that post-transitional justice outcomes are rooted in a combination of the transitional legacy (patterns of human rights organizing and types of transition) and subsequent developments in the actor, strategy, and institutional environments surrounding contestation over justice claims. The impact of international (transnational) intervention in this constellation is also considered.

Finally, the broader theoretical contributions and implications of the post-transitional justice framework are briefly explored.

Comparative Conclusions

In Chile, a strongly "legalistic" human rights response early in the dictatorship provided a useful springboard for a renewal of accountability activity and claim-making in the mid to late 1990s. Despite declining financial and human resources, Chilean human rights organizations can draw on early-acquired legal habits as well as on a strong case universe of multiple HRVs over which previous judicial, as well as denunciatory, action had been taken. Although until recently there was no marked innovation in legal strategy or thinking on the part of Chilean accountability actors, high levels of lawyer persistence and legal continuity were notable features. Although early legal pressure from accountability actors did not result in an immediate judicial response, it provided subsequent logistical advantages for dealing with technical obstacles such as prescription.

The drivers of accountability in Chile have thus been a mixture of this consistent legally framed pressure (albeit of varying intensity), serendipity, actions taken by pro-accountability actors around significant anniversaries, and favorable judicial decisions. This last has been particularly in evidence since the late 1990s, when courts began to reinterpret amnesty legislation to permit full investigation and declared disappearance an essentially non-amnestiable crime. Somewhat surprisingly, judicial change seems to have been pivotal to post-transitional accountability change in Chile, as a relatively unreformed judiciary adopted an activist approach toward this specific rights issue (and this issue alone). While no widespread or general move toward judicial activism has occurred in Chile, accountability progress has been both shored up and made possible by judicial change. This change has included demonstrable, although still modest, advances in recognition by judges of the validity and justiciability of international law.

From 1998 onward, the "Pinochet effect" certainly had an influence on the pace and outcomes of subsequent accountability claim-making in Chile. But the 1998 arrest was not itself the cause of the accountability debate's domestic reemergence. This began instead in the mid to late 1990s, coinciding with the first judicial decisions reinterpreting amnesty. Renewed domestic actor pressure in Chile in the post-1998 period has come from old and new groups. The latter are often consciously pursuing essentially political goals through the courts, due to a perception that the courts are now more responsive to accountability claims than the legislature or executive. Organized groups of survivors, rather than, as previously, groups formed predominantly by relatives of the victims of HRVs, have often taken a much more identifiably political approach to the justice issue. A political dynamic can also be observed in the January 1998 legal action that triggered the recent wave of investigations and claims against Pinochet in the domestic courts. That particular action was sponsored by the Communist Party, which displays a dual identity as both aggrieved "survivor" and the only left-wing party (self-)excluded from the political coalition that negotiated the 1990/91 transition and preserved the 1978 amnesty law.

In addition to hundreds of new criminal claims made against Pinochet and others in the new period, a modest but significant wave of civil claims for compensation were brought against individual perpetrators or the present-day state. New groups also seem keener than older groups to take their claims to the Inter-American Commission on Human Rights. Experts are generally dubious as to the permeability of Chilean institutions—particularly the judicial branch—to pressure exerted in this way, as they are about the openness of the domestic legal setting to invocations of international law. The 2004 Valech commission, related legislative proposals, and recent memorialization activities appeared to reverse previous executive neglect of the justice issue. They can also be read, however, as betraying an executive preference for "soft" policy options, rather than throwing official weight behind private claim-making in the courts. Executive policy over accountability in Chile is shaped by established practices of compromise and caution, or by pressure from the right and the military to honor specific transitional agreements. In particular, there appears to be a general consensus among these actors that the 1978 amnesty law should be preserved. The political right and even the military have begun to distance themselves from overt identification with the figure of Pinochet, as evidenced by their response to 2004 financial scandals. The increasingly indefensible human rights legacy of the dictatorship has undoubtedly been pivotal in this movement, likely to prove the most lasting and significant change of the post-1998 period. The principle of amnesty still appears to be nonnegotiable, however, and judicial innovation on amnesty interpretation has come under pressure from official and other elite sources at various points in the post-1998 "revival."

In El Salvador, a considerably reformed judicial and wider institutional setting has produced virtually no discernible accountability movement in almost two decades. There are certain contingent, structural reasons for this. The reformed postwar justice system gives almost uncontested discretion over prosecutions to the Fiscalía, whose current incumbent has implacably opposed accountability efforts. The reformed justice system in El Salvador also represents a relatively clean break with the past, something that has not favored pro-accountability actions. Improved due process guarantees and attempts to strengthen protection of defendants' rights have also, somewhat ironically, impeded retrospective opening of cases. But there are also more specific, political reasons for the lack of accountability movement in post-war El Salvador. Both major parties in El Salvador have an active interest in the preservation of the transitional amnesty, and the Fiscalía's current attitude derives in large part from the fact that it remains an essentially political appointment.

Apparent political consensus in favor of amnesty in El Salvador reflects domestic and international actor (UN and U.S.) positions at the time of peace negotiations in the early 1990s. The high priority placed on ending a devastating civil conflict meant that many were genuinely prepared to consider amnesty a price worth paying and worth preserving. The particular victim profile of El Salvador's civil war also meant that, although victims were numerous, sustained legal pressure on the transitional justice settlement from relatives and survivors was weaker in El Salvador than in some Southern Cone settings. Crucially, the Salvadorean human rights community never evolved what might be called "legal habits" during the conflict itself. The courts were not even theoretically open to claim-making at that time, and human rights activism focused principally on political lobbying via Washington to end the war.

These circumstances gave rise to a pattern, characteristic in wartime El Salvador, whereby only a very few HRV cases were ever dealt with judicially. Moreover, such judicial treatment as was afforded to these cases tended to be extremely cursory and did not lead to a more generalized opening of judicial channels to human rights claims. Occasional convictions of relatively low-level perpetrators did not, therefore, represent breakthrough judicial precedents. They served as one-off displays, essentially for outside consumption, while impunity remained the general rule. The Jesuit trial of 1991, flawed as it was, nonetheless represented the Salvadorean justice system's finest hour in regard to accountability. No subsequent accountability claims have prospered, and challenges to the constitutionality of the amnesty law have produced no significant or enforceable breakthroughs in judicial interpretation.

Subsequent attempts to reopen the Jesuit case domestically, using it as the thin end of a wedge to allow the beginnings of a cumulative, case-by-case attack on impunity, have so far foundered. This failure can be attributed to a combination of extremely successful gatekeeping by the Fiscalía and the lack of sustained or widespread actor enthusiasm for such initiatives. Additionally, any such case-by-case litigation strategy in El Salvador faces technical obstacles, including prescription due to the almost complete absence of early judicial activity. Finally, El Salvador is the country setting that perhaps most comprehensively gainsays transnational justice enthusiasts. A set of civil claims brought in the U.S. courts, whose initial stated aims included triggering accountability change inside El Salvador, has to date found very little echo among domestic human rights groups. Recent attempts from within El Salvador to access regional mechanisms—specifically the Inter-American Court of Human Rights—aroused more domestic actor optimism, but these efforts have met with an equally negative reception from political and judicial authorities to date.

CHILE AND EL SALVADOR COMPARED THEMATICALLY

Two historical elements are key for understanding Chilean and Salvadorean post-transitional justice outcomes. These are, firstly, the type of human rights organizing that was possible during the respective dictatorship and civil war periods; and, second, the type and political context of transition in each setting.

Human Rights Organizing Histories

The very different outcomes in Chile and El Salvador with regard to post-transitional accountability—high levels in Chile, virtually none in El Salvador—have their roots in the very different pre-transitional spaces that the two settings offered for human rights organizing. In Chile, legal strategies formed a significant part of domestic HRO responses to repression from very early on. El Salvador provides an illuminating counter-case, where legal activity either could not or did not become the primary response to HRVs. Human rights organizing in El Salvador was secondary to the logic of armed political conflict. It was also highly shaped by reference to the United States—to the point, indeed, of being mostly carried out there. Lobbying activities in the United States were possible, whereas in-country organizing and legal activity often were not. Thus, despite an extensive and internationally brokered

Table 3   Transitional and Post-transitional Justice in Chile and El Salvador

Chile	El Salvador
Transitional Justice	**Transitional Justice**
Transition	*Transition*
Internally pacted in 1990 after military dictatorship (1973–90)	UN-supervised accords in 1991–92 after 1980–92 civil war
Transitional truth measures	*Transitional truth measures*
Rettig commission report, Feb 1991	Truth commission report, Mar 1993
National commission	UN-sponsored, external commissioners
Focused on deaths or disappearance	Focused on paradigmatic cases
Did not name perpetrators	Named some perpetrators
Publication overshadowed by May assassination of right-wing politician Jaime Guzmán	Recommendations theoretically binding
	Called for Supreme Court mass resignation
Amnesty law	*Amnesty law*
Military self-amnesty law, Decreto 2.191 of 18 Apr 1978	Ley de Amnistía General para la Consolidación de la Paz, Decreto 486, 20 Mar 1993
Letelier assassination specifically exempted	Genuinely (if unequally) benefited both sides
Transitional accountability (justice) measures	Extinguished civil as well as criminal liability
Letelier case reopened at Aylwin's initiative, 1991	*Transitional accountability (justice) measures*
Attempt to have amnesty law reinterpreted to permit investigation ("Aylwin Doctrine") resisted by judges	Some military purges
	Early (1993) release under amnesty of only HRV-convicted officer (Jesuit case, 1992)
Post-transitional Milestones	**Post-transitional Milestones**
Domestic	*Domestic*
1993: Contreras and Espinoza convictions for Letelier killing	Mar 2000: IDHUCA attempts to have the Jesuit case reopened by accusing ex-president Cristiani and others of intellectual authorship
Jan 1998: First criminal complaints against Pinochet	Sep 2000: Supreme Court verdict: 1997/98 challenges to amnesty law constitutionality fail
Mar 1998: Pinochet enters Senate; acquires immunity	Dec 2003: Victims' monument unveiled
Sep 1998: Poblete-Córdoba verdict: amnesty requires investigation, and disappearance is an ongoing crime	Jan 2004: Supreme Court refuses to reopen Jesuit case
Oct 1998: Pinochet detained in London	
1999–2000: Mesa de Diálogo	
Mar 2000: Pinochet returns to Chile	
Jun and Aug 2000: Pinochet is stripped of immunity for Caravana	
Jan 2001: Pinochet is processed for Caravana	
Apr 2001: Naming of first dedicated HRV case judges	

(*continued*)

Table 3   Transitional and Post-transitional Justice in Chile and El Salvador (*continued*)

Chile	El Salvador
Apr 2003: Contreras sentenced for "amnestiable" disappearance Jun and Aug 2004: Pinochet stripped of immunity again; Cóndor case Jul 2004: Riggs bank scandal Aug 2004: Supreme Court finds Pinochet fit for trial Nov 2004: Valech report released Oct 2006: Almonacid verdict, Inter-American Court Dec 2006: Pinochet dies Oct 2009: First sentence for torture	
Transnational Sep 1998: Pinochet detention in London Nov 2000: Prats case: Argentina asks for extradition; Chile opens a case Oct 2003: CJA case against Fernández-Larios (Caravana) won in United States	*Transnational* June 2002: CJA/LCHR civil case lost in United States July 2002: CJA Romagoza case won in United States Sep 2004: CJA Saravia case won in United States Nov 2005: CJA Carranza case won in United States Mar 2005: Serrano case verdict, Inter-American Court Nov 2008: Complaint filed in Spain for Jesuit murders

institutional overhaul following the peace settlement (which included judicial reform), the Salvadorean amnesty law was apparently the most successful of the whole region in extinguishing accountability. A recent renewal of domestic accountability efforts, in the shape of attempts to revive legal action over the Jesuit killings, has been largely restricted to the initiative of a single actor and has in any case met with only limited success. Transnational efforts, such as recent civil cases in the United States, have nowhere to take root.

Kinds of Transition

Chile's transition was marked by apparent political renewal, with Pinochet replaced by a center-left opposition coalition. Yet no active government accountability agenda was forthcoming, since a heavily pacted transition left subsequent administrations both practically and, it seems, imaginatively

constrained in their approach to the issue. Early setbacks to a reasonably vigorous initial policy meant that although there was some progress on truth, it
was a truth-for-justice dynamic that was established early on. This dynamic
seems to have prevailed through to the present day. Cautious executive and
legislative approaches to accountability and to constitutional issues meant
that Chile's self-amnesty law was preserved intact. They also contributed to a
slow, gradualist approach to institutional reform, including judicial reform.
As far as formal political actors were concerned, only the extra-parliamentary
left, as represented by the Communist Party, elaborated a vocal and consistent pro-accountability agenda during the 1990s.

Unlike its Southern Cone counterparts, El Salvador at transition was effectively facing the challenge of building democratic institutions from scratch.
But high levels of international intervention with a stated democratizing
intent promised, if anything, a swifter and more comprehensive transformation than could have been expected in the case of purely domestically pacted
change. Compared to Chile, little political renewal was evident: the ARENA
party, which presided over the last years of the peace, retained power until
early 2009. Major judicial and other institutional reforms were undertaken
in the early 1990s, however, sponsored and overseen by the UN and other
international players in the peace process. Innovations included a drastic reduction of military strength, police reform, the creation of a human
rights ombudsperson, and the setting of ambitious judicial reform targets.
Initial institutional change in El Salvador was, correspondingly, swifter and
more comprehensive than the much more muted institutional overhaul that
accompanied Chile's gradual transfer of power.

Indeed, this is one of the paradoxes most immediately apparent in a
comparison of the two settings. In Chile, a recalcitrant judiciary in a little-
reformed institutional setting nonetheless began to produce startling levels of
change over accountability in the late 1990s. In El Salvador, site of one of the
earliest experiments of the international community in peace brokerage and
institutional engineering, significant levels of judicial change have produced
virtually no visible accountability impact.

Very different transitional patterns thus produced mixed, and sometimes counterintuitive, accountability outcomes. El Salvador's institutional
change was initially promising for accountability but did not take root, or
was countermanded, since political continuity allowed the continued blocking of accountability claims. Chile's initial political renewal appeared to be
more favorable to accountability, but incoming politicians did not hold, or
did not play, a strong hand, so continued military influence was allowed to

dampen or quash the accountability impulse. Institutional change in Chile was gradual, but in the event it was the essentially conservative judiciary that shifted first, and apparently furthest, over accountability in the late 1990s.

The Post-transitional Period

Comparing and contrasting Chile and El Salvador in terms of their human rights organizing histories and their particular transitional experiences allows us to begin to see how such legacies underpin the future evolution of account-ability in each setting in comprehensible albeit not entirely predictable ways. In Chile, strong human rights organizing gave rise to pro-accountability pressure, which was able to survive despite the strictures of a heavily pacted transition. After transition, accountability actors were therefore reasonably well placed to take advantage of subsequent institutional change. In El Sal-vador, by contrast, historically weak human rights organizing, faced with almost nonexistent legal opportunities, could not significantly evolve after transition. On the one hand institutional change signaled rupture—and thus abandonment of wartime issues and claims—and, on the other, it favored the continued influence of those political forces with a strong interest in pre-serving impunity. The following sections examine in more detail comparative actor, strategy, and institutional aspects of accountability change or continu-ity in the post-transitional period.

The Accountability Actor Scene After Transition

El Salvador arguably had few accountability actors, in the strict sense, in both the pre- and post-transitional periods, since many HROs—perceiving a negative opportunity structure for legal claims—pursued alternative legis-lative or campaigning goals outside the courts. By contrast, more of Chile's pre-transitional HROs could and can still be accurately described as pursu-ing an active accountability agenda through the courts. Nonetheless, even in Chile accountability claim-making became the preserve of a few in the post-transitional period, a time when HROs in both countries became resource-poorer and experienced reduced levels of international networking interest and support. Although the accountability actor scene remains extremely sparsely populated in El Salvador, in Chile it saw an influx in the late 1990s of new actors responding to domestic and third-country success in having crim-inal complaints against Pinochet and others upheld. Additionally, in Chile one political actor—the PC—has supported the accountability agenda, both in its own right and through the main relatives' group, the AFDD, by organiz-ing around events such as the twenty-fifth and thirtieth coup anniversaries and the accession of Pinochet to the Senate. In El Salvador, by contrast, no political actor has consistently pushed for accountability.

The Resulting Strategic Environment

The environment in Chile for accountability claim-making is in many senses more developed than in El Salvador. A previous case universe exists in Chile, and despite the persistence of amnesty some legal obstacles have been evaded or at least temporarily surmounted. The historical choice of legal strategy in preference to other possible mechanisms for human rights activism was heavily influenced by cost-benefit analyses and perceptions of likely success. Other factors also contributed to this choice, and legal channels were habitually used in Chile even at times when no positive outcomes were likely. Nonetheless the adoption of a long-term perspective, plus the relatively minor risk of immediate retaliation, made use of the courts a particularly logical strategy choice for HROs. More recently, increased resort to legal strategies was partly driven by "success breeding success," as the judiciary seemed to outperform political institutions in resolving justice claims. The possibility of overloading the judicial system, risking stagnation or even reversal of recent progress, has been recognized but not, perhaps, otherwise managed by lawyers and HROs.

The particular legal strategy followed in Chilean accountability actions often varied according to HRV type and individual (lawyer) idiosyncrasy. Nevertheless, the three principal legal obstacles of amnesty, *cosa juzgada,* and prescription have been tackled in broadly similar ways for many years. Early (1973–74) resort to international law was restricted to use of the Geneva Conventions to invoke wartime protection for prisoners. In more recent claims international law has been cited more often, although both human rights lawyers and relevant experts note continuing limits on the Chilean judicial system's openness to international standards and jurisprudence. A reluctance to launch a direct challenge to the constitutionality of the amnesty law derives from the strategic calculation that there is a high risk of a negative outcome: lawyers and other accountability actors fear that the existing law would only be reaffirmed or strengthened. Accountability actors were skeptical about the likelihood that either the Supreme Court or the legislature would overturn the amnesty law, even after the 2006 promise of an interpretive bill. Accordingly, individual cases and claims have been generated or pursued in an apparently haphazard fashion. This could, however, be interpreted as the essentially strategic use of a cumulative, attritional approach. The risks of producing overload are perhaps weighed against the view that avoiding an all-or-nothing legal onslaught may effect change "under the radar" of possible opponents. Innovations such as civil claims against the state have nonetheless already provoked defensive official reactions, as they touch directly on state economic interests.

El Salvador's few accountability actors have struggled to establish themselves in a much less permissive climate than that prevailing in Chile. Thus the first and most notable legacy of the Salvadorean wartime context was to dissuade potential claimants from the very adoption of legal recourse as a strategy. Those who do wish to use judicial routes have attempted to surmount the principal legal obstacle by having the amnesty law ruled unconstitutional. A minor victory in the shape of a September 2000 Supreme Court ruling that theoretically opens the way for certain prosecutions has not subsequently been tested. Moreover, even if more structural receptivity could be achieved, whether in the Fiscalía or within the judicial branch, very real practical hurdles remain, such as prescription problems and a lack of courtroom-quality proof. Efforts by Salvadorean HROs to resort to regional mechanisms and to explore the possibilities of transnational criminal action appear essentially as a triumph of hope over experience, since a history of official rejection of external censure offers no real grounds for optimism.

This apparently indeterminate impact of regional mechanisms on state behavior is one obvious similarity between the two settings. Domestic actors in both countries who used or considered using such mechanisms were far from convinced about the utility or enforceability of the resulting rulings and reports, even though they continued to count them as a strategic alternative. Another similarity in strategic thinking was a strongly expressed preference for domestic, rather than transnational or regional mechanism cases. Outside cases of either type were often, therefore, seen as a last resort or primarily as a "threat" used to indirectly prompt the judicial receptivity, or political will, considered necessary for domestic prosecutions to prosper. A third similarity was the perceived lack of national judicial enthusiasm for, or even full understanding of, arguments based on international law, whether being invoked in individual cases or to argue against the validity of amnesty laws per se. Finally, actors in both countries spoke of legal strategies as principally a means for retrospectively taking advantage of perceived judicial or political change. Few actors viewed their particular strategic choices as instrumental in driving lasting judicial change, although more saw the judicial setting as a possible channel for influencing medium-term executive policy preferences.

Judicial Receptivity/Justice System Issues

Judicial receptivity is one of various possible drivers of post-transitional accountability. It has been argued in this book that in Chile it was pivotal, providing the impetus to restore movement to a "gridlocked" accountability scene, formerly characterized by actor pressure held in check by political ambivalence and military defensiveness. Improved judicial receptivity to accountability claims was preceded in Chile by gradual judicial reform: in particular, by Supreme Court replacement. Hence consideration of the Chilean experience in isolation might suggest that judicial reform is a necessary, if not sufficient, condition for accountability progress. Judicial reform and judicial accountability changes in Chile, however, were not intentionally or explicitly causally connected. The aims of judicial reform did not include the promotion of a pro-accountability or pro-rights agenda. Judicial performance to date on accountability has been significantly at variance with performance on other liberal-democratic rights issues, such as freedom of speech. The possibility of forward linkages, or multiplier effects, emerging from recent Chilean judicial change on accountability will repay further investigation, much in the same way that scholars such as Hilbink and Huneeus have recently addressed its underlying causes. For the present, however, it can be argued that pressure exerted and legal strategies adopted by accountability actors in Chile were unable to produce favorable accountability case outcomes until they were matched in the mid-1990s by judicial change. This change served in turn to increase actor demand, since it enhanced the perceived likelihood of a satisfactory outcome to legal action.

In El Salvador, some HROs do perceive a limited increase in the Supreme Court's openness toward accountability claims. This perception is, however, mostly fuelled by the entry to the bench of judges associated with the human rights community. It has not yet been tested at the level of individual cases. Actor perception of judicial shifts will, moreover, remain untested for as long as accountability claims continue to be first filtered through self-limiting HROs and then comprehensively blocked by the Fiscalía. In this sense, although some aspects of judicial reform or replacement initially appeared promising, in overall terms justice system reforms have proved (for the time being) hostile to prospects for successful accountability claims in postwar El Salvador.

Both performance and perception of performance on accountability are, moreover, affected by previous institutional histories in each setting. The contrast in prior expectations of the justice sector in both countries is instructive.

High levels of initial legal response in Chile were driven in part by perceptions of a functional system temporarily made unresponsive for specific ideological reasons. In El Salvador, by contrast, one human rights activist spoke for many when she declared: "We've never believed in the courts, in justice" (Alicia García, interview 5 August 2003). The combination of perceived and real historical limitations on judicial capacity with the type and depth of posttransitional judicial change help to explain why Chile, despite experiencing a less thoroughgoing transformation of its judicial apparatus, has nonetheless experienced more favorable judicial change over the issue of accountability.

Moreover, both judicial systems have long been characterized—albeit to different degrees—as susceptible to direct political manipulation or as unduly deferent to executive policy preferences. Although the Chilean judiciary at times exceeded or ignored political signals urging moderation, it has to date kept its pro-accountability change within the bounds of the restrictive 1978 amnesty statute. In addition, in early 2005 the Supreme Court attempted to set a six-month upper time limit for the processing of ongoing cases, essentially the same kind of "guillotine" measure that the executive has also periodically tried to introduce since 1991. El Salvador's judiciary is essentially powerless in the matter of individual cases as long as the Fiscalía stands in the way. Nonetheless, the Salvadorean justice system as a whole clearly supports ARENA's vigorous anti-accountability stance, as evidenced by the political direction of Fiscalía appointments as well as by the Supreme Court's 2000 constitutionality ruling on the 1993 amnesty law.

The Impact of Transnational Activity

Transnational accountability action from the late 1990s was clearly not enough by itself to kick-start domestic accountability in these cases. Only Chile has been the setting or source for successful claims at both transnational and domestic levels, while transnational civil claims over El Salvador have not to date been matched by significant domestic change. One possible conclusion is that a strong preexisting accountability actor community improves the chances that transnational activity will have a domestic impact—or, more probably, that the existence of such a community is a prerequisite for such an outcome. The precise effect of the Spanish case against Pinochet on the outcomes of domestic cases in the Chilean courts after 1998 is a moot point, and is indeed impossible to establish. It may well have been an additional influence on Chilean judges faced with subsequent accountability case decisions. Since most domestic judges deny any connection, however, the nature of that influence remains a matter for conjecture. Overall the Pinochet case can more plausibly be held to have contributed to the destruction of Pinochet personally as a political force, not least by making clear within Chile the extent of international opprobrium for the would-be "elder statesman."

The experience of El Salvador, meanwhile, supports the contention that domestic progress on accountability cannot be achieved by transnational activity alone. Admittedly, Salvadorean transnational activity has so far had a much lower profile than that enjoyed by the Spanish case against Pinochet. The recent Spanish case for the Jesuit murders may yet gain some traction, and yet it does not promise a single, instantly identifiable face of repression whose detention might be likely to spark a media frenzy analogous to that triggered by the Pinochet case. Completed U.S. cases over El Salvador to date have moreover been civil rather than criminal, awakening less media interest in the host venue despite the fact that actions have centered on high-profile incidents, raising major question marks over U.S. policy and intervention. Some of the actors behind these claims harbored specific hopes of triggering a domestic domino effect. Yet there has to date been minimal domestic impact beyond very specific institutional contacts between two Salvadorean organizations and the U.S.-based CJA. This suggests, perhaps, that national and transnational accountability activity can only become mutually reinforcing where both are already established.

Theoretical Implications

This book has traced accountability histories in post-transitional Chile and El Salvador. It has analyzed who is acting in these cases and with what objectives, identified factors that contribute toward the presence or absence, success, or failure of long-term accountability strategies, and tested the assertion that transnational networks can produce "demonstration" or "domino" effects in which third-country prosecutions spur domestic judicial activity. It has argued that the existence of previous legal experience and strategic awareness among domestic accountability actors, plus changed domestic judicial receptivity, are particularly significant factors shaping post-transitional accountability trajectories. Little evidence was found of international initiatives having a discernible national impact where one of these factors was absent. It can therefore be concluded that post-transitional justice trajectories are primarily internally driven. Transnational initiatives, although occasionally successful in their own right, have shown themselves unable to interrupt or foreshorten domestic post-transitional trajectories to the extent of independently creating favorable accountability conditions.

Although transitional trade-offs certainly matter, it seems that they do not inevitably determine subsequent movement over accountability. Apparently unpropitious transitional conditions such as those prevailing in Chile can, in certain circumstances, give way to substantial change; while transitions apparently offering greater potential for institutional refounding can provide very little in the way of observable shifts over the interpretation of amnesty legislation or the treatment of accountability claims. Although the form and content of early amnesty legislation are important factors in post-transitional accountability outcomes, so too are wider justice system change and the presence, skill sets, and strategic attitudes of accountability actors. The potential multiplier effects of actor networking, whether at the domestic or international level, may exist in some form. But the content of law and, particularly, the domestic institutional context within which law is interpreted and applied act as real constraints.

Although it is perhaps the transnational facet of post-transitional justice that has hitherto been most visible on the world stage, it is contended here that post-transitional justice happens (or not) according to the presence and relative weight of the other, principally domestic, components the post-transitional justice framework identifies. Nonetheless, since current post-transitional justice claims are made within a context where there are certain enhanced possibilities for transnational action, transnationalism is one possible expression of the ongoing search for accountability for past HRVs. Transnationalism properly understood should thus be considered as one form, rather than an essential or constitutive element, of post-transitional justice. It might even be argued that transnational justice is properly epiphenomenal: that is, it cannot "really" happen, or take practical effect, unless it grows out of existing national actions and demand (rather than being copied from other transnational actions). The fact that such copying has taken place—particularly, as we have seen, in the United States—may serve only to increase the possibility of mismatched or patchy accountability action, in which external change is neither indicative of nor necessarily conducive to domestic accountability progress (El Salvador would appear to be a case in point).

The analytical framework of post-transitional justice adopted in this book can profitably be applied to other settings, whether in Latin America or beyond. Grounded in domestic accountability trajectories and legal repertoires, this approach offers a useful starting point for a critical examination of claims about the operation of globalized activism or transnational "civil society networks." It allows for observation of the effects of global activism on local systems and settings and, conversely, of the contributions and constraints that local opportunity structures, framing discourses, and political contexts transmit to the inter- or supra-state level. The observable re-irruption of accountability pressures after transition, and the theoretical framework presented here for understanding it, signal the analytical and practical significance of the use civil society groups make of law, and the importance of the law as an arena of state-citizen interaction in democracies. It thus contributes to a political perspective on law and the social uses of law, a growing but still-neglected field of inquiry.

Future work should seek to refine and develop the post-transitional justice framework further through its application to other country settings. Argentina presents itself as an obvious and intriguing choice: the addition of political will to the accountability mix in recent years is coming to be viewed as a mixed blessing by some private actors and HROs. Guatemala, the last in the early wave of Latin American transitions, escaped overt blanket amnesty but demonstrated for many years the equivalent or greater ability of de facto powers to preserve impunity through informal and illegal channels, including continued violence and selective assassination. The interaction of Spanish and Guatemalan venues in sending accountability cases back and forth from venue to host country since 2000 also promises to offer further insights into this dimension of post-transitional justice. Peru, the region's first transitional country of the new millennium, offers unique conditions—such as the predominance of non-state actors in fatal political violence—which may offer useful lessons for possible future cases, including Colombia. The state-led prosecution of former autocrat Alberto Fujimori in his own country for human rights and corruption crimes stands for what Chile never quite achieved, and may offer insights into whether institutional strengthening can be a product of, and not just a prerequisite for, accountability change. It has become a commonplace to remark on the negative effects of 9/11 on the prospects for minimally credible international justice. Nonetheless, the retreat from effective multilateralism does perhaps make it more urgent to pay sustained attention to what Latin America is now teaching us about delivering late, but local, responses to atrocity.

APPENDIX A: TRANSITIONAL JUSTICE IN SELECTED LATIN AMERICAN COUNTRIES

Country	Truth Commission	Mandate and Powers	Other Measures	Amnesty Law
ARGENTINA Transition via government collapse in 1983 after military dictatorship (1976–83)	**Comisión Nacional sobre la Desaparición de Personas (CONADEP)** Established by presidential decree, 15 Dec 1983 Dates of work: Dec 1983–Sep 1984 Report: "Nunca más," Nov 1984 Names of perpetrators were supposedly confidential. Passed all information to courts Named approximately 9,000 victims of death or disappearance A higher figure of 30,000, which later gained wide currency, is an estimate by relatives' associations and human rights groups	Investigate 1976–83 HRVs; document disappearance and kidnapping in that period Could require information, documents, and access to buildings from any public servant or member of the security forces Legal framework not specified Many of 1,300 written requests to the security forces went unanswered	Televised trial of nine junta members in 1985 1986 and 1987 amnesty measures: Prosecutions suspended and presidential pardons given Some financial reparations for forced exile and to relatives of the disappeared	Military self-amnesty annulled by Law 23.040, Dec 1983 Subsequently introduced: Ley de Punto Final, 23 Dec 1986, and Ley de Obediencia Debida, 5 June 1987 Status: Annulled by legislature Aug 2003, with retroactive effect
URUGUAY Transition via elections in 1984 after military dictatorship from 1973 (effective self-coup: civilian government handed power to military)	**(1) Comisión Investigadora sobre la Situación de Personas Desaparecidas y Hechos que la Motivaron (official)** Dates of work: 1985 (seven-month duration)	Restricted to disappearance, relatively rare	Around transition, none	Pre-transition amnesty for opposition Tupamaro guerrillas. Impunity

Report: "Informe final de la comisión investigadora sobre la situación de personas desaparecidas y hechos que la motivaron," 1985

Reported execution or disappearance of 164 Uruguayan citizens, 80 percent while in exile in Argentina

(2) Servicio de Paz y Justicia (SERPAJ)* (unofficial) (*NGO also active in other countries of the region)

Report: "Uruguay nunca más: Informe sobre la violación a los derechos humanos, 1972–1985," 1989

Excluded much more widespread practices of torture and prolonged detention

Later: Comisión para la Paz created by presidential decree in 2000 to investigate the fate of the remaining disappeared

Final report in 2003 suggested 26 of 28 disappeared Uruguayans, and 5 of 6 Argentinians disappeared in Uruguay, should be considered dead. Recommended reparations, but made no reference to the 1986 amnesty law (Ley de Caducidad)

Prosecution of two former presidents and a small number of former officers, 2009

Financial reparations law passed, 2009

policy agreed between Colorado party and military in "Club Naval" discussions preceding 1984 elections

Ley de Caducidad de las Pretensiones Punitivas del Estado, Law No. 15.848, Dec 1986

Excludes civilians and high command, but allows executive discretion over prosecution

Uniquely, reaffirmed by plebiscite on 16 Apr 1989

Article 4 (never applied) requires investigations

Status: Still in force

New plebiscite in October 2009 did not reach the required majority for repeal

Declared unconstitutional in one case by the Supreme Court in Oct 2009

(*continued*)

Country	Truth Commission	Mandate and Powers	Other Measures	Amnesty Law
CHILE Negotiated transition after 1990 after military dictatorship (1973–90)	**(1) Comisión Nacional de Verdad y Reconciliación ("Comisión Rettig")** Established by presidential Supreme Decree no. 355, 25 Apr 1990 Dates of work: May 1990–Feb 1991 Report: "Rettig Report," Feb 1991 Documented and named victims of disappearance and fatal political violence. Dealt with torture only in general terms Could not name perpetrators. Passed information to the courts about illegal burials or cases already in progress **(2) Comisión Nacional Sobre Prisión Política y Tortura** Established 2003 Report: "Valech Report," Nov 2004	Document gravest HRVs between 11 Sep 1973 and 11 March 1990 Identify and locate victims; recommend reparations and "other measures considered necessary for the purposes of justice and prevention" Legal framework: International human rights law, international humanitarian law, and "other norms relating to the use of force" Could request but not oblige information from private individuals and the armed forces	Reparations (pensions) for relatives of disappeared, financial assistance for returning exiles, medical program for survivors of torture Later: Sep 1998 onward: Renewed trials 1999–2000: Mesa de Diálogo: Military, church representatives, and lawyers met government authorities to recover information about the remaining disappeared 2004: Financial reparations extended to previously excluded relatives of fatal victims (a pension of approx US$170/month) Valech commission reparations (a pension) for named survivors	1978 military self-amnesty, Decreto Ley 2.191 Status: Still in force Reinterpreted from 1998 to allow full investigation 2008: "Interpretive" secondary legislation promised in response to an Inter-American Court finding that the statute contravened international obligations (Almonacid case)

2007: Government accepted reopening of Valech commission lists (7,000 original testimonies had been considered not substantiated enough for initial inclusion)

Nongovernment initiative: Survivors could claim from a compensation fund recovered from Riggs Bank

2009: Government again announced intention to reopen official lists. State memory museum built

Documented and named 28,000 survivors of torture, including 90 children

Did not name perpetrators. Testimonies to be kept secret for fifty years and not submitted to courts

EL SALVADOR

Transition 1991/92 via peace accords after 1980–92 conflict between armed left (FMLN) and a civilian-military government

Comisión de la Verdad

Agreed in principle as part of peace accord negotiations. Composition and caseload left to UN discretion

Report: "From Madness to Hope," Mar 1993

Investigate grave acts of violence since 1980

Consider the need to create public confidence in the peace process

Ad Hoc Commission and military purges, significant military and police restructuring. Introduction of HR ombudsperson (PDDH)

Ley de Amnistía General para la Consolidación de la Paz, Decreto 486, Mar 1993

Passed by majority vote in national assembly

(*continued*)

Country	Truth Commission	Mandate and Powers	Other Measures	Amnesty Law
	UN-sponsored, international composition to promote objectivity and minimize reprisals	Produce (supposedly binding) recommendations for preventive measures and initiatives to promote reconciliation	Reparations largely undelivered, except to ex-combatants	Uniquely, extinguished both criminal and civil liability: Article 4e
	Included violence by non-state forces (the FMLN and right-wing death squads)	Legal framework: International human rights law and international humanitarian law	Later: 2001: Third-country civil cases in the United States since 2001	Previous amnesty laws in 1983, 1987, and 1992 had freed political prisoners and allowed FMLN commanders to participate in peace negotiations and elections
	Named perpetrators for 40 cases examined in depth	Invited but could not compel testimony; offered anonymity but no protection	2003: Serrano sisters case in the Inter-American Court	Status: Still in force
	Recommendations were theoretically binding		2004/5: Nongovernment initiative: Memorial to victims unveiled in a San Salvador park in 2003	1993: Attempted challenges to constitutionality rejected
	Followed three days later by sweeping amnesty law			2008: Salvadorean government defends the amnesty law as the "cornerstone of peace" in an Inter-American Commission hearing

GUATEMALA		Mandate of official commission	Attempted domestic prosecutions	Law / Status
Transition in 1997 after civil war between armed left (URNG) and civilian-military government	**(1) REMHI, Catholic Church (unofficial)** Report: "Guatemala: Nunca Más," presented Apr 1998 by bishop Juan Gerardi	Mandate of official commission: Investigate alleged genocide against the Maya population; disappearance, massacres, and other killings by military and guerrillas; acts of violence by *poderes económicos*; mass forced displacement by the army between Jan 1962 and Dec 1996	Attempted domestic prosecutions under Article 8 to date unsuccessful: include 2000 complaint against Lucas García and 2001 complaint against Ríos Montt (then president of Congress) for genocide and war crimes	Ley de Reconciliación Nacional, Decreto no. 145, 27 Dec 1996
Final peace accord of Dec 1996 incorporated a 1994 Oslo Accords agreement to establish a truth commission	Named 52,000 of 200,000 civilians killed or disappeared; found army responsible for 80 percent			Article 8 excludes serious crimes, as designated by international or specific domestic human rights law
Under the peace accords, both sides had agreed to a general amnesty	Gerardi was murdered two days after publication		Menchú Foundation attempt to bring Spain genocide case rejected in 2000, finally accepted in 2006	This is the only Latin American domestic amnesty law to explicitly recognize international law limitations to its scope
	(2) Comisión de Esclarecimiento Histórico (official) Report: "Memory of Silence," published June 1999, a year after REMHI	Satisfy the "right to truth," "eliminate all types of vengeance or retribution"	June 2001: three soldiers and a priest convicted of Gerardi killing. Convictions overturned in 2002, reinstated in Feb 2003	Status: Still in force
	Dates of work: Aug 1997–Feb 1999	Encouraged but could not compel testimony		
	Found state responsible for over 93 percent of HRVs	Prioritized isolated regions; hearings were secret, anonymity and protection offered to sources		
	Found army responsible for genocide against rural indigenous populations			

(continued)

Country	Truth Commission	Mandate and Powers	Other Measures	Amnesty Law
		No judicial powers but information could be freely used for judicial purposes		
PERU	**Comisión de la Verdad y Reconciliación (CVR)**			
Internal conflict, 1980–2000, between armed left, especially Maoist group Sendero Luminoso, and state security forces	Report: "Informe Final de la CVR," 2003	Investigate political violence between 1980 and 2000 in context of army counterinsurgency war against Shining Path guerrillas	Approx. 45 case dossiers sent to Fiscalía by CVR. Some investigations ongoing, but generally cases have languished	First transitional administration, then Supreme Court, applied Apr 2001 Inter-American Court Barrios Altos verdict to invalidate Fujimori-era (self) amnesties and allow investigations to proceed
	Documented 28,000 but estimated 69,280 deaths between 1980 and 2000, with typical victim an indigenous, illiterate young male. Figure of 69,000 deaths became politically significant—"no-one noticed" the deaths of almost 40,000 people in Peru's remote, and poorest, highland areas	Analyze the political, social, and cultural conditions underlying the conflict	Fujimori named as individually indictable for Grupo Colina; current president García mentioned as having political responsibility for El Frontón prison massacre during his first term as president (1980–85),	Status: No amnesty
President Fujimori, democratically elected 1990, became increasingly authoritarian, then fled country in 2000 after corruption scandal	Recommended collective reparations in indigenous communities.			

Discussed the social and racial fault lines underlying the conflict

but not recommended for prosecution

First commission to find guerrillas responsible for more deaths than state (55.5 percent)

Fujimori detained in Chile in late 2005 and extradited to Peru, at the Peruvian government's request, in Sep 2007. Stood trial in Lima in 2008/9. Convicted in April 2009

Material produced and promoted in all main languages, via video, photo exhibition, and in electronic, book, and newspaper formats

Nongovernment initiative: Monument El Ojo Que Llora installed in a Lima park in 2003. Controversy over inclusion of Senderistas among names of victims. Monument vandalized Sep 2007

García's second administration (2006—) initially refused overseas offers to fund a memory museum, but finally convened a museum commission in 2009

(continued)

Country	Truth Commission	Mandate and Powers	Other Measures	Amnesty Law
PARAGUAY	**Comisión de Verdad y Justicia**			
Unipersonalist dictatorship of Alfredo Stroessner, 1954–1989	Established by Law 2225, Oct 2003	Investigate all serious HRVs by state and "parastate" agents between 1954 and 2003	A few cases were opened after 1989 against Stroessner-era functionaries. Pastor Coronel, head of the political police, was imprisoned but most fled into exile	No formal amnesty legislation
Date of transition is disputed: Stroessner was ousted in a palace coup in 1989, but his Colorado party continued in power until 2008. The Truth Commission investigated HRVs right through to its date of establishment, in 2003	Dates of work: 2004–8 (initial mandate extended in 2005 and 2006) Report: "Informe final: Anive haguã oiko," 2009 Named approximately 396* victims of illegal execution and disappearance, almost a third of whom disappeared in neighboring countries, mainly Argentina. Around 10 percent of disappearances within Paraguay were of foreign nationals.	No juridical status, but was to preserve judicial-standard proof and hand it to the courts Final recommendations included a genetic database, public archive (to complement the "Terror Archive," now housed in the main court building), and some prosecutions	In 1992 an abandoned police archive detailing coordinated Southern Cone repressive activities was discovered (and became known as the Terror Archive)	
Stroessner died in exile in Brazil in 2006	(*The report is internally inconsistent, with a figure of 395 also mentioned. Breakdowns by gender, age, and so forth give further inconsistencies when totalled, but none exceeds 396) Documented 2,691 testimonies of torture and extrapolated to estimate a total of 18,772 victims of the practice		A 2000 financial reparations package prompted some survivors to come forward	

NOTE: Table presented chronologically by date of transition.

APPENDIX B: LIST OF INTERVIEWS

Interview subjects are listed alphabetically within country sections: Chile, El Salvador, United States, Argentina, UK, and Peru. Job titles are at the time of the interview, although former and/or subsequent posts are included where particularly relevant.

Chile

Martin Abregú, Program Officer for Rights and Citizenship, Ford Foundation Office for the Andean Region and Southern Cone; formerly of the Centro de Estudios Legales y Sociales (CELS), Argentina. Santiago, 22 October 2002 and 7 February 2003

Oscar Acuña, Executive Secretary, Council for National Monuments (Consejo de Monumentos Nacionales). Santiago, November 2006

Federico Aguirre, Legal Team Coordinator, Corporación de Promoción y Defensa de los Derechos del Pueblo (CODEPU). Santiago, 24 October 2002, 3 and 7 April 2003, 13 December 2008

Oscar Azócar, Central Committee of the Chilean Communist Party. Santiago, 26 November 2002

Eduardo Bahamondes, Servicio de Paz y Justicia (SERPAJ-Chile). Santiago, 4 September 2003

Pascale Bonnefoy, journalist and human rights researcher. Santiago, 22 January 2003

Delia Bravo, librarian, Chilean Library of Congress; survivor and plaintiff. Santiago, 19 March 2003

Sebastian Brett, researcher, Human Rights Watch Americas Division. Santiago, 15 October 2002

Adil Brkovic, human rights lawyer; former legal director of the Corporación de Promoción y Defensa de los Derechos del Pueblo (CODEPU). Santiago, 23 January 2003 and 8 April 2003

Mariana Cáceres, archivist, Fundación de Documentación y Archivo de la Vicaría de la Solidaridad, Arzobispado de Santiago. Santiago, 4 April 2003

Diego Carrasco, lawyer, Area de Acciones Ciudadanas de Interés Público y Exigibilidad de Derecho, Formación Jurídica para la Acción. Santiago, 27 March 2003

Luciano Carrasco, HIJOS-Chile. Santiago, 5 September 2003 (conversation)

Nelson Caucoto, human rights lawyer, Fundación de Ayuda Social de las Iglesias Cristianas (FASIC). Santiago, 30 October 2002 and 15 November 2002

Carlos Cerda, judge, President, Santiago Court of Appeals. Santiago, 23 October 2002 and 7 November 2002

Alberto Chaigneau, judge, Chilean Supreme Court. Santiago, 6 January 2003

Sergio Concha, human rights lawyer, formerly of the Fundación de Ayuda Social de las Iglesias Cristianas (FASIC); Poblete Córdoba case lawyer. Santiago, 30 January 2003

Thomas Connolly, information officer, Chilean Library of Congress. Valparaíso, 26 December 2002

Eduardo Contreras, human rights lawyer; Communist Party lawyer; Caravana case litigant. Santiago, 3 December 2002 and 18 December 2002

Enrique Correa Ríos, consultant; former member of president Patricio Aylwin's cabinet. Santiago, 22 January 2003

Francisco Cox, lawyer; representative for Argentina, Chile, and Paraguay of the Center for Justice and International Law. Santiago, 28 October 2002

Luz Maria Cuadrado, granddaughter of Carlos Prats. Santiago, 23 January 2003 (conversation)

Viviana Díaz, Agrupación de Familiares de los Detenidos Desaparecidos (AFDD). Santiago, 26 November 2006

Mauricio Duce, law faculty, Universidad Diego Portales (UDP). Santiago, 14 April 2003

Gloria Elgueta, President, Colectivo Londres 38. Santiago, 3 January 2007

Jorge Escalante, journalist and author. Santiago, 11 November 2002

Victor Espinoza, Executive Secretary, Corporación de Promoción y Defensa de los Derechos del Pueblo (CODEPU). Santiago, 20 March 2003

Claudio Fuentes, researcher, Facultad Latinoamericana de Ciencias Sociales (FLACSO-Chile). Santiago, 20 March 2003

Yuri Gahona, HIJOS-Chile. Santiago, 5 September 2003

Magdalena Garcés, lawyer, Programa de Derechos Humanos del Ministerio del Interior. Santiago, 16 December 2008

Mireya García, Vice-President, Agrupación de Familiares de Detenidos Desaparecidos (AFDD). Santiago, 18 November 2002

Roberto Garretón, human rights lawyer, formerly of the Vicaría de la Solidaridad; Regional Representative for Latin America and the Caribbean, Office of the UN High Commissioner for Human Rights; member of the Mesa de Diálogo. Santiago, 10 January 2003 and 21 March 2003, September and November 2004

Alejandro González, retired; former legal director of the Vicaría de la Solidaridad; former director of the Programa de Derechos Humanos del Ministerio del Interior (ex Programa de Continuación de la Ley 19.123; ex Corporación Nacional de Reparación y Reconciliación). Santiago, 14 January 2003

Felipe González, Director, Clínica de Acciones de Interés Público y Derechos Humanos; law faculty, Universidad Diego Portales (UDP). Santiago, 8 September 2003

Hugo Gutiérrez, human rights lawyer. Santiago, 14 November 2002 and 12 March 2003

Juan Guzmán, judge, Caravana and other human rights cases. Santiago, 21 November 2002

Alfonso Insunza, human rights lawyer; Caravana case litigant. Santiago, 13 December 2002

Federico Joannon, editor, *El Mostrador* electronic newspaper. Santiago, 7 November 2002

Milton Juica, judge, Sala Penal, Chilean Supreme Court. Santiago, 6 November 2002

Humberto Lagos, Programa de Derechos Humanos del Ministerio del Interior. Santiago, January 2007

Sergio Laurenti, Director Ejecutivo, Amnesty International, Chile section. Santiago, 20 November 2002

Raquel Lermanda, judge exclusively dedicated to human rights cases (*jueza de dedicación exclusiva*), 9° Juzgado del Crimen de Santiago. Santiago, 16 April 2003

Fabiola Letelier, human rights lawyer; founder and former staff member of the Corporación de Promoción y Defensa de los Derechos del Pueblo (CODEPU). Santiago, 21 January 2003

Elizabeth Lira, Universidad Alberto Hurtado, member of the Mesa de Diálogo; member of the Valech commission. Santiago, August 2001

Maxine Lowy, researcher, Memoria y Justicia project and Web site. Santiago, 12 December 2002

Maria Luisa Sepúlveda, President's Representative, Presidential Commission on Human Rights. Santiago, 3 January 2007

Gladys Marín, President, Chilean Communist Party. Santiago, 20 November 2002

Daniel Martorell, Prats case lawyer for the Consejo de Defensa del Estado (CDE). Santiago, 23 April 2003

Juan Maureira, President, Agrupación de Familiares de Paine. Paine, 26 November 2006

Raquel Mejías, Head of Legal Team, Programa de Derechos Humanos del Ministerio del Interior. Santiago, 17 January 2003

Hugo Montero, Head of Legal Team, Programa de Derechos Humanos del Ministerio del Interior. Santiago, 7 November 2008

Enrique Nuñez, Agrupación de Ex-Presos Políticos de Valparaíso. Valparaíso, 1 September 2003

Roberto d'Orival, President, Colectivo 119, Familiares y Compañeros. Santiago, 21 December 2006

Juan Pavín, human rights lawyer, representative of the American Association of Jurists (Asociación Americana de Juristas). Santiago, 18 March 2003

María Paz Vergara, Executive Secretary, Fundación de Documentación y Archivo de la Vicaría de la Solidaridad, Arzobispado de Santiago. Santiago, 4 April 2003

Alfredo Pérez Esquivel, founder, Servicio de Paz y Justicia (SERPAJ), Argentina. Santiago, 7 November 2002

Sofia Prats, daughter of Carlos Prats, plaintiff in Prats case. Santiago, 7 February 2003

Hernán Quezada, human rights lawyer; plaintiffs' lawyer in the Prats case. Santiago, 13 January 2003

Veronica Reyna, human rights lawyer, Fundación de Ayuda Social de las Iglesias Cristianas (FASIC). Santiago, 10 October 2002 and 16 April 2003

Alfredo Riquelme, Pontificia Universidad Católica de Chile. Santiago, 8 January 2003

Victor Rosas, lawyer; member of the Agrupación Nacional de Ex-Presos Políticos (ANEPP). Santiago, 14 January 2003

Fulvio Rossi, Chair, Chilean Parliamentary Deputies' Commission on Human Rights, Nationality, and Citizenship (Comité Derechos Humanos, Nacionalidad, y Ciudadanía). Santiago, 14 April 2003

Héctor Salazar, human rights lawyer, Fundación de Ayuda Social de las Iglesias Cristianas (FASIC). Santiago, 17 October 2002

Patricia Silva, President, Agrupación de Familiares de Ejecutados Políticos (AFEP). Santiago, 15 October 2002

Juan Subercaseaux, human rights lawyer, member of Caravana case legal team. Santiago, 18 March 2003

Julia Urquieta, human rights lawyer; formerly of the Corporación de Promoción y Defensa de los Derechos del Pueblo (CODEPU); convener of the Asamblea por los Derechos Humanos. Santiago, 5 December 2002

Patricia Verdugo, journalist and author. Santiago, 18 November 2002

Tomás Vial, lawyer, Secretaría General de la Presidencia, División Jurídica. Santiago, 24 October 2002 (conversation)

Hiram Villagra, human rights lawyer, Corporación de Promoción y Defensa de los Derechos del Pueblo (CODEPU); litigant in cases Letelier, Caravana, Cóndor, Colombo, Villa Grimaldi. Santiago, 13 November 2002 and 7 November 2008

José Zalaquett, Co-director, Human Rights Center, Law Faculty, Universidad de Chile; member of the Rettig commission; member of the Mesa de Diálogo. Santiago, 28 November 2002

El Salvador

Chamba Acosta, photographer/archivist. San Salvador, 10 June 2003

Alberto Arene, consultant; former FMLN spokesman in Washington, D.C. San Salvador, 29 July 2003 (conversation)

Argentine Forensic Anthropology Team (Equipo Argentino de Antropología Forense, EAAF). San Salvador, 29 May 2003 (group interview)

Victoria de Avilés, Supreme Court judge; formerly *procuradora* of the Procuraduría para la Defensa de los Derechos Humanos (PDDH). San Salvador, 25 August 2003

Sidney Blanco, judge, Juzgado 5° de Instrucción de San Salvador; formerly state prosecutor (*fiscal*), then plaintiffs' lawyer, in the Jesuit case. San Salvador, 12 June 2003

Antonio Cañas, Program Officer, Area Fortalecimiento del Estado de Derecho, United Nations Development Program. San Salvador, 22 July 2003

Camelia Cartagena, educator in Human Rights, Centro de Formación en ddhh de la UCA; IDHUCA representative on the Comisión Pro-Memoria Histórica. San Salvador, 15 August 2003

Ernesto Chacón, Comisión de Derechos Humanos de El Salvador (CDHES) (nongovernmental). San Salvador, 14 and 18 August 2003

Eugenio Chicas, Parliamentary Deputy for the FMLN in the Central American Parliament. San Salvador, 17 July 2003

Pedro Cruz, lawyer, Instituto de Derechos Humanos de la Universidad Centroamericana "José Simeon Cañas" (IDHUCA); Jesuit case lawyer. San Salvador, 27 June 2003 and 13 August 2003

Benjamín Cuellar, Director, Instituto de Derechos Humanos de la Universidad Centroamericana "José Simeon Cañas" (IDHUCA). San Salvador, 25 June 2003

Héctor Dada, Parliamentary Deputy for the CDU party; formerly of the Facultad Latinoamericana de Ciencias Sociales (FLACSO–El Salvador). San Salvador, 18 July 2003

Alejandro Díaz, lawyer, Tutela Legal. San Salvador, 9 June 2003

Luis Domínguez Parada, Coordinator, Educación Judicial Popular, Supreme Court of Justice. San Salvador, 25 August 2003

Francisco Eliseo Ortíz, judge, Cámara Segunda of Sonsonate; President, Instituto de Estudios Jurídicos de El Salvador (IEJES). San Salvador, 22 July 2003

Nora Franco, journalist, Mujeres y Memoria Histórica. San Salvador, 23 July 2003

Fr. Mauricio Gaborit, S.J., Department of Psychology, Universidad Centroamericana "José Simeon Cañas" (UCA). San Salvador, 13 August 2003

Alicia García, President, Comité de Madres y Familiares de Presos, Desaparecidos y Asesinados Políticos de El Salvador "Oscar Arnulfo Romero" (COMADRES). San Salvador, 5 August 2003

Leonel Gómez; former Moakley commission researcher. San Salvador, 29 July 2003 and 14 and 27 August 2003

Ana Guadalupe Martínez, former FMLN commander; former FMLN peace negotiator. San Salvador, 15 August 2003 (conversation) and 24 August 2003 (interview)

David Holiday, Director, Proyecto de Participación Ciudadana y Gobernabilidad, CREA Internacional de El Salvador; formerly Human Rights Watch (HRW) representative in El Salvador. San Salvador, 21 May 2003

Claudia Interiano, legal team, Centro para la Promoción y Defensa de los Derechos Humanos "Madeleine Lagedec." San Salvador, 20 June 2003

Juan José Dalton, journalist. San Salvador, 27 August 2003

María Julia Hernández, Director, Tutela Legal. San Salvador, 18 June 2003

Marlon López, legal team, Asociación Comité de Familiares de Víctimas de Violaciones a los Derechos Humanos "Marianella García Villas" (CODEFAM). San Salvador, 16 July 2003

Neftalí López, legal team, Comisión de Derechos Humanos de El Salvador (CDHES) (nongovernmental). San Salvador, 18 August 2003

Sandra Lovo, Area Incidencia y Organización, Asociación Pro-Búsqueda de Niñas y Niños Desaparecidos (Pro-Búsqueda). San Salvador, 9 June 2003

José María Méndez, Jr., lawyer. San Salvador, 26 June 2003

Fr. José María Tojeira, S.J., Rector, Universidad Centroamericana "José Simeon Cañas" (UCA). San Salvador, 2 July 2003

Roxana Marroquín, legal team, Centro para la Promoción y Defensa de los Derechos Humanos "Madeleine Lagedec." San Salvador, 20 June 2003

Jaime Martínez, Director, Centro de Estudios Penales de El Salvador (CEPES); Fundación de Estudios para la Aplicación del Derecho (FESPAD). San Salvador, 3 June 2003

Carmen Medina, El Salvador Country Representative, International Cooperation for Development, Catholic Institute for International Relations (now Progressio). San Salvador, 10 June 2003

David Morales, Assistant Procurator, Procuraduría para la Defensa de los Derechos Humanos (PDDH). San Salvador, 18 August 2003

Walter Navarette, Fundación Salvadoreña para la Reconstrucción y el Desarrollo. San Salvador, 2 July 2003

Armando Pérez Salazar, Executive Director, Asociación Comité de Familiares de Víctimas de Violaciones a los Derechos Humanos "Marianella García Villas" (CODEFAM). San Salvador, 16 July 2003

Mirna Perla, Supreme Court judge; formerly of the Comisión de Derechos Humanos de El Salvador (CDHES) (nongovernmental); formerly of the Comisión para la Defensa de los Derechos Humanos en Centroamérica in Costa Rica. San Salvador, 24 July 2003

Gustavo Piñeda, lawyer, Procuraduría para los Derechos Humanos (PDDH). San Salvador, 6 and 17 June 2003

Ovidio Portillo, Head of Section, División para la Defensa de los Intereses de la Sociedad, Fiscalía General de la República. San Salvador, 24 July 2003

Carlos Ramos, researcher, FLACSO–El Salvador. San Salvador, 29 May 2003

José Roberto Burgos, lawyer, Oficina de Procuración de Justicia, Instituto de Derechos Humanos de la Universidad Centroamericana "José Simeon Cañas" (IDHUCA). San Salvador, 12 June 2003

Melvin Tebbutt, Fundación Salvadoreña para la Reconstrucción y el Desarrollo. San Salvador, 29 May 2003

Mauricio Vargas, former general in the El Salvador armed forces; armed forces negotiator for the peace accords. San Salvador, 15 July 2003

Ricardo Zamora, judge, Cámara de la 4a Sección del Centro, Nueva San Salvador; former investigating magistrate in the Romero and Jesuit cases. San Salvador, 31 July 2003 and 14 and 21 August 2003

United States

Sarah Anderson, Institute for Policy Studies (IPS). Washington, D.C., 9 August 2002

Louis Bickford, Senior Associate, International Center for Transitional Justice. New York, 23 July 2002

Patty Blum, Boalt Law School; now Senior Legal Advisor, Center for Justice and Accountability (CJA). 20 November 2002 (telephone interview)

Rafael Cohen, National Security Archive Chile Information Project. Washington, D.C., 6 August 2002

John Dinges, journalist and author. Washington, D.C., 6 August 2002 (telephone interview)

Matt Eisenbrandt, Staff Attorney, Center for Justice and Accountability (CJA). 24 September 2004 (telephone interview)

Priscilla Hayner, Program Director, Research and Technical Assistance, International Center for Transitional Justice. New York, 23 July 2002

Ken Hurwitz, International Justice Program, Lawyers' Committee for Human Rights (LCHR). New York, 26 July 2002

Stacie Jonas, Project Director, "Bring Pinochet to Justice" project, Institute for Policy Studies (IPS). Santiago, 27 April 2003

Peter Kornbluh, National Security Archive. 7 August 2002 (telephone interview)

Saul Landau, journalist and author. 5 August 2002 (e-mail exchange)

José Miguel Vivanco, Americas Director, Human Rights Watch. Washington, D.C., 6 August 2002

Gail Pellett, filmmaker and producer. New York, 22 July 2002

Maggie Popkin, Executive Director, Due Process of Law Foundation; formerly of the Instituto de Derechos Humanos de la Universidad Centroamericana "José Simeon Cañas" (IDHUCA), El Salvador. Washington, D.C., 7 August 2002; San Salvador, 13 July 2003

Juan Romagoza, CJA case plaintiff. 10 August 2002 (telephone interview)

Paul Seils, Senior Associate, International Center for Transitional Justice. New York, 29 July 2002

Argentina

Jorge Berlanda, State Prosecutor, Juzgado Federal no. 1, Buenos Aires; state prosecutor in the Prats trial in Argentina. Buenos Aires, 5 March 2003

Marcel Bertolesi, archivist, Centro de Documentación, Servicio de Paz y Justicia (SERPAJ-Argentina). Buenos Aires, 17 February 2003

Hugo Cañón, State Prosecutor, district of Bahía Blanca; permanent member of the Comisión Provinciana por la Memoria, province of La Plata; originator of truth trials. La Plata, 3 March 2003

Alejandro Carrío, lawyer; representative of the Chilean government in the Prats case trial in Argentina. Buenos Aires, 25 February 2003

Ana Chávez, lawyer, Servicio de Paz y Justicia (SERPAJ-Argentina). Buenos Aires, 17 February 2003 and 3 March 2003

Diego Díaz, educator, Programa "Comunidad e Identidad," Comisión Provinciana por la Memoria, province of La Plata. La Plata, 3 March 2003

Maria Ester Alonso, lawyer, Abuelas de la Plaza de Mayo, La Plata branch. La Plata, 5 March 2003

Eduardo Freiler, State Prosecutor, Juzgado Federal no. 6. Buenos Aires, 25 February 2003

Ariel Garrido, lawyer, representative for the Prats family in legal proceedings in Argentina. Buenos Aires, 4 March 2003

Mabel Gutiérrez, Familiares de Detenidos y Desaparecidos por Razones Políticas. Buenos Aires, 20 February 2003

Alba Lanzillotto, Abuelas de la Plaza de Mayo. Buenos Aires, 24 February 2003

Carmen Lapacó, Madres de la Plaza de Mayo Linea Fundadora; board member of the Centro de Estudios Legales y Sociales (CELS). Buenos Aires, 24 February 2003

Ernesto Lejderman, HIJOS-Argentina; plaintiff in Chilean criminal complaint. Buenos Aires, 22 February 2003 and 4 March 2003

Stella Maris Ageitos, lawyer and author. Buenos Aires, 20 February 2003

Silvina Ramírez, Executive Director, Instituto de Estudios Comparados en Ciencias Penales y Sociales. Buenos Aires, 7 March 2003

Horacio Ravenna, Asamblea Permanente por los Derechos Humanos. Buenos Aires, 17 February 2003

Marcos Salgado, journalist, covered the Prats trial in Argentina for Chilean electronic newspaper *El Mostrador*. Buenos Aires, 18 February 2003

Catalina Smulovitz, Universidad Torcuato di Tella. Buenos Aires, 4 March 2003

Beinusz Szmukler, President for Latin America, Asociación Americana de Juristas; member of the National Judicial Council (Consejo de la Magistratura). Buenos Aires, 26 February 2003

Rubén Vaena, Digitalization of Police Archives Project, Comisión Provinciana por la Memoria/Universidad de La Plata. La Plata, 3 March 2003

Carolina Varsky, lawyer, Centro de Estudios Legales y Sociales (CELS). Buenos Aires, 7 March 2003

UK

Dina Coloma, researcher, Mexico and Central America Desk, Amnesty International, International Secretariat. London, 21 August 2002

Osvaldo Vásquez, Central America Joint Programme Manager, International Cooperation for Development, Catholic Institute for International Relations. London, 24 June 2002

Peru

Fr. José Manuel Miranda, founder, Comisión de Derechos Humanos de Ica. Ica, 24 June 2004

Charo Huayanca Zapata, journalist, Area Comunicación, Comisión de Derechos Humanos de Ica. Ica, 24 June 2004

Carlos Rivera, Head of Legal Area, Proyecto Justicia Viva, Instituto de Defensa Legal. Lima, 28 June 2004

Francisco Soberón Garrido, Executive Secretary, Coordinadora Nacional de Derechos Humanos. Lima, 30 June 2004

Susana Villarán, Head, Area Seguridad Ciudadana, Instituto de Defensa Legal. Lima, 30 June 2004

REFERENCES

Main Printed Sources

Abregú, Martín. 2000. "Human Rights After the Dictatorship: Lessons from Argentina." *NACLA* 34, no. 1: 12–18.

Aceves, William J. 2000. "Liberalism and International Legal Scholarship: The Pinochet Case and the Move Toward a Universal System of Transnational Law Litigation." *Harvard International Law Journal* 41, no. 1: 129–84.

Acuña, Carlos H., and Catalina Smulovitz. 1997. "Guarding the Guardians in Argentina." In A. James McAdams, ed., *Transitional Justice and the Rule of Law in New Democracies*, 93–122. Notre Dame: University of Notre Dame Press.

Agüero, Felipe, and Claudio Fuentes, eds. 2009. *Influencias y resistencias: Militares y poder en América Latina*. Santiago: Catalonia.

Ahumada, E., et al. 1989. *Chile: La memoria prohibida*. 3 vols. Santiago: Pehuen.

Alvarez, Sonia, Evelina Dagnino, and Arturo Escobar, eds. 1998. *Cultures of Politics, Politics of Cultures: Revisioning Latin American Social Movements*. Boulder, Colo.: Westview Press.

Americas Watch. 1985. Report. "Managing the Facts: How the Administration Deals with Reports of Human Rights Abuses in El Salvador." New York: Americas Watch.

———. 1987. "Observaciones de Americas Watch a la situación de derechos humanos en Chile." New York: Americas Watch.

Amnesty International. 2001a. Annual report. Document ref. POL 10/001/2001. Available at http://www.amnesty.org/.

———. 2001b. "Legal Brief on the Incompatibility of Chilean Decree Law no. 2191 of 1978 with International Law." AI document ref. AMR 22/002/2001. Available at http://www.amnesty.org/.

———. 2003. Press release. Document ref. AMR 29/011/2003. Available at http://www.amnesty.org/.

Angell, Alan. 1993. "Chile Since 1958." In L. Bethell, ed., *Chile Since Independence*, 192–202. Cambridge: Cambridge University Press.

———. 2003a. "The Pinochet Factor in Chilean Politics." In M. Davis, ed., *The Pinochet Case: Origins, Progress, and Implications*, 63–84. London: ILAS.

———. 2003b. Review of R. Barros, *Constitutionalism and Dictatorship. Bulletin of Latin American Research* 22, no. 3: 385–86.

———. 2007. *Democracy After Pinochet: Politics, Parties, and Elections in Chile*. London: Institute for the Study of the Americas.

Anguita, Eduardo. 2001. *Sano juicio: Baltasar Garzón, algunos sobrevivientes, y la lucha contra la impunidad en Latinoamérica.* Buenos Aires: Editorial Sudamericana.

APRODEH (Asociación pro-Derechos Humanos). 2003. "La judicialización de las violaciones a los derechos humanos en el Perú, 1980–2000." Report of conference "La judicialización de las violaciones a los derechos humanos en el Perú, 1980–2000," held in Lima, Peru, 23–25 July 2002.

Arnson, Cynthia, ed. 1999. *Comparative Peace Processes in Latin America.* Stanford: Stanford University Press.

Arriagada, Genaro. 1998. *Por la Razón o la Fuerza: Chile bajo Pinochet.* Santiago: Editorial Sudamericano.

Aylwin, Andrés. 2003. *Simplemente lo que vi: 1973–1990.* Santiago: LOM Ediciones.

Aylwin, Patricio. 1998. *El reencuentro de los demócratas: Del golpe al triunfo del no.* Santiago: Ediciones Grupo Zeta.

Barcella, E. Lawrence. 1998. "Pursuing Pinochet: The Case We Made, 22 Years Ago." *Washington Post,* 6 December.

Barros, Robert. 2002. *Constitutionalism and Dictatorship: Pinochet, the Junta, and the 1980 Constitution.* Cambridge: Cambridge University Press.

Baytelman, Andrés, ed. 2002. *Evaluación de la reforma procesal penal chilena.* Santiago: Facultad de Derecho, Universidad Diego Portales.

Beckett, Andy. 2002. *Pinochet in Piccadilly.* London: Faber and Faber.

Benomar, J. 1995. "Justice After Transitions." In N. Kritz, ed., *Transitional Justice: How Emerging Democracies Reckon with Former Regimes,* 1:32–41. Washington, D.C.: United States Institute of Peace Press.

Bethell, Leslie, ed. 1993. *Chile Since Independence.* Cambridge: Cambridge University Press.

Bickford, Louis. 2000. "Human Rights Archives and Research on Historical Memory: Argentina, Chile, and Uruguay." *Latin American Research Review* 35, no. 2: 160–82.

Binford, Leigh. 2001. (First edition 1997.) *El Mozote: Vidas y memorias.* San Salvador: UCA Editores.

Bradley, Curtis A., and Jack L. Goldsmith. 1999. "Pinochet and International Human Rights Litigation." *Michigan Law Review* 97, no. 7: 2129–84.

Brett, Sebastian. 2009. "The Pinochet Effect: Ten Years On from London, 1998." Report of the conference "El efecto Pinochet," held in Santiago, Chile, 8–10 October 2008. Electronic publication by the Universidad Diego Portales available via http://www.icso.cl/.

Brinkmann, Beatriz. 1999. *Itinerario de la impunidad: Chile, 1973–1999.* Santiago: Colección CINTRAS.

de Brito, Alexandra Barahona. 1997. *Human Rights and Democratization in Latin America: Uruguay and Chile.* Oxford: Oxford University Press.

———. 2001. "Bibliographic Survey." In A. de Brito, C. González-Enríquez, and P. Aguilar, eds., *The Politics of Memory: Transitional Justice in Democratizing Societies,* 315–51. Oxford: Oxford University Press.

———. 2003. "The Pinochet Case and the Changing Boundaries of Democracy." In M. Davis, ed., *The Pinochet Case: Origins, Progress, and Implications,* 212–30. London: ILAS, University of London.

de Brito, Alexandra Barahona, Carmen González-Enríquez, and Paloma Aguilar, eds. 2001. *The Politics of Memory: Transitional Justice in Democratizing Societies.* Oxford: Oxford University Press.

Brody, Reed. 2001. "Justice: The First Casualty of Truth?" *The Nation,* 30 April: 25–32.

Brody, Reed, and Michael Ratner, eds. 2000. *The Pinochet Papers*. The Hague: Kluwer Law International.

Brysk, Alison. 1994. *The Politics of Human Rights in Argentina: Protest, Change, and Democratization*. Stanford: Stanford University Press.

———. 2000. "Introduction: When Worlds Collide." In A. Brysk, ed., *From Tribal Village to Global Village: Indian Rights and International Relations in Latin America*, 8–27. Stanford: Stanford University Press.

———, ed. 2002a. *Globalization and Human Rights*. Berkeley and Los Angeles: University of California Press.

———. 2002b. "Transnational Threats and Opportunities." In A. Brysk, ed., *Globalization and Human Rights*, 1–16. Berkeley and Los Angeles: University of California Press.

Buergenthal, Thomas. 1995. "The United Nations Truth Commission for El Salvador." In N. Kritz, ed., *Transitional Justice: How Emerging Democracies Reckon with Former Regimes*, 1:292–325. Washington, D.C.: United States Institute of Peace Press.

Burbach, Roger. 2003. *The Pinochet Affair: State Terrorism and Global Justice*. New York: Zed Books.

Burgerman, Susan. 1998. "Mobilizing Principles: The Role of Transnational Activists in Promoting Human Rights Principles." *Human Rights Quarterly* 20, no. 4: 905–23.

———. 2001. *Moral Victories: How Activists Provoke Multilateral Action*. Ithaca: Cornell University Press.

Burke-White, William. 2001. "Reframing Impunity: Applying Liberal International Law Theory to an Analysis of Amnesty Legislation." *Harvard Law Journal* 42, no. 2: 467–533.

Burt, Jo-Marie. 2009. "Guilty as Charged: The Trial of Former Peruvian President Alberto Fujimori for Human Rights Violations." *International Journal of Transitional Justice* 3, no. 3: 384–405.

Byers, Michael, ed. 2000. *The Role of Law in International Politics*. Oxford: Oxford University Press.

Call, Charles. 2002. "Assessing El Salvador's Transition from Civil War to Peace." In E. Cousens, D. Rothchild, and S. Stedman, eds., *Ending Civil Wars: The Implementation of Peace Agreements*, 383–420. Boulder, Colo.: Lynne Rienner Publishers.

———. 2003. "Democratisation, War, and State-Building: Constructing the Rule of Law in El Salvador." *Journal of Latin American Studies* 35, no. 4: 827–62.

Cañas, Antonio, and Héctor Dada. 1999. "Political Transition and Institutionalization in El Salvador." In C. Arnson, ed., *Comparative Peace Processes in Latin America*, 69–95. Stanford: Stanford University Press.

Capponi, Ricardo. 1999. *Chile: Un duelo pendiente: Perdón, reconciliación, acuerdo social*. Santiago: Editorial Andrés Bello.

Carocca, Alex, et al., eds. 2000. *Nuevo proceso penal*. Santiago: Editorial Cono Sur.

Carranza, Salvador, ed. 2001. (First edition 1990.) *Mártires de la UCA*. San Salvador: UCA Editores.

Caucoto, Nelson, and Héctor Salazar. 1994. *Un verde manto de impunidad*. Santiago: FASIC/Ediciones Academia.

Cavallo, Ascanio. 1998. *La historia oculta de la transición*. Santiago: Editorial Grijalbo.

Cavallo, Ascanio, Manuel Salazar, and Oscar Sepúlveda. 1990. *La historia oculta del régimen militar*. Santiago: Editorial Antártica.

Cavanaugh, William. 1998. *Torture and Eucharist*. Oxford: Blackwell.

CDHES (Comisión de Derechos Humanos de El Salvador). 1993. "Boletín: Resumen noticioso." San Salvador: CDHES.

Charney, Jonathan. 1999. "Progress in International Law?" Editorial comment. *American Journal of International Law* 93, no 2: 452–64.

Clapham, Andrew. 2003. "Issues of Complexity, Complicity, and Complementarity: From the Nuremberg Trials to the Dawn of the New International Criminal Court." In P. Sands, ed., *From Nuremberg to The Hague: The Future of International Criminal Justice*, 30–67. Cambridge: Cambridge University Press.

CNRR (Corporación Nacional de Reparación y Reconciliación). 1996. "Informe sobre calificación de víctimas de violaciones de derechos humanos y de la violencia política." Santiago: CNRR.

CODEPU (Corporación de Promoción y Defensa de los Derechos del Pueblo). 2003a. *Comisiones de la verdad: ¿Un camino incierto?: Estudio comparativo de comisiones de la verdad en Argentina, Chile, El Salvador, Guatemala, y Sudáfrica desde las víctimas y las organizaciones de derechos humanos.* Santiago: CODEPU.

———. 2003b. "Informe de derechos humanos, 2002." Santiago: CODEPU.

Collins, Cath. 2006. "Grounding Global Justice: International Networks and Domestic Human Rights Accountability in Chile and El Salvador." *Journal of Latin American Studies* 38, no. 4: 711–38.

———. 2008. "State Terror and the Law: The (Re)judicialization of Human Rights Accountability in Chile and El Salvador." *Latin American Perspectives* 162, no. 5: 20–37.

———. 2010. "Human Rights Trials in Chile During and After the 'Pinochet Years.'" *International Journal of Transitional Justice* 4, no. 1: 67–86.

Comisión Chilena de Derechos Humanos/Fundación Ideas. 1999. "Nunca más en Chile: Síntesis corregida y actualizada del informe Rettig." Santiago: LOM Ediciones.

CONADEP (Comisión Nacional sobre la Desaparición de Personas). 1986. "Nunca Más: A Report by Argentina's National Commission for Disappeared People." London: Faber and Faber.

Concertación de Partidos por la Democracia. 1989. "Programa de gobierno." Santiago: Editorial Jurídica Publiley.

Cooper, Marc. 2001. *Pinochet and Me.* London: Verso.

Corporación Justicia y Democracia. 2001. "Las comisiones de verdad y los nuevos desafíos en la promoción de los derechos humanos." Report of conference "Las comisiones de verdad y los nuevos desafíos en la promoción de los derechos humanos," held in Santiago, Chile, 9–11 April 2001.

Corradi, Juan, Patricia Weiss Fagen, and Manuel Antonio Garretón, eds. 1992. *Fear at the Edge: State Terror and Resistance in Latin America.* Berkeley and Los Angeles: University of California Press.

Correa Sutil, Jorge. 1992. "Dealing with Past Human Rights Violations: The Chilean Case After Dictatorship." *Notre Dame Law Review* 67, no. 5: 455–94.

———. 1997. "'No Victorious Army Has Ever Been Prosecuted . . .': The Unsettled Story of Transitional Justice in Chile." In A. James McAdams, ed., *Transitional Justice and the Rule of Law in New Democracies*, 123–54. Notre Dame: University of Notre Dame Press.

———. 1999. "Cenicienta se queda en la fiesta: El poder judicial chileno en la década de los 90." In P. Drake and I. Jaksić, eds., *El modelo chileno: Democracia y desarrollo en los noventa*, 281–315. Santiago: LOM Ediciones.

Couso, Jaime. 2002. "Competencia de la justicia militar: Una perspectiva político-criminal." In J. Mera, ed., *Hacia un reforma de la justicia militar*, 73–146. Santiago: Escuela de Derecho, Universidad Diego Portales.

Couso, Javier. 2005. "The Judicialization of Chilean Politics: The Rights Revolution that Never Was." In Rachel Sieder, Line Schjolden, and Alan Angell, eds., *The Judicialization of Politics in Latin America*, 105–29. London: Palgrave Macmillan.

Crocker, David. 1999. "Reckoning with Past Wrongs: A Normative Framework." *Ethics and International Affairs* 13: 43–64.

CVR (Comisión de la Verdad y Reconciliación). 2003a. "Informe Final." Available at http://cverdad.org.pe/ifinal/index.php, last accessed 2 November 2009.

———. 2003b. "Yuyanapaq: Para recordar: Relato visual del conflicto armado interno en el Perú." Lima: Fondo Editorial de la Pontificia Universidad Católica del Perú.

———. 2004a. "Hatun Willakuy: Versión abreviada del informe final de la CVR Perú." Lima: Comisión de Entrega de la CVR.

———. 2004b. "Informe final: Perú, 1980–2000: Tomo I." Lima: Universidad Nacional Mayor de San Marcos and the Pontificia Universidad Católica del Perú.

Dakolias, M. 1996. "The Judicial Sector in Latin America and the Caribbean: Elements of Reform." World Bank Technical Paper no. 319. Washington, D.C.: World Bank.

Danner, Mark. 1994. *The Massacre at El Mozote: A Parable of the Cold War*. New York: Vintage Books.

Davis, Madeleine. 2000. "The Pinochet Case." Research Paper no. 53. London: ILAS, University of London.

———. 2003a. "Introduction: Law and Politics in the Pinochet Case." In M. Davis, ed., *The Pinochet Case: Origins, Progress, and Implications*, 1–21. London: ILAS, University of London.

———, ed. 2003b. *The Pinochet Case: Origins, Progress, and Implications*. London: ILAS, University of London.

Dezalay, Yves, and Bryant Garth. 2001. "Constructing Law Out of Power: Investing in Human Rights as an Alternative Political Strategy." In A. Sarat and S. Scheingold, eds., *Cause Lawyering and the State in a Global Era*, 354–81. Oxford: Oxford University Press.

———, eds. 2003a. *Global Prescriptions: The Production, Exportation, and Importation of a New Legal Orthodoxy*. Ann Arbor: University of Michigan Press.

———. 2003b. "Legitimating the New Legal Orthodoxy." In Y. Dezalay and B. Garth, eds., *Global Prescriptions: The Production, Exportation, and Importation of a New Legal Orthodoxy*, 306–34. Ann Arbor: University of Michigan Press.

Dinges, John. 2004. *The Condor Years: How Pinochet and His Allies Brought Terrorism to Three Continents*. New York: The New Press.

Dinges, John, and Saul Landau. 1980. *Assassination on Embassy Row*. New York: Pantheon Books.

Dodson, M. 2002. "Assessing Judicial Reform in Latin America." *Latin American Research Review* 37, no. 2: 200–220.

Doggett, Martha. 1993. *Death Foretold: The Jesuit Murders in El Salvador*. Washington, D.C.: Georgetown University Press.

Domingo, Pilar. 1999. "Judicial Independence and Judicial Reform in Latin America." In A. Schedler, L. Diamond, and M. Plattner, eds., *The Self-Restraining State:*

Power and Accountability in New Democracies, 151–75. Boulder, Colo.: Lynne Rienner Publishers.

Domingo, Pilar, and Rachel Sieder, eds. 2001. *Rule of Law in Latin America: The International Promotion of Judicial Reform.* London: ILAS, University of London.

Domínguez, Jorge, and Marc Lindenberg, eds. 1997. *Democratic Transitions in Central America.* Gainesville: University Press of Florida.

Domínguez, Jorge, and Abraham Lowenthal, eds. 1996. *Constructing Democratic Governance: Latin America and the Caribbean in the 1990s: Themes and Issues.* Baltimore: Johns Hopkins University Press.

Drake, Paul, and Iván Jaksić, eds. 1995. (First edition 1991.) *The Struggle for Democracy in Chile.* Lincoln: University of Nebraska Press.

———. 1999. *El modelo chileno: Democracia y desarrollo en los noventa.* Santiago: LOM Ediciones.

Duce, Mauricio. 2004. "La reforma procesal penal chilena: Gestación y estado de avance de un proceso de transformación en marcha." In L. Pásara, ed., *En busca de una justicia distinta: Experiencias de reforma en América Latina,* 195–248. Lima: Consorcio Justicia Viva, Instituto de Defensa Legal.

Duce, Mauricio, and Cristián Riego. 2002. *Introducción al nuevo sistema procesal penal.* Santiago: Escuela de Derecho, Universidad Diego Portales.

Dunkerley, James. 1982. *The Long War: Dictatorship and Revolution in El Salvador.* London: Verso.

———. 1988. *Power in the Isthmus: A Political History of Modern Central America.* New York: Verso.

———. 1994. *The Pacification of Central America: Political Change in the Isthmus, 1987–1993.* New York: Verso.

EAAF (Equipo Argentino de Antropología Forense). 2001. "Annual Report, 2001." Buenos Aires: EAAF.

ECA (Estudios Centroamericanos). 2000a. "Editorial: Dar cuenta y asumir responsabilidades." *Estudios Centroamericanos* 625–26 (November–December): 1095–1118.

———. 2000b. "Editorial: El paso no dado aún: La justicia debida." *Estudios Centroamericanos* 615–16 (January–February): 3–17.

Eckstein, Susan. 2001. "Epilogue: Where Have All the Movements Gone?" In S. Eckstein, ed., *Power and Popular Protest,* 351–401. Berkeley and Los Angeles: University of California Press.

Eckstein, Susan, and Timothy Wickham-Crowley, eds. 2003. *What Justice? Whose Justice? Fighting for Fairness in Latin America.* Berkeley and Los Angeles: University of California Press.

Editorial 30 Años. 2003. *Allende vive.* Santiago: Editorial 30 Años.

Ekaizer, Ernesto. 2003. *Yo, Augusto.* Buenos Aires: Editorial Aguilar.

Elster, John. 2004. *Closing the Books: Transitional Justice in Historical Perspective.* Cambridge: Cambridge University Press.

Ensalaco, Mark. 1994. "Truth Commissions for Chile and El Salvador: A Report and Assessment." *Human Rights Quarterly* 16, no. 4: 656–75.

———. 2000. *Chile Under Pinochet: Recovering the Truth.* Philadelphia: University of Pennsylvania Press.

———. 2005. "Pinochet: A Study in Impunity." In S. Nagy-Zekmi and F. Leiva, eds., *Democracy in Chile: The Legacy of September 11, 1973.* Sussex: Sussex University Press.

Epp, Charles. 1998. *The Rights Revolution: Lawyers, Activists, and Supreme Courts in Comparative Perspective.* Chicago: University of Chicago Press.

Escalante, Jorge. 2000. *La misión era matar: El juicio a la caravana Pinochet-Arellano.* Santiago: LOM Ediciones/Colección Nuevo Periodismo.

Estella Nagle, Luz. 2000. "The Cinderella of Government: Judicial Reform in Latin America." *California Western International Law Journal* 30, no. 2: 345–79.

Falk, Richard. 2000. *Human Rights Horizons: The Pursuit of Justice in a Globalizing World.* New York: Routledge.

Farer, Tom. 1997. "The Rise of the Inter-American Human Rights Regime: No Longer a Unicorn, Not Yet an Ox." *Human Rights Quarterly* 19, no. 3: 510–46.

FASIC (Fundación de Ayuda Social de las Iglesias Cristianas). 1999. "Mesa de Diálogo exposiciones." Santiago: FASIC Colección Documentos.

Fernández, Karinne, and Pietro Sferrazza. 2009. "La aplicación de la prescripción gradual en casos de violaciones de derechos humanos." In *Anuario de Derechos Humanos* (Universidad de Chile) 5:183–92.

FESPAD (Fundación de Estudios para la Aplicación del Derecho). 2002. "Reforma penal y acuerdos de paz." San Salvador: FESPAD/CEPES.

———. 2003. "Informe de seguimiento de la reforma procesal penal en El Salvador." San Salvador: FESPAD/CEPES.

Filippini, Leonardo. 2005. "El prestigio de los derechos humanos." Unpublished manuscript on file with author.

FLACSO (Facultad Latinoamericana de Ciencias Sociales). 1999. *Entre la II cumbre y la detención de Pinochet: Chile, 1998.* Santiago: FLACSO-Chile.

———. 2000. *Nuevo gobierno: Desafíos de la reconciliación: Chile, 1999–2000.* Santiago: FLACSO-Chile.

Foweraker, Joe, and Todd Landman. 1997. *Citizenship Rights and Social Movements.* Oxford: Oxford University Press.

Fuentes, Claudio A. 2009. "La pausada des-pinochetizatión de las Fuerzas Armadas en Chile." In Felipe Agüero and Claudio Fuentes, eds., *Influencias y resistencias: Militares y poder en América Latina,* 299–327. Santiago: Catalonia.

Gaborit, Mauricio. 2002. "Memoria histórica: Relato desde las víctimas." *Estudios Centroamericanos* 649–50 (November–December): 1021–32.

Gallardo Silva, Mateo. 2003. *Intima complacencia.* Santiago: FRASIS Editores/El Periodista.

Garretón, Manuel Antonio. 1994. "Human Rights in Processes of Democratisation." *Journal of Latin American Studies* 26, no. 1: 221–34.

———. 1995. "The Political Opposition and the Party System Under the Military Regime." In P. Drake and I. Jaksić, eds., *The Struggle for Democracy in Chile,* 211–50. Lincoln: University of Nebraska Press.

———. 1996. "Human Rights in Democratization Processes." In E. Jelín and E. Hershberg, eds., *Constructing Democracy,* 39–55. Boulder, Colo.: Westview Press.

Garretón, Roberto. 2004. "Educando a los jueces en derecho internacional." Available at http://www.memoriayjusticia.cl/espanol/sp_memoria-garreton.htm, last accessed 4 March 2009.

Goldstone, Richard. 2001 *For Humanity: Reflections of a War Crimes Prosecutor.* New Haven: Yale University Press.

Golob, Stephanie. 2002a. "'Forced to Be Free': Abroad and At Home." *Democratization* 9, no. 4: 25–57.

———. 2002b. "'Forced to Be Free': Globalized Justice, Pacted Democracy, and the Pinochet Case." *Democratization* 9, no. 2: 21–42.

———. 2003. "Rule of Law in Transition: The Chilean Judiciary, Globalized Norms, and the Repatriation of the Pinochet Case." Paper presented at the Latin American Studies Association Annual Conference, Dallas, Tex., 27–29 March 2003.

González, Miriam. 2002. "Los archivos del terror del Paraguay: La historia oculta de la represión." In L. da Silva Catela and E. Jelín, eds., *Los archivos de la represión: Documentos, memoria, y verdad,* 85–114. Madrid: Siglo Veintiuno.

González, Mónica, and Edwin Harrington. 1987. *Bomba en una calle de Palermo.* Santiago: Editorial Emisión.

Goodale, Mark. 2002. "Legal Ethnography in an Era of Globalization." In J. Starr and M. Goodale, eds., *Practicing Ethnography in Law,* 50–71. New York: Palgrave Macmillan.

de Grieff, Pablo, and Ciaran Cronin, eds. 2002. *Global Justice and Transnational Politics.* Cambridge: MIT Press.

Hammergren, Linn. 1998a. "Fifteen Years of Judicial Reform in Latin America . . . Where We Are and Why We Haven't Made More Progress." Available at http://www.uoregon.edu/~caguirre/hammergren.html, last accessed 3 November 2009.

———. 1998b. *The Politics of Justice and Justice Reform in Latin America: The Peruvian Case in Comparative Perspective.* Boulder, Colo.: Westview Press.

———. 2007. *Envisioning Reform: Improving Judicial Performance in Latin America.* University Park: Pennsylvania State University Press.

Hayner, Priscilla. 1995. "Fifteen Truth Commissions, 1974–1993: A Comparative Study." In N. Kritz, ed., *Transitional Justice: How Emerging Democracies Reckon with Former Regimes,* 1:225–61. Washington, D.C.: United States Institute of Peace Press.

———. 1996. "Commissioning the Truth." *Third World Quarterly* 17, no. 1: 19–29.

———. 2001. *Unspeakable Truths: Confronting State Terror and Atrocity.* New York: Routledge.

Hesse, Carla, and Robert Post, eds. 1999. *Human Rights in Political Transitions: Gettysburg to Bosnia.* New York: Zone Books.

Hilbink, Lisa. 1999. "Un estado de derecho no liberal: La actuación del poder judicial en los años 90." In P. Drake and I. Jaksić, eds., *El modelo chileno: Democracia y desarrollo en los noventa,* 317–37. Santiago: LOM Ediciones.

———. 2000. Review of W. Prillaman, *The Judiciary and Democratic Decay in Latin America.* In *Latin American Politics and Society* 44, no. 1: 169–74.

———. 2003. "An Exception to Chilean Exceptionalism?" In S. Eckstein and T. Wickham-Crowley, eds., *What Justice? Whose Justice? Fighting for Fairness in Latin America,* 64–97. Berkeley and Los Angeles: University of California Press.

———. 2007. *Judges Beyond Politics in Democracy and Dictatorship: Lessons from Chile.* Cambridge: Cambridge University Press.

Hitchens, Christopher. 2001. *The Trial of Henry Kissinger.* London: Verso.

Hite, Katherine, and Paolo Cesarini. 2004. *Authoritarian Legacies and Democracy in Latin America and Southern Europe.* Notre Dame: University of Notre Dame Press.

Hite, Katherine, and Cath Collins. 2009. "Memorial Fragments, Monumental Silences, and Re-awakenings in Twenty-first Century Chile." *Millennium: Journal of International Studies* 38, no. 2.

HRW (Human Rights Watch). 1998. "Los límites de la tolerancia: Libertad de expresión y debate público en Chile." Santiago: LOM Ediciones.

———. 2004. "Beyond The Hague: The Challenges of International Justice." In Human Rights Watch, "2004 World Report." Available at http://hrw.org/wr2k4/10.htm#_Toc58744959, last accessed October 2004.

Hume, Mo. 2008. "The Myths of Violence: Gender, Conflict, and Community in El Salvador." *Latin American Perspectives* 162, no. 35: 59–76.

Huneeus, Alejandra. 2010. "Judging from a Guilty Conscience: The Chilean Judiciary's Human Rights Turn." *Law and Social Inquiry* 35, no. 1: 99–135.

Huntington, Samuel. 1991. *The Third Wave: Democratization in the Late Twentieth Century*. Norman: University of Oklahoma Press.

———. 1995. "The Third Wave: Democratization in the Late Twentieth Century." In N. Kritz, ed., *Transitional Justice: How Emerging Democracies Reckon with Former Regimes*, 1:65–81. Washington, D.C.: United States Institute of Peace Press.

IDHUCA (Instituto de Derechos Humanos de la Universidad Centroamericana). 2000. "Comentario." *Estudios Centroamericanos* 617 (March): 289–303.

———. 2003a. "Cumplimiento de las recomendaciones de la comisión de la verdad en El Salvador." *Estudios Centroamericanos* 655 (May): 415–24.

———. 2003b. "Informe sobre los derechos humanos en el 2002." Available at http://www.derechos.org/nizkor/salvador/doc/infodho2.html, last accessed 2 November 2009.

IEJES (Instituto de Estudios Legales de El Salvador). 1993. "Special Edition no. 1." San Salvador: IEJES.

Insunza Bascuñan, Alfonso. n.d. "La amnistía de 1978 y los tratados internacionales." http://www.memoriayjusticia.cl/espanol/sp_home.html, section "Temas de la Actualidad," last accessed 4 March 2009.

Inter-American Commission of Human Rights (IACHR). 1996. Report no. 34/96 in case 11.228. Available at http://www.cidh.oas.org/annualrep/96eng/Chile11.228.htm, last accessed 2 November 2009.

———. 1999. Report no. 133/99 in case 11.725 and report no. 136/99 in case 10.488. Available at http://www.cidh.oas.org/annualrep/99eng/Merits/ElSalvador10.488.htm, last accessed 2 November 2009.

———. 2000. Report no. 37/00 in case 11.481. Available at www.cidh.oas.org/annualrep/99eng/Merits/ElSalvador11.481.htm, last accessed 2 November 2009.

IPS (Institute for Policy Studies). n.d. "TNI and the Pinochet Precedent." Available at http://www.tni.org/primer/tni-and-pinochet-precedent, last accessed 2 November 2009.

IPS/Washington College of Law. 2004. "Confronting Challenges to the Pinochet Precedent." Transcript of roundtable "Confronting Challenges to the Pinochet Precedent and the Globalization of Justice," held at Washington College of Law, Washington, D.C., 3 February 2004. Available at http://tni-archives.org/acts/roundtable.pdf, last accessed 2 November 2009.

Jelín, Elizabeth, and Eric Hershberg, eds. 1996. *Constructing Democracy*. Boulder, Colo.: Westview Press.

Joignant, Alfredo. 2007. *Un día distinto: Memorias festivas y batallas conmemorativas en torno al 11 de septiembre en Chile (1974–2006)*. Santiago: Editorial Universitaria.

Juhn, Tricia. 1998. *Negotiating Peace in El Salvador*. New York: St. Martin's Press.

Kaldor, Mary. 2003. *Global Civil Society*. Cambridge: Polity Press.

Kamminga, Menno T. 2001. "Lessons Learned from the Exercise of Universal Jurisdiction in Respect of Gross Human Rights Offenses." *Human Rights Quarterly* 23, no. 4: 940–74.

Keck, Margaret, and Kathryn Sikkink. 1998. *Activists Beyond Borders: Advocacy Networks in International Politics*. Ithaca: Cornell University Press.

Kochavi, Arieh. 1998. *Prelude to Nuremberg: Allied War Crimes Policy and the Question of Punishment*. Chapel Hill: University of North Carolina Press.

Kritz, Neil, ed. 1995. *Transitional Justice: How Emerging Democracies Reckon with Former Regimes*. 3 vols. Washington, D.C.: United States Institute of Peace Press.

Kymlicka, Will, and Wayne Norman, eds. 2000. *Citizenship in Diverse Societies*. Oxford: Oxford University Press.

Lacabe, Margaret. 1998. "The Criminal Procedures Against Chilean and Argentine Repressors in Spain: A Short Summary." Available at http://www.derechos.net/marga/papers/spain.html, last accessed 4 March 2009.

Landau, Saul, and S. Anderson. 1998. "The Autumn of the Autocrat." *Covert Action Quarterly* 64 (Spring): 33–40.

LCHR (Lawyers' Committee for Human Rights). 1984. "Summary of the Cases of the U.S. Citizens Who Have Been Killed in El Salvador." New York: LCHR.

———. 1987. "From the Ashes: A Report on the Effort to Rebuild El Salvador's System of Justice." New York: LCHR.

———. 1989. "Underwriting Injustice: AID and El Salvador's Judicial Reform Program." New York: LCHR.

———. 1995. "Improvising History: A Critical Evaluation of the United Nations Observer Mission in El Salvador." New York: LCHR.

———. 2002. "Universal Jurisdiction: Meeting the Challenge Through NGO Cooperation." Report of the conference "Universal Jurisdiction: Meeting the Challenge Throughout NGO Cooperation," held in New York, 3–5 April 2002.

Lira, Elizabeth, and Brian Loveman. 2000a. *Las ardientes cenizas del olvido: Vía chilena de reconciliación política, 1932–1994*. Santiago: LOM Ediciones.

———. 2000b. *Las suaves cenizas del olvido: Vía chilena de reconciliación política, 1814–1932*. Santiago: LOM Ediciones.

———. 2002. *El espejismo de la reconciliación política: Chile, 1990–2002*. Santiago: LOM Ediciones.

Little, David. 1999. "A Different Kind of Justice: Dealing with Human Rights Violations in Transitional Societies." *Ethics and International Affairs* 13, no. 2: 65–80.

Loveman, Mara. 1998. "High-Risk Collective Action: Defending Human Rights in Chile, Uruguay, and Argentina." *American Journal of Sociology* 104, no. 2: 477–525.

Lowden, Pamela. 1996. *Moral Opposition to Authoritarian Rule in Chile (1973–1990)*. Basingstoke: Macmillan.

Lutz, Ellen, and Kathryn Sikkink. 2000. "International Human Rights Law and Practice in Latin America." *International Organization* 54, no. 3: 633–59.

———. 2001. "The Justice Cascade: The Evolution and Impact of Foreign Human Rights Trials in Latin America." *Chicago Journal of International Law* 2, no. 1: 1–33.

Macedo, Stephen J., ed. 2003. *Universal Justice, National Courts, and the Prosecution of Serious Crimes Under International Law*. Philadelphia: University of Pennsylvania Press.

Macleod, Morna. 1986. "GAM-Comadres, un análisis comparativo." *CITGU [Ciencia y Tecnología para Guatemala]*, Serie Cuadernos 12, no. 3.

Malamud, Carlos, ed. 2000. "El caso Pinochet: Un debate sobre los límites de la impunidad." Madrid: Instituto Universitario Ortega y Gasset.

Malamud-Goti, Jaime. 1995. "Transitional Governments in the Breach." In N. Kritz, ed., *Transitional Justice: How Emerging Democracies Reckon with Former Regimes*, 1:189–202. Washington, D.C.: United States Institute of Peace Press.

———. 1996. *Game Without End: State Terror and the Politics of Justice*. Norman: University of Oklahoma Press.

Martorell, Francisco. 1999. *Operación Cóndor: El vuelo de la muerte*. Santiago: LOM Ediciones.

Matus, Alejandra. 1999. *El libro negro de la justicia chilena*. Santiago: Editorial Planeta.

Matus, Alejandra, and Francisco Artaza. 1996. *Crimen con castigo*. Santiago: Ediciones Diario La Nación.

McAdam, Doug, Sidney Tarrow, and Charles Tilly. 2001. *Dynamics of Contention*. Cambridge: Cambridge University Press.

McAdams, A. James, ed. 1997. *Transitional Justice and the Rule of Law in New Democracies*. Notre Dame: University of Notre Dame Press.

Meili, Stephen. 2001. "Latin American Cause-Lawyering Networks." In A. Sarat and S. Scheingold, eds., *Cause Lawyering and the State in a Global Era*, 307–33. Oxford: Oxford University Press.

Méndez, Juan. 1997. "Accountability for Past Abuses." *Human Rights Quarterly* 19, no. 2: 255–82.

Méndez, Juan, Guillermo O'Donnell, and Paulo Sérgio Pinheiro, eds. 1999. *The (Un)rule of Law and the Underprivileged in Latin America*. Notre Dame: University of Notre Dame Press.

Mera, Jorge, ed. 2002. *Hacía una reforma de la justicia militar*. Santiago: Escuela de Derecho, Universidad Diego Portales Serie Cuadernos de Análisis Jurídico.

Mertus, Julie. 1999. "From Legal Transplants to Transformative Justice: Human Rights and the Promise of Transnational Civil Society." *American University International Law Review* 14, no. 5: 1335–89.

Minow, Martha. 1998. *Between Vengeance and Forgiveness: Facing History After Genocide and Mass Violence*. Boston: Beacon Press.

Nino, Carlos Santiago. 1996. *Radical Evil on Trial*. New Haven: Yale University Press.

O'Donnell, Guillermo, and Philippe Schmitter. 1986. *Transitions from Authoritarian Rule: Tentative Conclusions About Uncertain Democracies*. Baltimore: Johns Hopkins University Press.

O'Donnell, Guillermo, Philippe Schmitter, and Laurence Whitehead, eds. 1986. *Transitions from Authoritarian Rule: Comparative Perspectives*. Baltimore: Johns Hopkins University Press.

Orentlicher, Diane. 1991a. "A Reply to Professor Nino." *Yale Law Journal* 100, no. 8: 2641–43.

———. 1991b. "Settling Accounts: The Duty to Prosecute Human Rights Violations of a Prior Regime." *Yale Law Journal* 100, no. 8: 2537–615.

———. 1993. "The Role of the Prosecutor in the Transition to Democracy in Latin America." In I. Stotzky, ed., *Transition to Democracy in Latin America: The Role of the Judiciary*, 249ff. Boulder, Colo.: Westview Press.

———. 2002. "The Role of Domestic Courts and Judges in the Implementation and Enforcement of International Humanitarian Law." Draft paper for the U.S. Institute of Peace Working Group on International Humanitarian Law, Washington, D.C.

———. 2003. "The Future of Universal Jurisdiction in the New Architecture of Transnational Justice." In S. Macedo, ed., *Universal Justice, National Courts, and the Prosecution of Serious Crimes Under International Law*, 214–39. Philadelphia: University of Pennsylvania Press.

Osiel, Mark. 2000a. (First edition 1997.) *Mass Atrocity, Collective Memory, and the Law*. New Brunswick, N.J.: Transaction Publishers.

———. 2000b. "Why Prosecute? Critics of Punishment for Mass Atrocity." *Human Rights Quarterly* 22, no. 1: 118–47.

———. 2002. *Mass Atrocity, Ordinary Evil, and Hannah Arendt: Criminal Consciousness in Argentina's Dirty War*. New Haven: Yale University Press.

Oxhorn, Philip. 1995. *Organizing Civil Society: The Popular Sectors and the Struggle for Democracy in Chile*. University Park: Pennsylvania State University Press.

———. 2003. "Social Inequality, Civil Society, and the Limits of Citizenship in Latin America." In S. Eckstein and T. Wickham-Crowley, eds., *What Justice? Whose Justice? Fighting for Fairness in Latin America*, 35–63. Berkeley and Los Angeles: University of California Press.

Oyarzún, María Eugenia. 1999. *Augusto Pinochet: Diálogos con su historia*. Santiago: Editorial Sudamericana.

Pacheco, Máximo. 1983. *Lonquén*. Santiago: Editorial Aconcagua.

Paley, Julia. 2001. *Marketing Democracy: Power and Social Movements in Post-dictatorship Chile*. Berkeley and Los Angeles: University of California Press.

Panizza, Francisco, and David Beetham. 1995. "Human Rights in the Processes of Transition and Consolidation of Democracy in Latin America." Special issue, *Political Studies* 43, no. 4: 168–88.

Pásara, Luis, ed. 2004. *En busca de una justicia distinta: Experiencias de reforma en América Latina*. Lima: Consorcio Justicia Viva/Instituto de Defensa Legal.

Pasqualucci, Jo M. 1994. "The Whole Truth and Nothing but the Truth: Truth Commissions, Impunity, and the Inter-American Human Rights System." *Boston University International Law Journal* 12, no. 2: 321–70.

Payne, Leigh. 2003. "Perpetrators' Confessions: Truth, Reconciliation, and Justice in Argentina." In S. Eckstein and T. Wickham-Crowley, eds., *What Justice? Whose Justice? Fighting for Fairness in Latin America*, 158–84. Berkeley and Los Angeles: University of California Press.

———. 2007. *Unsettling Accounts: The Politics and Performance of Confessions by Perpetrators of Authoritarian State Violence*. Durham: Duke University Press.

PDDH (Procuraduría para la Defensa de los Derechos Humanos). 2002. "Recopilación de Resoluciones e Informes Especiales, Enero-Diciembre 2002." San Salvador: PDDH.

Pearce, Jenny. 1981. *Under the Eagle: U.S. Intervention in Central America and the Caribbean*. London: Latin America Bureau.

Pérez, Mónica, and Felipe Gerdtzen. 2000. *Augusto Pinochet: 503 días atrapado en Londres*. Santiago: Editorial Los Andes.

Pion-Berlin, David. 1995. "To Prosecute or to Pardon?" In N. Kritz, ed., *Transitional Justice: How Emerging Democracies Reckon with Former Regimes*, 1:82–103. Washington, D.C.: United States Institute of Peace Press.

————. 2004. "The Pinochet Case and Human Rights Progress in Chile: Was Europe a Catalyst, Cause, or Inconsequential?" *Journal of Latin American Studies* 36, no. 3: 479–505.

Plataforma Argentina contra la Impunidad. 1997. "Contra la impunidad." Report of the conference "Simposio contra la impunidad y en defensa de los derechos humanos," held in Barcelona, Spain, 24–27 October 1997.

PNUD (Programa de las Naciones Unidas para el Desarrollo). 1998. "Instrumentos internacionales." Buenos Aires: Editoriales del Puerto.

Popkin, Margaret. 2000. *Peace Without Justice: Obstacles to Building the Rule of Law in El Salvador*. University Park: Pennsylvania State University Press.

————. 2004. "The Serrano Sisters: El Salvador in the Inter-American Court of Human Rights." Available at http://www.dplf.org/uploads/1190407226.pdf, last accessed 4 March 2009. Republished in 2005 in *Revista CEJIL* 1, no. 1: 41–56.

Popkin, Margaret, and Nehal Bhuta. 1999. "Latin American Amnesties in Comparative Perspective: Can the Past Be Buried?" *Ethics and International Affairs* 13, no. 1: 99–122.

Popkin, Margaret, and Naomi Roht-Arriaza. 1995. "Truth as Justice." In N. Kritz, ed., *Transitional Justice: How Emerging Democracies Reckon with Former Regimes*, 1:262–89. Washington, D.C.: United States Institute of Peace Press.

Portales, Felipe. 2000. *Chile: Una democracia tutelada*. Santiago: Editorial Sudamericana.

Prillaman, William. 2000. *The Judiciary and Democratic Decay in Latin America*. Westport, Conn.: Praeger.

Pro-Búsqueda (Asociación Pro-Búsqueda). 2000a. "Memoria 'reencuentros impostergables.'" Report of the conference "Reencuentros impostergables: Seminario sobre niñez desaparecida como consecuencia de los conflictos armados en Centroamérica," held in San Salvador, El Salvador, 23–25 November 2000.

————. 2000b. "Reconstruyendo identidades: Hacia la creación de la Comisión Nacional de Búsqueda de Niñas y Niños Desaparecidos." San Salvador: Pro-Búsqueda.

————. 2001. *El día más esperado: Buscando a los niños desaparecidos en El Salvador*. San Salvador: UCA Editores.

————. 2003. "La paz en construcción: Un estudio sobre la problemática de la niñez desaparecida por el conflicto armado en El Salvador." San Salvador: Pro-Búsqueda.

Propper, Eugene, and Taylor Branch. 1982. *Labyrinth*. New York: Viking Press.

Przeworski, Adam, ed. 1995. *Sustainable Democracy*. Cambridge: Cambridge University Press.

Ratner, Michael, and Beth Stephens. 1996. *International Human Rights Litigation in U.S. Courts*. New York: Transnational Publishers.

Remiro Brotóns, Antonio. 1999. *El caso Pinochet: Los límites de la impunidad*. Madrid: Biblioteca Nueva.

————. 2003. "International Law After the Pinochet Case." In M. Davis, *The Pinochet Case: Origins, Progress, and Implications*, 231–51. London: ILAS, University of London.

Rettig (Comisión Nacional de Verdad y Reconciliación). 1993. "Report of the Chilean National Commission on Truth and Reconciliation." English translation published by the Center for Civil and Human Rights, Notre Dame Law School. Available at http://www.usip.org/files/resources/collections/truth-commission-Chile-90, last accessed 2 November 2009.

Risse, Thomas, Stephen C. Ropp, and Kathryn Sikkink, eds. 1999. *The Power of Human Rights: International Norms and Democratic Change.* Cambridge: Cambridge University Press.

Roberts, Kenneth. 1998. *Deepening Democracy? The Modern Left and Social Movements in Chile and Peru.* Stanford: Stanford University Press.

Robertson, Geoffrey. 2000. (First edition 1999.) *Crimes Against Humanity.* London: Penguin Books.

Rodríguez Elizondo, José. 1995. *La ley es más fuerte.* Buenos Aires: Grupo Editorial Zeta.

Roht-Arriaza, Naomi. 1995. *Impunity and Human Rights in International Law and Practice.* Oxford: Oxford University Press.

———. 2001. "The Role of International Actors in National Accountability Processes." In A. de Brito, C. González-Enríquez, and P. Aguilar, eds., *The Politics of Memory: Transitional Justice in Democratizing Societies,* 40–64. Oxford: Oxford University Press.

———. 2003. "Of Catalysts and Cases: Transnational Prosecutions and Impunity in Latin America." In M. Davis, ed., *The Pinochet Case: Origins, Progress, and Implications,* 191–212. London: ILAS, University of London.

———. 2005. *The Pinochet Effect: Transnational Justice in the Age of Human Rights.* Philadelphia: University of Pennsylvania Press.

Roht-Arriaza, Naomi, and Javier Mariezcurrena, eds. 2006. *Transitional Justice in the Twenty-First Century: Beyond Truth Versus Justice.* Cambridge: Cambridge University Press.

Rojas, Francisco. 2001. "La detención del General Pinochet: Notas para su interpretación y evaluación del impacto en el sistema político chileno." In F. Rojas and C. Stefoni, eds., *El "Caso Pinochet": Visiones hemisféricas de su detención en Londres,* 21–40. Santiago: FLACSO-Chile.

Rojas, Francisco, and Carolina Stefoni, eds. 2001. *El "Caso Pinochet": Visiones hemisféricas de su detención en Londres.* Santiago: FLACSO-Chile.

Roniger, Luis. 1997. "Paths of Citizenship and the Legacy of Human Rights Violations: The Cases of Redemocratized Argentina and Uruguay." *Journal of Historical Sociology* 10, no. 3: 270–309.

Roniger, Luis, and Mario Sznajder. 1999. *The Legacy of Human Rights Violations in the Southern Cone: Argentina, Chile, and Uruguay.* New York: Oxford University Press.

Ropp, Stephen C., and Kathryn Sikkink. 1999. "International Norms and Domestic Politics in Chile and Guatemala." In T. Risse, S. Ropp, and K. Sikkink, eds., *The Power of Human Rights: International Norms and Democratic Change,* 172–204. Cambridge: Cambridge University Press.

Salazar, Manuel. 1995. *Contreras: Historia de un intocable.* Santiago: Editorial Grijalbo.

Samayoa, Salvador. 2002. *El Salvador: La reforma pactada.* San Salvador: UCA Editores.

Sands, Philippe. 2003a. "After Pinochet: The role of national courts." In P. Sands, ed., *From Nuremberg to The Hague: The Future of International Criminal Justice,* 68–108. Cambridge: Cambridge University Press.

———, ed. 2003b. *From Nuremberg to The Hague: The Future of International Criminal Justice.* Cambridge: Cambridge University Press.

Sarat, Austin, and Stuart Scheingold. 2001. "State Transformation, Globalization, and the Possibilities of Cause Lawyering." In A. Sarat and S. Scheingold, eds., *Cause Lawyering and the State in a Global Era,* 3–31 Oxford: Oxford University Press.

Schedler, Andreas, Larry Diamond, and Marc Plattner, eds. 1999. *The Self-Restraining State: Power and Accountability in New Democracies.* Boulder, Colo.: Lynne Rienner Publishers.

Seils, Paul. 2003. "La justicia transicional." In APRODEH report of conference "La judicialización de las violaciones a los derechos humanos en el Perú, 1980–2000," held in Lima, Peru, 23–25 July 2002.

Siavelis, Peter. 2000. *The President and Congress in Postauthoritarian Chile.* University Park: Pennsylvania State University Press.

Sieder, Rachel. 2001. "War, Peace, and Memory Politics in Central America." In A. de Brito, C. González-Enríquez, and P. Aguilar, eds., *The Politics of Memory: Transitional Justice in Democratizing Societies,* 161–89. Oxford: Oxford University Press.

Sieder, Rachel, and Patrick Costello. 1996. "Judicial Reform in Central America." In R. Sieder, ed., *Central America: Fragile Transition,* 169–211. London: ILAS.

Sieder, Rachel, Line Schjolden, and Alan Angell, eds. 2005. *The Judicialization of Politics in Latin America.* London: Palgrave Macmillan.

Siegel, Richard Lewis. 1998. "Transitional Justice: A Decade of Debate and Experience." *Human Rights Quarterly* 20, no. 4: 431–54.

Sikkink, Kathryn. 2003. "Transnational Advocacy Networks and the Social Construction of Legal Rules." In Y. Dezalay and B. Garth, eds., *Global Prescriptions: The Production, Exportation, and Importation of a New Legal Orthodoxy,* 37–64. Ann Arbor: University of Michigan Press.

———. 2004. "The Transnational Dimension of the Judicialisation of Politics in Latin America." Draft paper presented at the conference "Judicialisation of Politics," Institute of Latin American Studies, London, 17–18 March 2004. Revised version published in R. Sieder, L. Schjolden, and A. Angell, eds., 2005, *The Judicialization of Politics in Latin America,* 263–92. London: Palgrave Macmillan.

da Silva Catela, Ludmila, and Elizabeth Jelín, eds. 2002. *Los archivos de la represión: Documentos, memoria, y verdad.* Madrid: Siglo Veintiuno.

Slaughter, Anne-Marie. 2003. "Breaking Out: The Proliferation of Actors in the International System." In Y. Dezalay and B. Garth, eds., *Global Prescriptions: The Production, Exportation, and Importation of a New Legal Orthodoxy,* 12–36. Ann Arbor: University of Michigan Press.

Smulovitz, Catalina. 1995. "Constitución y poder judicial en la nueva democracia Argentina: La experiencia de las instituciones." In C. Acuña, ed., *La nueva matriz política argentina,* 71–114. Buenos Aires: Ediciones Nueva Visión.

Sobrino, Jon. 2003. "La verdad de las víctimas." *Estudios Centroamericanos* 655 (May): 461–72.

Spooner, Mary Helen. 1994. *Soldiers in a Narrow Land: The Pinochet Regime in Chile.* Berkeley and Los Angeles: University of California Press.

Stanley, William. 1996. *The Protection Racket State: Elite Politics, Military Extortion, and Civil War in El Salvador.* Philadelphia: Temple University Press.

Steiner, Henry, and Philip Alston. 1996. *International Human Rights in Context.* Oxford: Oxford University Press.

Stern, Steve. 2006. *Remembering Pinochet's Chile* and *Battling for Hearts and Minds* (books 1 and 2 of the trilogy *The Memory Box of Pinochet's Chile*). Durham: Duke University Press.

Stirton Weaver, Patrick. 1994. *Inside the Volcano: The History and Political Economy of Central America.* Boulder, Colo.: Westview Press.

Stotzky, Irwin P., ed. 1993. *Transition to Democracy in Latin America: The Role of the Judiciary.* Boulder, Colo.: Westview Press.

Sugarman, David. 2001a. "Bringing Pinochet to Justice: Transnational Alliances and the Practice of International Politics." Paper presented at the conference "The Pinochet Case," Institute of Latin American Studies, London, 15–16 November.

———. 2001b. "The Pinochet Case: International Criminal Justice in the Gothic Style?" *Modern Law Review* 64, no. 6: 933–44.

———. 2002. "From Unimaginable to Possible: Spain, Pinochet, and the Judicialisation of Power." *Journal of Spanish Cultural Studies* 3, no. 1: 107–24.

Tarrow, Sidney. 2005. *The New Transnational Activism.* Cambridge: Cambridge University Press.

Teitel, Ruti G. 1995. "How Are the New Democracies of the Southern Cone Dealing with the Legacy of Past Human Rights Abuses?" In N. Kritz, ed., *Transitional Justice: How Emerging Democracies Reckon with Former Regimes,* 1:146–54. Washington, D.C.: United States Institute of Peace Press.

———. 1997. "Transitional Jurisprudence: The Role of Law in Political Transformation." *Yale Law Journal* 106, no. 7: 2009–80.

———. 1999. "Bringing the Messiah Through the Law." In C. Hesse and R. Post, eds., *Human Rights in Political Transitions: Gettysburg to Bosnia,* 177–93. New York: Zone Books.

———. 2000. *Transitional Justice.* Oxford: Oxford University Press.

———. 2003. "Transitional Justice Genealogy." *Harvard Human Rights Journal* 16 (Spring): 69–94

Tepperman, J. 2002. "Truth and Consequences." *Foreign Affairs* 81, no. 2: 128–45.

Tojeira, José María, S.J. 2000. "El sistema judicial en El Salvador." *Estudios Centroamericanos* 625–26 (November–December): 1119–27.

UDP (Universidad Diego Portales). 2003. "Verdad y justicia respecto de las violaciones del pasado." In *Informe anual sobre derechos humanos en Chile,* 135–206. Santiago: Universidad Diego Portales, Facultad de Derecho.

UN Truth Commission for El Salvador. 1993. "From Madness to Hope: The 12-Year War in El Salvador." UN Publication S/25500, Spanish and English versions available via http://www.un.org/. English version at http://www.usip.org/files/file/ElSalvador-Report.pdf.

Ungar, Mark. 2002. *Elusive Reform: Democracy and the Rule of Law in Latin America.* Boulder, Colo.: Lynne Rienner Publishers.

U.S. Secretary of State's Panel on El Salvador. 1993. "Report of the Secretary of State's Panel on El Salvador." Washington, D.C.: U.S. Department of State.

Verbitsky, Horacio. 1995. *El vuelo.* Buenos Aires: Editorial Planeta.

Verdugo, Patricia. 1989. *Los zarpazos del puma.* Santiago: LOM.

———. 1998. *Interferencia secreta: 11 de septiembre de 1973.* Santiago: Editorial Sudamericana.

———. 1999. *Bucarest 187.* Santiago: Editorial Sudamericana.

———. 2000. *Pruebas a la vista: La caravana de la muerte.* Santiago: Editorial Sudamericana, Serie Crónicas y Testimonios.

Vial, Gonzalo. 2002. *Pinochet: La biografía.* Santiago: El Mercurio/Aguilar.

Wehr, Ingrid. 2001. "Soberanía estatal vs. justicia universal: El caso Pinochet y la discusión sobre la extraterritorialidad de la ley." In F. Rojas and C. Stefoni. eds., *El "caso Pinochet"*: *Visiones hemisféricas de su detención en Londres,* 49–63. Santiago: FLACSO-Chile.

Weiss, Peter. 1998. "Punishing Pinochet." *Covert Action Quarterly* 64 (Spring): 39–40.

Weschler, Lawrence. 1990. *A Miracle, A Universe: Settling Accounts with Torturers.* New York: Pantheon.

Whitfield, Teresa. 1998. *Pagando el precio: Ignacio Ellacuría y el asesinato de los jesuitas en El Salvador.* San Salvador: UCA Editores.

———. 1999. "The Role of the United Nations in El Salvador and Guatemala: A Preliminary Comparison." In C. Arnson, ed., *Comparative Peace Processes in Latin America,* 257–90. Stanford: Stanford University Press.

Wilde, Alex. 1999. "Irruptions of Memory: Expressive Politics in Chile's Transition to Democracy." *Journal of Latin American Studies* 31, no. 2: 473–500.

Williams, S., ed. 2002. *Light Among Shadows.* Washington, D.C.: IPS.

Wilson, Richard. 1996. "Spanish Criminal Prosecutions Use International Human Rights Law to BattleImpunity in Chile and Argentina." Available at http://www .derechos.org/koaga/iii/5/wilson.html, last accessed 4 March 2009.

———. 1999. "Prosecuting Pinochet: International Crimes in Spanish Domestic Law." *Human Rights Quarterly* 21, no. 4: 928–79.

Yañez, Sol. 2002. "Apoyo social en tiempo de oscuridad: Una experiencia compartida en El Salvador." *Estudios Centroamericanos* 649–50 (November–December): 1103–20.

Yashar, Deborah. 2002. "Globalization and Collective Action." *Comparative Politics* 34, no. 3: 355–75.

Zalaquett, José. 1995a. "Confronting Human Rights Violations Committed by Former Governments: Principles Applicable and Political Constraints." In N. Kritz, ed., *Transitional Justice: How Emerging Democracies Reckon with Former Regimes,* 1:3–31. Washington, D.C.: United States Institute of Peace Press.

———. 1995b. "The Dilemma of New Democracies Confronting Past Human Rights Violations." In N. Kritz, ed., *Transitional Justice: How Emerging Democracies Reckon with Former Regimes,* 1:203–6. Washington, D.C.: United States Institute of Peace Press.

———. 1999a. "La reconstrucción de la unidad nacional y el legado de violaciones de los derechos humanos." *Perspectivas.* Facultad de Ciencias Físicas y Matemáticas, Universidad de Chile; Vol. 2, Número Especial.

———. 1999b. "Truth, Justice, and Reconciliation." In C. Arnson, ed., *Comparative Peace Processes in Central America,* 341–62. Stanford: Stanford University Press.

———. 2000. "La Mesa de Diálogo sobre derechos humanos y el proceso de transición política en Chile." *Estudios Públicos* 79 (Winter): 5–30.

Zamora, Rubén. 2001. "Participación y democracia en El Salvador." In G. Maihold, S. Kurtenbach, and R. Córdova Macías, eds., *Pasos hacia una nueva convivencia: Democracia y participación en Centroamérica,* 59–94. San Salvador: FUNDAUNGO.

Zamora, Rubén, and David Holiday. 2007. "The Struggle for Lasting Reform: Vetting Processes in El Salvador." In Pablo De Greiff and Alexander Mayer-Rieckh, eds., *Justice as Prevention: Vetting Public Employees in Transitional Societies,* 80–119. New York: SSRC.

Other Sources

WEB SITES

http://www.amnesty.org/
http://www.cels.org/
http://www.chipsites.com/derechos/
http://www.cidh.org/
http://www.cja.org/
http://www.codepu.cl/
http://www.cverdad.org.pe/
http://www.ddhh.gov.cl/
http://www.derechos.org/nizkor/
http://www.doj.gov.za/trc/
http://www.dplf.org/
http://www.elmostrador.cl/
http://www.fasic.org/
http://www.iachr.org/
http://www.icj-cij.org/
http://www.memoriayjusticia.cl/
http://www.tni.org/pinochet/
http://www.uca.edu.sv/
http://www.udp.cl/
http://www.un.org/
http://www.usip.org/
http://www.vicariadelasolidaridad.cl/
Closed e-discussion group on Universal Jurisdiction: uj-info@yahoogroups.com

PRINT MEDIA

Clarín, Buenos Aires, Argentina
El Diario de Hoy, San Salvador, El Salvador
Mensaje, Santiago de Chile
El Mercurio, Santiago de Chile
El Mostrador, Santiago de Chile
New York Times, New York, U.S.
Página 12, Buenos Aires, Argentina
Qué Pasa, Santiago de Chile
Santiago Times, Santiago de Chile
La Segunda, Santiago de Chile
Siete mas Siete, Santiago de Chile
La Tercera, Santiago de Chile

FILM

Caravan of Death. 2001, UK. BBC Television documentary in the "Correspondent" series by Isabel Hilton. First broadcast on 27 January 2001, BBC.

Estadio nacional. 2000, Chile. Documentary film by Carmen Luz Parot.

Fernando ha vuelto. 1999, Chile. Documentary film by Silvio Caiozzi.

The Judge and the General. 2008, Chile/U.S. Documentary film by Patricio Lanfranco and Elizabeth Farnsworth.

Justice and the Generals. 2002, U.S. Documentary film by Gail Pellett. First broadcast on 21 February 2002, PBS.

El muro de los nombres. 1999, Chile. Documentary film by Germán Liñero.

INDEX

Page numbers followed by "*t*" indicate tables.